Managing Human Resources

The management of human resources in the workplace is a matter of central concern to all managers and not only to HRM professionals. This new text, designed for the MBA student in particular, aims to show the central role of good human resource management strategies in giving a company competitive edge.

The ability to adapt to a constantly changing environment is what makes an organization successful: this ability to adapt and respond to change relies mainly on the motivation and efficiency of the people within the organization. The creation of an effective work culture through human resource strategies such as team building, performance appraisal, quality management, decentralized structures, and flexible working practices is central to the role of the manager.

This book shows how managers can develop the structures and processes necessary to achieve their goals. Its clear, up-to-date coverage of human resource issues, and demonstration of how these can contribute to successful business strategies, make this book an excellent introduction for business students and professional managers alike.

Christopher Molander and **Jonathan Winterton** are both senior lecturers at the University of Bradford's Management Centre.

Elements of Business Series
Series editor: David Weir
University of Bradford Management Centre

This important new series is designed to cover the core topics taught at MBA level with an approach suited to the modular teaching and shorter time frames that apply in the MBA sector. Based on current courses and teaching experience, these texts are tailor-made to the needs of today's MBA student.

Other titles in the series:

Business and Society
Edmund Marshall

Management Accounting
Leslie Chadwick

Business and Microeconomics
Christopher Pass and Bryan Lowes

Managerial Leadership
Peter Wright

Financial Management
Leslie Chadwick and Donald Kirby

Managing Human Resources

Christopher Molander and
Jonathan Winterton

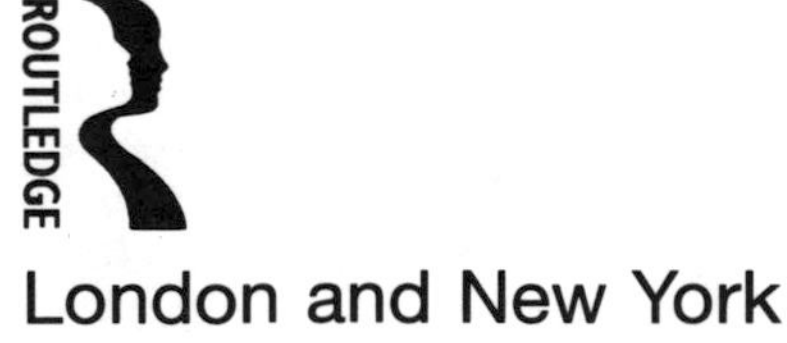

London and New York

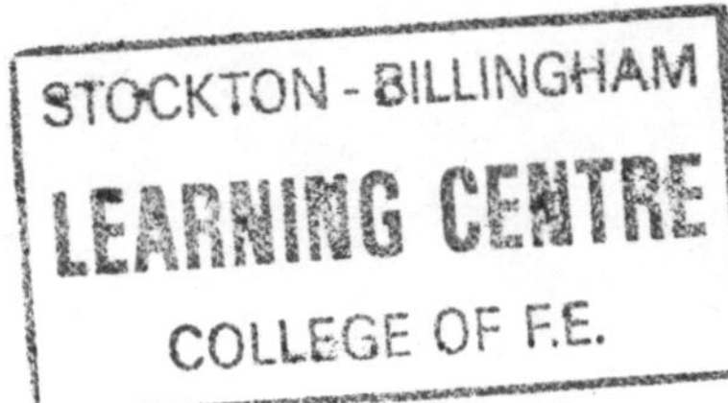

First published 1994
by Routledge
11 New Fetter Lane, London EC4P 4EE

Simultaneously published in the USA and Canada
by Routledge
29 West 35th Street, New York, NY 10001

Reprinted by International Thomson Business Press 1996

Typeset in Garamond by
J&L Composition Ltd, Filey, North Yorkshire
Printed and bound in Great Britain by
Biddles Ltd, Guildford and King's Lynn

British Library Cataloguing in Publication Data

A catalogue record for this book is available from the British Library

Library of Congress Cataloging in Publication Data
Molander, Christopher.
Managing human resources / Christopher Molander and Jonathan Winterton.
p. cm. – (Elements of business)
Includes bibliographical references.
ISBN 0-415-06853-3. – ISBN 0-415-06854-1 (pbk.)
1. Personnel management. I. Winterton, Jonathan, 1951–
II. Title. III. Series.
HF5549.M5657 1994
658.3–dc20 94–15560
CIP

ISBN 0-415-06853-3 (hbk)
0-415-06854-1 (pbk)

For Alan, Kate, Daisy, Ruth, Ben and Rachel

Contents

List of figures and tables viii
Preface ix
List of abbreviations x
1 What is human resource management? 1
2 Organization design and development 17
3 Human resource planning 32
4 Dealing with unions 44
5 Employee recruitment and selection 64
6 Training and management development 78
7 Equal opportunity 94
8 Performance appraisal 108
9 Payment 120
10 Quality of working life 132
11 Collective bargaining 155
12 Discipline, grievances and disputes 171
13 The working environment 185
Bibliography 196
Index 204

Figures and tables

FIGURES

1.1 The development of organization culture 7
2.1 Tall and flat organization structure 19
2.2 The functional organization structure 21
2.3 The divisional organization structure 22
2.4 A mixed organization structure 23
2.5 Direct and functional reporting relationships 24
2.6 A matrix structure 25
2.7 A group process questionnaire 29
3.1 The stages of human resource planning 35
3.2 Types of leaver by length of service (cohort analysis) 39
3.3 Survival rate 39
3.4 A Markov chain 41
4.1 Patterns of workplace relations 47
4.2 Union membership 1890–1990 53
4.3 Union structure 56
4.4 Union government 57
5.1 Stages in the recruitment and selection process 65
5.2 The seven-point plan 66
5.3 Person specification for military aircrew (based on the seven-point plan) 67
6.1 The stages in effective training provision 80
6.2 The learning cycle 92
8.1 Purposes of the parties to the appraisal process 109

TABLES

6.1 Types of management development activity 87
12.1 Annual statistics of stoppages of work 176

Preface

This is the second book concerned with human resource management produced in recent years by the Management Centre of the University of Bradford.

In the Foreword to the earlier work, Sir John Harvey-Jones, sometime Managing Director of ICI and Chancellor of the University of Bradford, commented:

> So many fundamental changes are occurring in our society that industry is inevitably faced with a massive period of adjustment to external change. Skills in different areas of business life tend to wax and wane in a cyclical fashion. I suspect that for many reasons the day of the professionally equipped human resource specialist may be about to dawn.

There is recognition that traditional approaches to the management of people at work have led the profession to sell itself short and to exclude the very people whose responsibility it is: operating managers. The result has been the emergence of a climate of mutual misunderstanding and lost opportunity. Professional human resource managers have been precluded from serious involvement in the development of strategy and operating managers have not infrequently surrendered control over employment processes which cannot be other than theirs.

All this is of course not new. In 1956 Pigors and Myers roundly asserted that 'Personnel administration is a basic function of management.' More than thirty years later Guest (1989) declared that 'if HRM is to be taken seriously, personnel managers must give it away.' The search for the competitive edge has, however, renewed the power of these assertions and line managers are thinking anew of more effective uses of human resource staff.

This book seeks to show what this effective use might be. We hope it will be of value to those students on management programmes and equally to those who wish to update their knowledge with regard to current thinking in this area.

Christopher Molander
Jonathan Winterton
Bradford

Abbreviations

ACAS	Advisory, Conciliation and Arbitration Service
AEU	Amalgamated Engineering Union (now AEEU)
AEEU	Amalgamated Engineering and Electrical Union
APEX	Association of Professional, Executive, Clerical and Computer Staff
ASE	Amalgamated Society of Engineers (now AEEU)
ASLEF	Associated Society of Locomotive Engineers and Firemen
ASTMS	Association of Scientific, Technical and Managerial Staffs
AUEW	Amalgamated Union of Engineering Workers
BACM	British Association of Colliery Management
BC	British Coal
BPS	British Psychology Society
BR	British Rail
CAC	Central Arbitration Court
CBI	Confederation of British Industry
COSHH	Control of Substances Hazardous to Health (Regulations)
CRC	Community Relations Council
CRE	Commission for Racial Equality
EC	European Commission
EEC	European Economic Community
EETPU	Electrical, Electronic, Telecommunication and Plumbing Union
EO	Equal Opportunities
EOC	Equal Opportunities Commission
EI	Equal Involvement
EqPA	Equal Pay Act, 1970
ERG	Existence, relatedness, growth
ETU	Electrical Trades Union (now EETPU)
FTAT	Furniture, Timber and Allied Trades Union
GMB	General, Municipal and Boilermakers' Union
GMWU	General and Municipal Workers' Union (now GMB)
HRM	Human resource management

HRP	Human resource planning
HSC	Health and Safety Commission
HSE	Health and Safety Executive
HSWA	Health and Safety at Work, etc. Act 1974
ILB	Industry Lead Body
IMS	Institute of Manpower Studies
IPM	Industry of Personnel Management
ITO	Industry Training Organization
JNNC	Joint National Negotiating Committee
JSSC	Joint Shop Stewards' Committee
LDC	Local Departmental Committee
MBA	Master of Business Administration
MBO	Management by Objectives
MD	Management development
MDW	Measured day work
MES	Multi-linear events sequencing
MORT	Managerial oversight and risk tree
MSF	Manufacturing, science, finance
NACODS	National Association of Colliery Overmen, Deputies and Shotfirers
NALGO	National and Local Government Officers' Association (now UNISON)
NCB	National Coal Board
NCVQ	National Council for Vocational Qualification
NEC	National Executive Committee
NJIC	National Joint Industrial Council
NJNC	National Joint Negotiating Committee
NPLA	National Power Loading Agreement
NUM	National Union of Mineworkers
NUPE	National Union of Public Employees (now UNISON)
NUR	National Union of Railwaymen (now RMT)
OD	Organizational development
PBR	Payment by results
PLA	Power Loading Agreement
PRP	Performance-related pay
PSBR	Public Sector Borrowing Requirement
QWL	Quality of working life
RMT	National Union of Rail, Maritime and Transport Workers
RRA	Race Relations Act, 1976
SCOTVEC	Scottish Vocational Education Council
SDA	Sex Discrimination Act, 1975
SRSC	Safety Representatives and Safety Committees (Regulations)
SVQ	Scottish Vocational Qualifications
TGWU	Transport and General Workers' Union

TQM	Total quality management
TUC	Trades Union Congress
UDCATT	Union of Construction, Allied Trades and Technicians
UDM	Union of Democratic Mineworkers
USDAW	Union of Shop, Distributive and Allied Workers
WTC	Workplace Training Committee

Chapter 1

What is human resource management?

INTRODUCTION

The purpose of this initial chapter is to persuade the reader – if persuasion is necessary – that the management of human resources in the workplace is a matter of central concern to all managers and not only to human resource management (HRM) professionals.

The last area of managerial activity to be adequately addressed is the more efficient use of people. Highly successful top managers have joined a procession of gurus in emphasizing that the effective deployment and motivation of employees at all levels is the crucial factor which will give or deny the competitive edge.

We shall explore the pressures for change in work organizations and review the impact these pressures have had on the development of HRM – particularly with regard to changing organizational cultures. This will be followed by a brief analysis of professional HRM, concentrating on the various levels in which it is to be found – strategic and functional – in large-scale organizations.

We shall then be in a position to explore three major areas in which HRM professionals have an important role to play. Throughout, particular attention will be paid to stressing the importance of integrated action between operating and HR managers.

THE CHANGING EXTERNAL ENVIRONMENT OF WORK ORGANIZATIONS

Anyone reading a daily newspaper cannot fail to be aware of the deteriorating economic environment with which work organizations are faced. There have been clear indications of increasing difficulty for firms in maintaining economic stability, largely in consequence of increasingly global competition, fragmentation of mass markets and a general decline in consumer demand. These difficulties are currently experienced not only in the UK but worldwide, not excluding Japan. The economic turmoil which is likely to follow political events in Eastern Europe is already aggravating economic and political instability.

Even those countries which by any standard of excellence have performed well economically – the young dragons of South East Asia such as Singapore – are keenly aware that economic growth will be maintained at present rates only if greater value added activity is generated. This implies the successful emergence of a new generation of technologically complex and desirable products together with a trained, motivated and efficient labour force to produce them.

One of the obvious effects of this turbulence is clearly visible in the increased level of competition which firms are experiencing in every market. The push for increasing efficiency – particularly with regard to the use of labour at all levels – is widely seen as one of the few remaining means whereby organizations can hold on to or regain the competitive edge. The consequences of under-investment in technology are well understood; the consequences of inefficient use of the human resource have begun to be realized with an increased sense of urgency.

We have argued that external economic pressures are a strong force for internal change. There are others. Although something like 80 per cent of all wage settlements are currently conducted on the basis of collective bargaining, few would deny the changing role of unions in the United Kingdom. Historically the traditional power of the unions has waxed and waned with turns of the economic cycle. During the 1980s in particular, management felt able to take a stronger position in relation to the unions, supported by the implied and actual threat of increased levels of redundancy.

It is likely that this decline in the traditional power of the unions will be replaced by a more strategic multinational approach to relations with management, following the development of the single European market. UK companies will have to adapt in particular to the principles expressed in the Social Charter. In the meantime economic conditions provide a managerial opportunity for replacing the adversarial model of union relationships with an alternative more within its control.

The public sector is not immune from these pressures for change as any teacher, health worker or local government administrator will testify. In both the private and public sectors the constant search for new markets and products has become a normal feature of work experience. Private sector firms are driven to look for ever wider markets – usually abroad. The internationalization of the productive process raises new problems of control and motivation across economic and cultural boundaries, the managerial implications of which are not always properly understood.

The final external change to be mentioned at this point is that relating to the quality of the work force. It does not always follow that in a free economy high unemployment levels will lead to low levels of job vacancies. We have argued already that the competitive edge will be won and secured through the most effective use of people. It is more than ever important then that firms should ensure that the selection, appraisal, training and reward systems are the best possible, so that they are able to attract and retain a high-quality labour force. Companies need to sell themselves to potential employees just as much as aspiring recruits must sell themselves to the organization.

We are talking of a change in culture. The change is concerned with customer satisfaction – that is the competitive edge; the means by which it is attained is the efficient use of the labour resource.

Such a change has to be understood, planned for and managed. It is far more than the introduction of management techniques such as Quality Circles. HRM professionals alongside line managers have a crucial role to play in the process of culture change. They have in the past frequently failed to think at the necessary strategic level.

It is easy to sympathize with managers who have memories of a less stressful economic period and claim that 'nowadays it is one damn thing after another'. But there is no promise of a return to stability in due course. Organizations which are likely to survive in the 1990s will be those which develop a view of change not as temporary turbulence but as the norm; and then go on to develop the structures and processes which will accommodate and exploit it.

THE CHANGING INTERNAL ENVIRONMENT

All organizations if they are to survive make an adjustment to the pressures on them from the external environment (Molander 1986). That they do survive implies that the adjustment is to some extent satisfactory. Many work organizations perish, however, and they do so because they are unable to adjust to the demands of the external environment.

In this section we shall attempt to define the elements of a satisfactory adjustment. They can be summed up in the word 'culture'.

The culture or climate of an organization is made up of traditions, habits, ways of organizing and patterns of relationships at work. Anyone who has spent time in a number of work organizations will have noticed how the 'climate' differs, the different ways in which things are done, differing levels of energy and individual freedom, and of course different kinds of people. Organizations have different sets of values, rules and beliefs, and these are reflected in different formal and informal relationships and systems of working. Culture is reflected in organization structure, power distribution, reward systems, development processes and motivational levels. In short, culture is the growing medium in which the personnel of an organization operate.

Some growing mediums are hostile and arid, producing personnel who are suspicious and unresponsive. Others offer a supportive climate, encouraging employees to develop and flourish.

Organization culture materializes in the systems and processes which have emerged over time and which are responsible for the output. 'Culture', an American once said, 'is the way we do things round here.'

It is possible to define some of the elements of an effective work culture, given the external environment reviewed above:

- *Flexible.* The rate of technological change and the change in economic conditions brought about by global trading has meant that companies must be able to adjust speedily to market forces. Traditional bureaucratic systems of planning and implementation are likely to result in responses which are too slow, are inappropriate and do not carry the commitment of trained and motivated employees.

  Instead we must look for new ways of 'lining up to get work done' (organization structure) which is alert to market needs and can adjust output accordingly. It is likely that flat decentralized structures will be appropriate in many instances.
- *Integrated.* Along with flexibility must go a greater degree of integration which the classical bureaucratic structure has always avoided. The various parts of the organization must work together in a coherent way to avoid the duplication and squandering of effort which obtains in companies which thrive on the promotion of narrow sectional interests (empire building) and internal politics. Corporate planning and the development of strategy are therefore prerequisites for survival.

  The organization structure most suitable for such integration is not the common functional division of labour with its built-in barriers to co-operation, but product- and project-based structures, both of which produce flexible as well as integrated activity.
- *Decentralized.* In Chapter 2 we look at the design of organizations. There we make the point that the maintenance of a competitive edge depends upon not only satisfying customers but delighting them (Deming 1986). Organizations which push the point of decision making as far down as possible are likely to find that they are more responsive to customer need – simply because decisions are more likely to be made by those who are in closest contact with the consumer. Decentralized structures are 'flat' rather than 'vertical' or hierarchical.
- *Performance-oriented.* Having obtained a strategy and clearly defined goals, the HRM culture is concerned with achievement of objectives. These are quantified and expressed in 'bottom line' terms. The danger of short termism is consequently a real one. One might expect to find in such organizations a concern with performance-related appraisal systems and other methods of close monitoring. There will be those who lack the

enthusiasm for such a 'shape up or ship out' culture and 'exiting' procedures will be in place.

There is then a strong element of individual responsibility best understood on the basis of a contract. The organization undertakes to provide the resources and the training for the individual to achieve objectives. Where these are persistently achieved employees will find themselves rewarded. Consistent underachievement may lead to redeployment or 'separation'.

- *Quality conscious.* Many of the functional activities to be mentioned in a later section of this chapter stem from this much espoused element in the emerging HRM culture. For example, moves to introduce flatter organization structures, perhaps based on product rather than functional lines, are designed to allow employees to respond more quickly to the needs of the customer. Recent interest in empowerment also has this as its objective by pushing down the organizational point at which decisions are made affecting the satisfaction level of the customer.

  In the search for quality, Total Quality Management (TQM) has become modish with the consequent interest in such techniques as Quality Circles and other employee-involving devices.
- *Cooperative.* In order for the cultural elements mentioned above to be achieved, the next factor in the changing culture relates directly to the management of people. The history of industrial relations in the United Kingdom has been characterized by pluralism (Fox 1971, amongst others). It has been long accepted that any large group of people consists of varying and irreconcilable interests. The function of management is therefore to manage the conflict so that the underlying common interest of keeping the organization running is achieved.

  Central to the HRM culture, however, is a return to an earlier managerial view that the organization is a unitary institution, the members of which share common interests. Since conflict is unnecessary and dysfunctional, the task of management is not the pluralist one of managing the conflict, but the unitary one of conflict avoidance. Accordingly the search is on for non-adversarial and non-collective systems of employee representation, through which the hearts and minds of employees can be won. Those whose parts are not negotiable are free to work elsewhere.

  Two consequences follow from this change in managerial philosophy. Firstly and most importantly, it has effects on negotiation procedures. One of the arguments against incremental payment systems is that employees have been known to demand an extra increment if they are to take on extra responsibility.

  This has led to managerial interest in individually negotiated wage and salary packages, as opposed to collectively negotiated incremental payment systems. Such packages are also related to appraisal or merit rating systems. Management expect that such payment systems will lead to greater scope to target rewards and also provide a greater degree of flexibility. Broad-band payment systems together with some form of group-based incentive system are likely to be of increasing interest to managers.

Secondly, with regard to relationships at work generally, managers will look to replace the former collective systems with more direct relationships. The forging of such direct relationships between managers and individual employees is more relevant to the intregrated HRM approach in which operating managers reassume the responsibility for those individuals who report to them. In sum, it is increasingly being seen as part of every manager's job and an important element in the new, more cooperative and individualistic culture.

This view will appear to some as a resurrection of an earlier management position which reflects a more 'macho' industrial relations policy much encouraged by the British Conservative government of the 1980s.

- *Empowered.* Central to the points listed above is the concept of empowerment – giving authority to those who lack it to make decisions which lead to greater customer satisfaction and through this to an increase in the level of personal motivation.

  It is important not to be swept away by a facile view of what empowerment entails. If it is not to be seen by a cynical work force as yet another way of getting more work done without increasing payment, it must be integrated into the culture and must be the end product of a lengthy organization-wide development programme. Appraisal, training and reward systems must be supportively in tune with the philosophy of empowerment (Molander 1994).
- *Segmented.* The desirability or otherwise of harmonization is increasingly a matter of concern for managers. It is not only a matter of the rights and wrongs of equalizing conditions of service between the various grade of employee on moral grounds.

  There are more substantial issues relating to the overall managerial attitude to various grades and types of employee. Increasingly, organizations are distinguishing between core and peripheral workers. The former group are those who are identified as being particularly important to the organization and need to be retained by the necessary rewards. The rest, often the easily replaceable, are kept, as Torrington (1988) asserts, 'at arm's length' and encouraged to move on by the conspicuous lack of reward and development opportunities.

  The possibility of such a new-style division of labour is inherent in the human resource management culture, which Torrington describes as 'demand driven'.

The major elements of HRM strategy and functions can be related to organization culture in the form of a flow chart (see Figure 1.1). It is

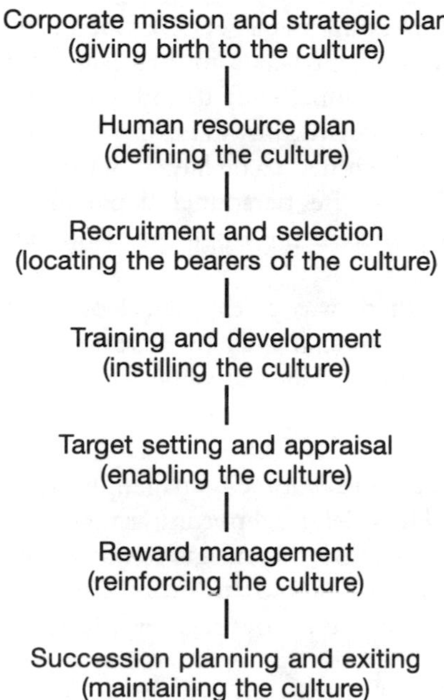

Figure 1.1 The development of organization culture

questionable whether there are many organizations which actually manage to achieve an integrated corporate and human resource plan, or whether HRM activities are as smoothly achieved as such models suggest. None the less, they indicate the philosophy of HRM in a tidy fashion.

STRATEGIC AND FUNCTIONAL ASPECTS OF HUMAN RESOURCE MANAGEMENT

Before embarking on a description of the broad areas in which professional HR staff might be expected to be involved, it is important to review the position of HR staff in the modern large-scale organization. Hopefully this will avoid confusion later on.

Typically in Britain before the 1980s the personnel department was heavily weighted numerically towards the centre. It was primarily seen as a 'staff' function which existed to advise managers as to best practice in handling people at work: expert advisers without operating responsibility.

This alone encouraged the development of a rather aloof attitude to operating managers and a mutual lack of sympathy between the two managerial types. Empire building was common and some larger organizations seemed unable to control either the growth in size of the personnel department or the growth in the gulf between what personnel considered their role and what operating managers considered the personnel people as actually achieving. The result was a mutual lack of respect and the widespread failure of the personnel staff to influence events to any noticeable degree. Some large-scale firms, however, saw the personnel department as inevitable and a cost which had to be largely written off. Few firms saw the possibility of developing the personnel department as a cost centre or describing its performance in the language of operating managers – profit and loss accounting.

During the 1980s there was a reappraisal of the role of the personnel department amongst others, fuelled by adverse economic conditions and the consequent need for managerial value for money. A consequence was the decentralizing of the department and the integration of its activities with corporate goals.

The core central human resource management group was vastly reduced in size and those HRM staff reporting to and working for operating managers were increased. By this means it was expected that the activities of the HRM professional would be more closely tied to the needs of operating managers who were now responsible for employing and paying their HRM staff.

Whilst the majority of HRM staff now found themselves working to the agenda of operating managers, the reduced central group were also encouraged to integrate their activities with those of other top managers. They were represented on the top team and began to have as powerful a role as any other director in the development of corporate policy.

The reader will have noticed a change in title which is now common. The abandonment of the term 'personnel management' in favour of 'human resource management' was designed to emphasize a new, harder-headed look at the handling of people at work. Employees were just as much a resource as any other asset and needed to be carefully acquired, used and maintained.

Care needs to be taken, however, to avoid the view that this change is universal and coherent. As Guest (1987) has pointed out, the change is uneven and there are no doubt firms which have simply changed the description on the door plate of the department, whilst within much continues as before.

From here onwards, the term 'human resource management' will be used in place of personnel management. Strategic HRM staff should be taken to mean those central specialists engaged in the development of HRM policy and working as part of the top management team, whilst HRM officers are those professionals working for and responsible to operating managers. This latter term refers to those managers who have an overall responsibility for and authority over others and who are not specialists – in the area of human resource management for example.

This distinction between the strategic and the functional role of the

HRM specialist is important if the reader is to understand fully the changing role of the human resource specialist.

HUMAN RESOURCE MANAGEMENT ISSUES

In this section we shall take a more detailed look at the various activities in which both HRM professionals and line managers may be expected to get involved and which stem from the cultural elements discussed above. Human resource management is not something which can be left to the professionals. We have already explored the importance of integration. The activities of both line manager and professional HR manager must also be integrated.

Corporate planning

It is essential that the HRM function carries directorial status and is represented at the top of the organization. It is here that corporate planning will take place and the HR director has a vital role to play in this process.

It is difficult to see how decisions affecting the activities of the organization can be properly made without a human resource input. Is the organization to move into new product areas? Is it to open a new plant in a different country and is it to decentralize? What are the implications of these possibilities for employees and are there enough of them to satisfy potential staffing requirements? What are the possible implications for recruitment, training, organization design and development?

This sample of questions should help to illustrate the need to have a technical HRM *input* into strategic decision making. HRM professionals also need to obtain information necessary for the development of human resource policy – to get an *output* from the strategic plan.

Human resource management policy

One should reasonably expect the top levels of HR management to concern themselves with the development of an HRM policy for use throughout the company. Its application arguably should be left to line managers. HRM specialists should concern themselves with the validation of the policy. Is it relevant to the needs of the organization? Does it promote a performance-oriented culture? This is not to imply that HRM staff lay down the operating details of the policy; it might well be that the central policy allows for the operating divisions to develop their own procedures within wide margins.

There will always be personnel-related issues which need central review and which require responses understood and wholly supported by board-level managers.

Human resource planning

This is an area in which centrally located HR staff might be expected to play an important role. Whatever the contents of the strategic plan, there will be human resource implications. In order for it to be developed adequately, top line managers will expect adequate information about the supply of labour now and in the future and also about the characteristics of the labour supply.

In its turn, the HR department will expect to glean sufficient relevant information about the possible growth and decline in company assets, and outlines of any plans to change the technology or develop the product. With the data obtained, personnel staff should encourage the production of a five-year rolling plan which will allow line managers together with their operating HR staff to develop recruitment, training and retention budgets.

Recruitment and selection

It is commonplace but true that if the wrong people are selected, then no amount of development through good management will make them effective. The whole of HRM specialist and operating manager activity hinges on this point. It is therefore important that the best selection methods are used.

Operating managers will doubtless want to make the final selection decision, since they will be responsible for new recruits and will need to find their wage or salary from their budget. No self-respecting manager would allow this selection function to fall into the hands of others and equally no self-respecting HRM officer would presume to make the decision on behalf of those responsible for the new employee. There is a good political reason for this. So long as operating managers can blame others for bad selection decisions, they will. It was common in the past, when personnel staff often made employment decisions, for the operating managers to give up trying to develop individual members of their teams, claiming that they should never have been selected and 'those personnel people have messed things up again'.

There is good reason why the functional HRM officer should take an active part in the proceedings, ensuring that there is a job description and that the short list is adequate and does not, for example, offend against employment legislation, and advising upon and administering selection tests. Even though the interviews for the short-listed candidates might be usefully attended by the HR specialist, the final decision must still be made by the operating manager whose commitment to making a good decision is the higher for being responsible for it.

Strategic HRM staff will want no doubt to develop operating procedures and encourage top management to follow their recommendations as to the use of various selection techniques. These professionals will no doubt also want to monitor the selection process to ensure that the head count remains in line with corporate planning.

Reward management

Generally the policy and mechanics of payment should be a responsibility of the operating manager rather than HR staff. None the less, questions such as the type of job evaluation scheme, if any, which is to be used, whether there is a policy regarding harmonization of terms and conditions of service, whether there is to be a general system of appraisal and any consequent performance-related payments will be matters for top management concern, including the top HRM managers. The latter will be expected to have the available data regarding national and international trends in reward management and have relevant statistics relating to payment trends.

Both the implementation of wage and salary systems and the policy decisions relating to the development of reward systems generally will always involve line managers. We should expect that the latter policy decisions will involve an input by specialist HRM staff. Even so, the responsibility for final policy decisions also rests with line management.

It is worth emphasizing that there are many strategic elements in the development of reward systems. White (1985) for example draws attention to the need to have a clear idea as to what the pay system is designed to achieve. Systems can encourage certain types of staff to remain loyal to the organization and at the same time discourage others from staying beyond a certain point – related to age or wage level. Such fiscal engineering requires strategic thinking and monitoring at the highest level and is an example of an area where top-level HRM professionals will be involved.

Training

It will be clear by now that almost all HRM issues involve operating managers. This is true of training. Operating managers must take responsibility for identifying the training needs of their staff – no doubt through some form of appraisal. In many instances, there is also no one better to carry out the training. We note in Chapter 6 that 'on the job' training is frequently the least expensive and the most effective form of development. It therefore makes sense to leave it to operating managers to decide in conjunction with the trainee what training is appropriate and when.

It is also important that the cost of training is borne by managers and not provided for by a central fund in the control of HRM staff. A cost centre approach will help ensure that money is not wasted on training and that some thinking takes place before expense is incurred.

By now the reader will be wondering just what responsibilities HRM staff have. We shall pursue this point in detail shortly. In the meantime, it may be said that the professional trainers if any are likely to be located in the operating divisions of the company and under the control of line managers. In the largest companies there may be some who will be located centrally and will sell their services on the market principle: managers will buy them as they would any material needed for production. In either case the responsibility for implementing training must rest with line managers. It is likely, however, that the strategic decisions as to training priorities, funding policies and provider contracting will be handled centrally by HRM professionals and much of the training itself will involve HRM officers who work in the operating divisions.

A particular contribution which HRM staff generally can make is to help managers think through training policy. There is a tendency for managers to rely heavily on training for the resolution of employee problems, the cause of which in fact lies elsewhere – in departmental structure and responsibilities, roles and job descriptions, motivation and rewards. In the past training has earned itself a poor reputation because it passed from the control of those who should have retained an interest; also partly because too much has been asked of it. Sending people on courses in particular might be all right as part of the reward system, but it has been the cause of much waste of money and consequent cynicism.

Management development

This last point relating to the overuse of training as the cure for problems at work is perhaps even more valid with regard to management development. A major skill of managers is the capacity to analyse and define problems and to delay the process of looking for solutions. Whilst training is of course important, there are many factors which affect the performance of managers other than technical competence. Accordingly, training ought not to be embarked upon without caution. There are many other ways in which managers can be developed, particularly changing the circumstances in which they are expected to produce: the internal environment of the organization or department. Much of managerial behaviour is a reflection of the prevailing culture.

Managers ought to be able to rely on up-to-date information on management development techniques from HR staff. Central staff will, as the reader might by now expect, be engaged in the production of policy as regards the development of managers. What ought to be the priorities?

What methods of development does the organization favour? Who are to be the providers? The administration of training is something which HRM officers in the operating departments will be able to provide for managers.

Industrial relations

Industrial relations continues to be an area of importance despite the shift in power from unions to managers which reflects changes in the economic environment. The vast majority of wage claims are settled on a collective basis. Quite apart from the settlement of wage and salary issues, there is much to be done regarding the devising and setting up of systems of communication and consultation.

Line managers will require support with regard to the handling of day-to-day conflict from their own personnel staff, for the whole arena is legally complex.

There are also policy issues which will require attention by top managers, including central HRM staff. The handling of pay negotiations is a strategic issue, as is policy regarding union recognition and the search for alternative forms of employee reward and also representation.

Organization design and development

As technology and the product or service change, or indeed as markets change, there will be a need to review the structure of the organization to ensure that it is best suited to the changing environment. Since the late 1980s there has been much talk of flatter decentralized structures which are said to be more responsive to customer need and in any event may be necessary in the emerging multinational firm.

Changing structures is only one method of achieving organizational change and there are those who would argue that it is overused and badly handled, being seen as the answer to all managerial problems. Certainly the process of structural change will in itself not win the hearts and minds of the employees. Without a degree of employee commitment even the most judicious of planned structural change will have little chance of succeeding in its objectives. Structural change requires the planning involvement of those who will be affected.

As markets, technology and processes change, so the organization will need to change or develop. Organization development is an area requiring knowledge of the social sciences and the managerial skills to plan and implement the change process. Increasingly, the change found to be the most significant is in organization culture. Not infrequently the objective of the change process is the development of a more customer-aware culture, with all that that implies for the development of the reward system, employee empowerment and so on.

The change effort might be directed instead at reducing the degree of bureaucracy by freeing up decision-making processes to allow decisions to be taken by those most competent to take them: an operating state which many practising managers would say is seldom present. Such changes rest on the commitment of top management and the inclusion of knowledge-based and skilled specialists in the top team. As much as any of the other areas explored in this section, analysis and design constitute an area in which the human resource professional will be expected to contribute to the efficiency of the organization.

Support services

It is hoped that the reader will have gathered that human resource management is a cooperative, strategic and hard-headed activity staffed by managers committed to the financial success of the organization. The role of honest broker, adopted in the past by personnel managers anxious to see themselves as poised between management and worker, interpreting the one to the other, has long gone. So also has the image of the personnel officer as the good fairy, primarily protecting the interests of the non-managerial employee.

There are residual issues which do not fit neatly into any of the areas described above, but which none the less are important. Health and safety are issues that few firms can ignore. Quite rightly, there is a mounting level of legislation to protect the employee which the organization ignores at its peril. In addition, all companies ought to have a developed policy with regard to health and safety which goes beyond the legal minimum requirements and which will doubtless vary from country to country for multinational organizations.

Issues such as company policy regarding the provision of social amenities, health services and health promotion require thought and a coherent strategy. Much may depend on the area in which the firm operates, and there are good arguments for and against, for example, the provision of sports facilities. These need to be made and decisions taken as policy matters. Human resource professionals should see that this process takes place but they should encourage others to participate in it.

This last point stretches to other issues such as the provision of canteens and general administrative activities of this kind. There is no reason to think that the modern HR professional is likely to be any better than any other manager in handling these issues. Drucker (1961) argued many years ago that personnel staff were in danger of becoming the 'corporate trash-can'. This danger still remains.

CONCLUSION: THE NEW PRAGMATISM

The following chapters in this book will alert the reader to the strategic and functional roles of the human resource specialist as they apply to the major areas of people management.

There are two myths which are difficult to dispel and are a historical consequence of the function and the early pioneering but social work-oriented activities of the 'social secretaries' in the late nineteenth century.

The first myth is concerned with the view that there is some middle ground for the human resource specialist to inhabit comfortably. The specialist no longer has a role to interpret the needs of managers to the unions and of the unions to managers in the manner of an honest broker. HR professionals are paid by managers to represent them in the most cost-effective manner. Their interests are clearly managerial. The liberalism of the 1950s and 1960s has been replaced by a new profit-oriented pragmatism which will lead the organization to adopt those HR policies and behaviours which contribute most successfully to profitability.

Much if not all of what HR staff do can be costed reasonably accurately. There is no fundamental difficulty in operating HR services on a cost centre basis in which HR staff will need to sell their services to operating managers on the basis of cost and quality and to compete with outside providers. Training services are an obvious example: it might be more cost-effective to use external resources on demand rather than keep up an expensive and often underused training resource.

The second myth which still prevails is that human resource specialists are blessed with a capacity to understand, like and work with people. This also is far from accurate. All management involves the motivation of others, or else it is the work of the machine or process minder. The effective management of others is not something that can be left to a limited number of HR specialists. Only alongside operating managers can they implement policies and systems which provide a more productive environment in which employees feel sufficiently motivated to spend most of their waking hours.

The most important element of HR management is contained in the day-to-day working relationships of manager and employee, rather than in the exercise of charm by a limited number of specialists.

Modern human resource management, then, is pragmatic in its concern with value for money rather than being tied to an employee-centred philosophy. It is also strategic in its concern with the integration of human resource planning with corporate strategy.

It is appropriate now to apply this overall view of the human resource role to specific managerial issues. We shall start by taking a closer look at organizational design and development.

FURTHER READING

Sisson, K. (1989) *Personnel Management in Britain*, Oxford: Blackwell.
Storey, J. (1989) *New Perspectives on Human Resource Management*, London: Routledge.
Guest, D.E. (1987) 'Human Resource Management and Industrial Relations', *Journal of Management Studies*, 24, 5, September.
Torrington, D. (1988) 'How Does Human Resources Management Change the Personnel Function?', *Personnel Review*, 17, 6.

QUESTIONS FOR DISCUSSION

1 What in your view are the major factors which have led to the reappraisal of personnel management?
2 Are the developments in the personnel function implied in the change of title to human resource management any more than cosmetic?
3 What are the salient elements in organizational culture which are said to have given rise to recent developments in human resource management?

Chapter 2

Organization design and development

INTRODUCTION

Elsewhere in this book the authors argue that a major determinant of an individual's behaviour is the environment in which he or she works. The immediate work environment sets explicit and implicit standards which embrace the pattern and quality of relationships, the management style, patterns of leadership and the systems for rewarding people at work.

Some of these elements in the internal climate are a function of the organization's structure; others are the result of its value system, from which day-to-day behaviour stems. Accordingly, the design and development of organizations are important managerial concerns. Much depends on choices made by management, choices about what to do and how to do it. Although these important decisions will involve the commitment of top line managers, HRM specialists will rightly be looked to as a source of analysis, diagnosis and plans for change.

This chapter introduces the basic issues involved in organization design and examines the relationship between it and organization development.

KEY DESIGN ISSUES

The way in which the organization is structured or designed is a major determinant of behaviour. The design encourages some forms of behaviour whilst making others difficult. For example, the wider the span of control of a manager – a function of the design of the organization – the less possible is it to exercise close day-to-day control.

Crucial to organization design are two issues: firstly, the degree of centralization, and secondly, the overall dimension – tall and narrow or squat and wide.

Centralization

Centralization relates to the degree to which decision making is limited to the higher echelons of the organization. In centralized structures, there is little participation in decision making by employees. In decentralized companies, there is less emphasis on monitoring and checking and more on employee empowerment to make decisions. It is not easy to measure the degree of centralization in a numerically precise manner. It is, however, possible to collect data as to the variety and magnitude of decisions made by various levels of management, for example, and to compare one structure with another in this regard. In some companies few managers can make decisions of any magnitude, a centralized structure ensuring that significant decisions are made only by a few individuals at or near the top of the managerial ladder. One might reasonably assume then that the lower the level at which broadly similar decisions are made, the greater is the degree of decentralization.

It is also possible to use a financial indicator of centralization. Which levels of management have the authority to make financial decisions and what upper limits are set for the various levels of management?

Modern managerial thinkers tend to indicate that decentralized structures – perhaps involving internationalization and globalization – are likely to be more effective. There are, however, pros and cons. In some cases it might be better for a firm to introduce a greater degree of needed control through centralization, whilst in others the loosening of control systems might lead to greater flexibility of response by the organization, and thus to increased satisfaction and higher levels of employee motivation.

Decentralized organizations tend to lack integration and coordination. The result might be a degree of 'short termism' in which no group feels any particular responsibility to think strategically or in the longer run. Current problems tend to become the focus of activity whilst organization-wide issues receive less attention.

Because decentralization pushes down the organizational point at which decisions are made, there is sometimes the risk of a lack of central coordination. For instance, disputes might arise about the allocation of shared data-processing facilities. This conflict potential is exacerbated by the relative independence of the various operating units. Any disputes are less likely to be detected or averted, and are less likely to be well managed if the activities of the operating units are not coordinated.

On the other hand decentralization can enhance employee motivation and increase creativity levels. It increases the chances of involvement in decision-making processes which, as has been argued elsewhere in this book (p. 115), is a major element in achieving employee commitment. It is argued that increased commitment will lead to more productive attitudes to work and hence to improved performance.

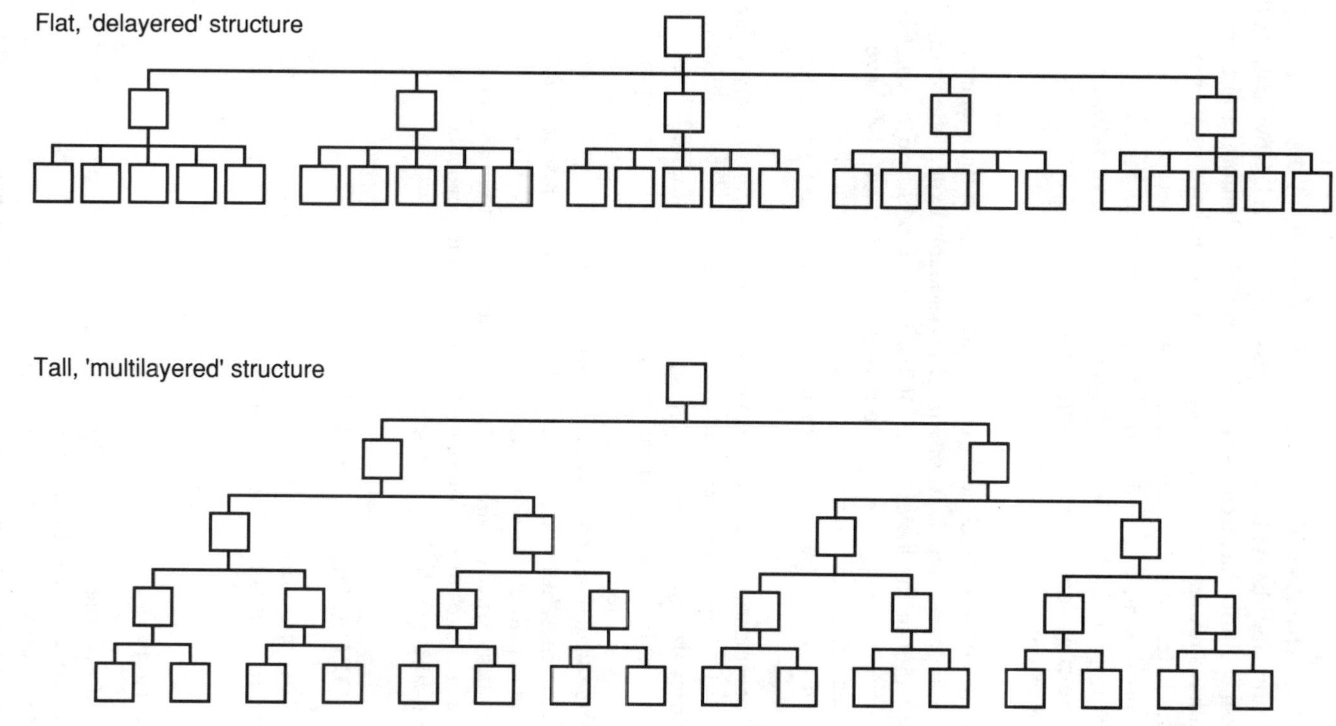

Figure 2.1 Tall and flat organization structure

Height and width

These two related characteristics of an organization refer to the number of levels of authority and the width or broadness of each level. Obviously, tall organizations have more hierarchical levels from top to bottom; and flatter organizations have fewer. The former organizations will have smaller spans of control; the latter, larger. Figure 2.1 illustrates the difference.

Span of control is an important concept and refers to the number of people reporting to a single manager. Previous writers have attempted to argue that there is an ideal span of control which varies between five and seven. See for example Fayol (1949).

It is now considered unrealistic to attempt to give a precise number for the ideal span of control. Much will depend on the level in the hierarchy at which the span appears. Generally, one might reasonably expect the span of control to be larger in the lower levels of the system, whilst in the higher reaches the reverse will be true. The technology in use will also have an impact on span. Routine machine-controlled operations allow a much greater span of control by a supervisor than is the case for 'one-off' production systems.

The taller organization with its narrower spans of control allows for closer control of subordinates and therefore discourages decentralization, whilst flatter organizations are more predisposed to decentralized decision-making processes. In so far as decentralization is said to have positive advantages and is at the root of many attempts to improve performance at work, the flatter structure is looked upon with favour.

Carried to extremes, however, the flat organization can present problems. When the many report to the few, there is a danger of loss of control and/ or an increase in the stress levels of those at the top of the hierarchy. It is important then to take into account the factors in any particular situation before coming to a conclusion.

CURRENT ORGANIZATION DESIGNS

By far the most common organization designs in use today are the 'functional', 'divisional' and what is often referred to as a 'hybrid' version of the two.

Functional structure

Employees and activities are grouped according to what they do: that is, their function. In this structure, coordination between the efforts of the various quasi-independent functions takes place at the top. It is argued that this structure is most effective when there is a need for collaboration in the organization and when there is a need for expertise in a defined set of

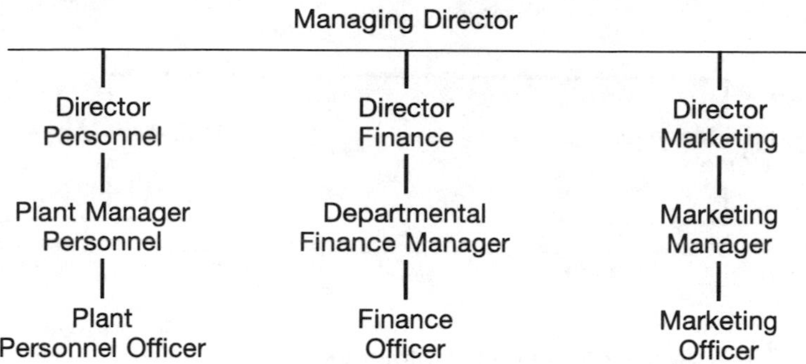

Figure 2.2 The functional organization structure

operations. It is often also felt that this structure is best suited to a stable operating environment and when the activities of the functions are relatively few in number.

The drawback of the functional structure is its slowness to change. The operating units or functions take a departmental rather than an organizational perspective and tend to react rather than be proactive in predicting the need to adjust to the external environment. The functional structure is not creative and tends to lack flexibility. There is a difficulty in coordinating activities across the boundaries of units or departments. It is difficult to measure the contribution of each unit, since the end product is an amalgam of the efforts of a number of discrete departments.

The control of this structure is exercised from the top, usually by a senior management group drawn from the operating functions. Since these people have worked their way up one or other of the functions, they are not necessarily in a position to think corporately, but choose rather to continue to represent their own function and fight hard for its interests in matters such as budget allocation. In any case they will not have the experience or knowledge to think corporately. The Chair of this group may well suffer from similar constraints.

Divisional or product structure

This organizational form groups employees and activities according to product or output. Each product line or division is provided with its own resources such as personnel, marketing and production facilities.

It will be readily appreciated that the coordination in this model takes place within divisions rather than between them. The necessary main line and support functions are dedicated to the activities of the various sectors rather than provided centrally or, as in Figure 2.2, by specialist functions in their own right.

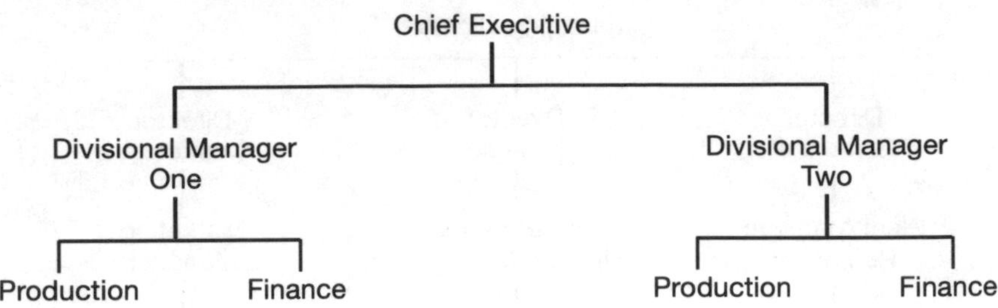

Figure 2.3 The divisional organization structure

The advantages of this structural form are that the various activities of the organization are responsive to the needs of the producing units. This enables a more efficient production process as far as each division is concerned and allows a more ready response to the recognition and satisfaction of the changing needs of the customer. Where consumer responsiveness is a critical element in survival, the divisional structure has much to commend it.

Where too the organization operates in a rapidly changing environment and needs to adapt to change readily, the divisional structure is said to be appropriate. Similarly where the organization produces many diverse products or services a greater degree of central control would be dysfunctional.

The disadvantage of the divisional form is that economy of scale is sacrificed to organizational responsiveness. In most cases, it would be more economical to provide many services centrally or to have the same organizational activity carried out by one unit, thus avoiding duplication. For example, it would be cheaper to have a personnel function providing services for all the divisions rather than have each division maintain its own.

This leads to another problem with this structural form. Cohesion between the divisions is much more difficult to maintain. Different policies will emerge in the different units leading to potential conflict and dissatisfaction. Sharing of needed competencies on an organization-wide basis is unlikely to occur in a structure which broadly speaking is a federation of quasi-independent empires. Technological advance will not be shared company-wide, and indeed energy may be spent on preventing the spread of information in an attempt to win power in the organization as a whole. Figure 2.3 is an example of a divisional structure.

Hybrid (or mixed) organization structure

As a consequence of the difficulties with the pure forms of the two types of structure outlined above, few companies remain true to either one or the

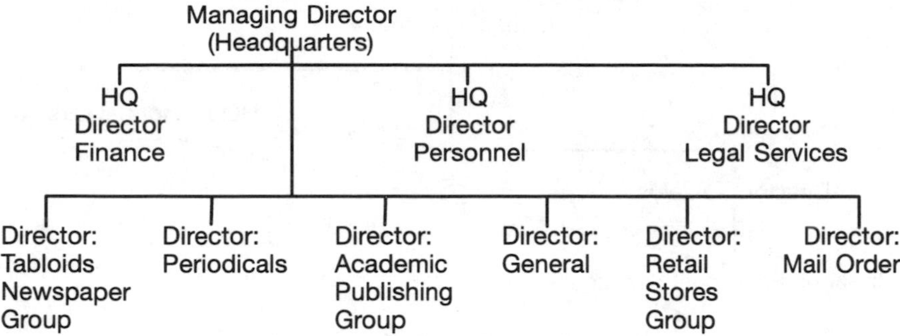

Figure 2.4 A mixed organization structure

other. Many firms combine the advantages of each. Indeed the hybrid structure is almost certainly the most prevalent.

Some activities may be highly specialized and located at the headquarters of the organization. These might include Human Resource Management, Finance, and Strategic Planning amongst other service functions. At the same time, there might be other more self-contained operating units working elsewhere more or less independently. This balance might provide the best of both worlds. Hybrids provide the product or divisional groups with the functional support they need *within the group*. At the same time economies of scale can be achieved by *central provision* of common services. Obviously there will be greater opportunity for central control in the hybrid as opposed to the divisional structure. This is clear in Figure 2.4.

No structure is without its difficulties. The mixed structure raises problems of dual reporting and the ambiguities which follow from them. For example, a personnel officer employed by the director of the periodicals division of the newspaper group may find that he or she has two masters: the director of the division and the HQ director of personnel. This duality is sometimes referred to as a 'line and staff ' reporting relationship. Whilst it will normally be the director of the newspaper group who will appoint the personnel officer, it is common for relevant HQ staff to lay down generalized conditions of employment, and in this case to provide the operating divisions with centrally generated policy statements covering most processes relevant to all the divisions.

Problems arise when, for example, a group director decides that a formal appraisal system will not be adopted although the central personnel people have encouraged the main board to accept it company-wide and expect local personnel staff to encourage its introduction.

Political skill and words in the right quarters can usually resolve these problems, but it is as well to note them as a fact of life in the hybrid organization. Figure 2.5 illustrates the dual reporting relationship.

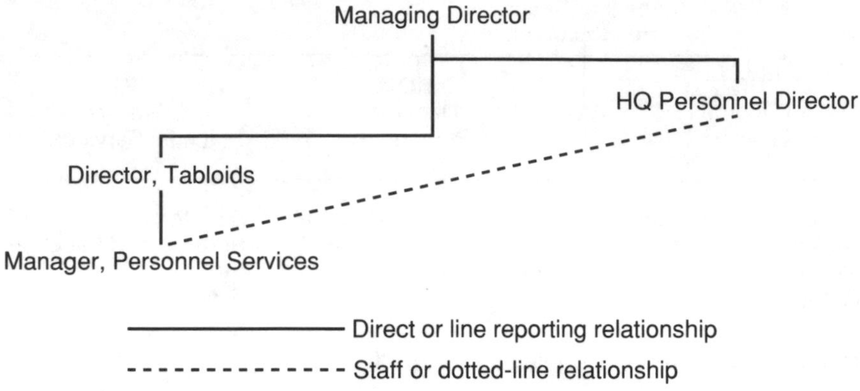

Figure 2.5 Line and staff reporting relationships

The matrix structure

When there is a need for continuous interchange between two or more functions a matrix structure will be useful. These are normally superimposed on top of one of the structural types already referred to in this chapter; so they should not be seen as an alternative but rather as a useful addition. What we have reviewed to date have been forms of pyramid structure. The matrix structure by its very nature is something different.

There are times in an organization's life when innovation is prevalent. Start-up situations for example come to mind; or occasions when novel problems arise and there is a strong need for creativity in unknown territory. The matrix design allows an employee, usually a manager, to report to two or more supervisors in one or more temporary groups drawn from different functions. Selection into such a group assumes that the manager has a significant though perhaps temporary role to play. By this means a form of decentralized coordination is achieved. It is thought to be particularly appropriate when project teams are needed.

If, for example, a product development team reports to both production and R. & D., it is likely that both production and research considerations can be entertained simultaneously, thus saving time, easing communication problems, gaining commitment and stimulating creative managerial behaviour.

In practice these structures not only have limited applicability, being placed alongside one or other of the traditional pyramid structures, but they are also not without their own problems. There is a lack of clarity in reporting relationships, caused by the duality of reporting inevitably involved – both to the manager of the project group and to the manager of the permanent group.

It is also frequently observed that the members of the temporary matrix

Project Group Membership	Production	Functions Marketing	Finance	R. & D.
Product A	√		√	√
Product B	√	√		
Product C	√		√	√
Product D		√	√	

Figure 2.6 A matrix structure

group are not always problem-based in their personal behaviour. They bring with them to the new group a set of values and loyalties derived from their permanent group. Accordingly, matrix groups can induce conflict and protectionist behaviour. Figure 2.6 indicates the nature of a matrix structure.

Structural change in perspective

Whether changes in the design of any organization work or not depends on the motives of the organizational members and their shared culture. History and tradition, politics, commitment and rewards are all important and can hinder or facilitate the introduction of a new structure (Child 1984).

Frequently structural change is seen as a panacea for organizational ills, almost on the principle that, all else having failed, a significant organizational shake-up should stimulate members. We have seen in this chapter that there is no one 'right' structure. It is essential that a thorough analysis of the organization is undertaken before decisions are made as to its size and shape.

It is also essential that employees are involved in the planning processes and have an understanding of the reasons for change. Without this commitment and involvement change is apt to follow change without the desired improvements in efficiency being achieved but with an increasing sense of alienation amongst employees (Bowey and Thorpe 1986).

Getting change in organizations

Attending to the structure of the organization – organization design or redesign – is one method of bringing about change. As we have observed, however, design responses to organizational problems are not always relevant. Altering structures and work flows will not in itself prove an adequate response to financial underfunding, poor-quality management, or technological obsolescence.

McGivering (1987) and others have used the term 'organization development' to describe the process of reducing the level of bureaucracy in an organization. As long ago as 1969, Beckhard spelt out the criteria against which it is possible to assess the health of a work organization. They constitute an admirable summary of the effective organization. The reader may find it interesting to contrast the characteristics of the mature rational problem-solving organization (■) with the bureaucracy (#).

■ The total organization and those who work in it operate within agreed goals and plans to achieve them.

Individual duties and responsibilities are defined in detail. These definitions are developed by the various functional groupings often using professional judgement rather than corporate planning processes.

■ 'Form follows function.' The task determines how human resources are used.

The organization has a relatively inflexible and well-defined structure and organizational goals are generated, accepted or rejected according to the extent to which they are compatible with that structure. That is, 'Function follows form.'

■ Decisions are made at or near the sources of information, wherever they are located.

There is a tendency for decisions to be made by those with authority rather than knowledge. Since the decision makers tend to be those with the longest service, and the furthest removed from the 'front line', the decision making is not always of the highest quality.

■ Managers are rewarded not only for short-term profitability, but also for fostering the growth and development of subordinate managers and for creating viable working groups.

Managers are rewarded for decision making which adheres to regulations and precedent and which is both observable and measurable. This tends to encourage short-term behaviour.

■ Communication systems are good, both laterally and vertically, encouraging openness and confrontation in working relationships.

Communications systems are poor laterally since there are many artificially erected boundaries between functions. Vertical communication is much more effective in a downward than an upward direction.

■ Minimum effort is spent on win/lose behaviour between individuals and groups. Conflict is subject to problem-solving techniques, both within and between groups.

Conflict is endemic and is handled by well-defined procedures which

depersonalize it. Compromise is often the outcome of what is in effect a 'conflict-averse' organizational posture.

- The organization takes a system view in the planning of change. It bases efforts to change on an understanding that the various parts of an organization interact, affect and reflect upon each other, also that the organization as a whole is affected by the external environment in which it operates.
- The organization operates on the basis of the interaction between quasi-independent fiefdoms loosely and precariously held together by a top coordinating body. Since this body consists of factional leaders, there is a built-in incapacity to think at an organization-wide level and a predisposition to fight for as large a share of power as can be won.

TECHNIQUES OF ORGANIZATION DEVELOPMENT

Before attempting to introduce change, the practitioner will ensure that a diagnostic process has been undertaken which allows for the drawing of conclusions as to what element in the working of the system requires change, what energy and commitment there are to introduce change and who is to take responsibility for the process. If the analysis, diagnosis and administration of change are half-hearted it may be assumed that the change effort will be at best irrelevant and at worst catastrophic. Many organizational development (OD) efforts have been one or the other, and in some cases have contrived to be both.

It is often wise to enlist the services of independent consultants who may have a stronger power base than anyone in the human resource department. It is normally the case that for political reasons insiders are inappropriate change agents. This is not to deny, however, that any change programme likely to succeed must be owned by top management and be seen to have its continued and practical support.

The techniques of OD can be usefully categorized as fitting into one of five levels of activity. It is important that the reader remembers that all OD activity is designed to improve organization competence.

Level one: personal skills

At this basic level, OD looks little different from management development. If, however, there is a coherent strategy for the general development of managerial skill based on some form of needs analysis, and assuming a degree of success, the result must be the development of the organization as a whole.

Individual counselling and appraisal are examples of OD interventions at the personal level. Specific development experiences following on appraisal, such as training course provision or planned job experience, also serve as examples. The important point to remember is that they constitute OD activities only in so far as they are an element in a planned effort leading to the improvement of organizational performance.

Level two: interpersonal relationships

It is a sociological truism that much conflict which exists in organizations is a result of role conflict rather than of personality differences. It is often possible therefore to reduce interpersonal conflict levels by a rational process, often involving a third party, or by redefining roles and job descriptions. This may lead to a reduction of the likelihood of incompatible goals and role ambiguities.

Level three: team development

This constitutes the major OD activity. It is sometimes said that the basic building block of organizations is not the individual but the work group. Increasingly managers and others work as members of small groups. It is therefore important that these groups work effectively and exploit the resources of all the members.

Typically the OD consultant will collect data individually from the group members as to how they feel the group is managed, how they personally perform in the group and what needs to be done to make the group more effective. These data are shared with all the members including, importantly, the group leader. Once difficulties have been explored, it should be possible to draw up a list of changes which need to be made to make the group more effective.

Normally all the information necessary to make appropriate changes resides in the group. The facilitator's role is one of legitimizing the activities of the group members in looking at the operating processes and ensuring that change does in fact take place. It is important to review progress on a regular basis to prevent backsliding. Figure 2.7 provides an example of the type of instrument often used to collect data regarding individual members' attitudes to the team.

Level four: intergroup relations

One of the unintended consequences of team development is that it can lead to the worsening of intergroup relationships. As the individual groups become stronger, they develop an exclusive identity which makes cooperation across departmental boundaries more difficult.

It is possible also to reduce the level of conflict by confronting the stereotypes on which this intergroup alienation is normally based. Conflict between groups is caused by their being physically separated. This

MEASURING THE GROWTH OF A GROUP

To help you to measure the development of this group, a number of dimensions have been listed below. The group can assess itself by its members generating these data – as individuals – and sharing the data for examination, to help to understand the growth and development process.

A MATURE GROUP POSSESSES:

1. Adequate mechanisms for getting feedback:

Poor feedback mechanisms	0.......1.......2.......3.......4.......5	Excellent feedback mechanisms

2. Adequate decision making procedure:

Poor decision making	0.......1.......2.......3.......4.......5	Very adequate decision making procedure

3. Optimal cohesion:

Low cohesion	0.......1.......2.......3.......4.......5	Optimal cohesion

4. Flexible organization and procedures:

Very inflexible	0.......1.......2.......3.......4.......5	Very flexible

5. Maximum use of member resources:

Poor use of resources	0.......1.......2.......3.......4.......5	Excellent use of resources

6. Clear communications:

Poor communication	0.......1.......2.......3.......4.......5	Excellent communication

7. Clear goals accepted by members:

Unclear goals – not accepted	0.......1.......2.......3.......4.......5	Very clear goals – accepted

8. Feelings of interdependence with authority persons:

No inter-dependence	0.......1.......2.......3.......4.......5	High interdependence

9. Shared participation in leadership functions:

No shared participation	0.......1.......2.......3.......4.......5	High shared participation

10. Acceptance of minority views and persons:

No acceptance	0.......1.......2.......3.......4.......5	High acceptance

Figure 2.7 A group process questionnaire

invariably leads to the generation of negative stereotypes. Where a degree of intergroup interaction is called for, these problems can be overcome by the setting up of multifunctional work groups or reduced dramatically by consultant-led intergroup confrontations in which the two or more alienated groups hammer out a more acceptable method of working together and in the process come to realize that members of rival groups are not markedly less able or effective than themselves.

Level five: systems and structures

Frequently there are design or structural reasons for the existence of more than normal degrees of intergroup conflict. Readers are referred to the earlier sections of this chapter.

The most complex level of OD is that which looks at the organization as a whole and collects data as to the overall pattern of internal relationships and gauges their effectiveness in the achievement of organizational goals. (It may be of course that the quality or indeed the absence of such realistic goals is a major problem in itself. Here the writer wishes to distinguish between the pious platitudes of mission statements – long on generalities and short on detail and strategic planning, geared to action, to which there are reasonable levels of commitment at all levels. It is depressing to witness the frequent confusion between the two.)

This most complex level of OD is also concerned with the interaction of the organization and its external environment. Now more than ever it is important for survival that the work organization develops an effective intelligence system which will allow it to gather up-to-date information about competitors, technological development and social change, so that it can introduce change before it is forced to do so – often too late.

Defined and attainable goals, appropriate internal structures, relevant reward systems and appropriate personal development systems need to be assessed in relation to each other and in terms of the corporate strategy if the competitive edge is to be attained and maintained.

This is not the place to go into detail about any one method of OD. The reader is referred to the recommended sources at the end of the chapter. It is well to conclude this brief overview with a consideration of the role of the internal human resource professional.

There are occasions when internal staff can be used as resources. There are also occasions when HR professionals can act indirectly through the process of introducing change via top line management. This ensures that change will take place and not simply be ignored.

On other occasions especially when sensitive political issues are involved, it will be more effective to use the services of external consultants. They normally have the power that comes from being outside 'experts' and they more easily obtain the ear of crucial decison makers from within. This does not mean that the HR professional has no role to play. The professionals' behavioural science knowledge, their capacity to take an organization-wide view and hopefully their access to top management will enable them to play a vital part in introducing and controlling the direction of change.

What is clear is that these professionals cannot achieve significantly by simply using their own position. They will need to earn the support of senior line managers through whom change will need to be introduced.

CONCLUSION

Organization design and development are increasingly seen as important weapons in the battle to maintain the competitive edge. Change has fundamental implications for 'the way people in the organization line up to get work done' (in the words of Sir John Harvey Jones who thus defines organization structure).

In the internal battle for survival, human resource professionals will need to demonstrate competence in the design and development area if they are to be seen as a relevant managerial group. It is an area above all which HR professionals can legitimately call their own since it rests so heavily on the application of the behavioural sciences.

It is as well to conclude this chapter with the warning that whether change 'sticks' and has the desired effect or not will depend almost totally on the goodwill of those who are expected to accept it. Unless their involvement in the planning of change is achieved, the necessary cooperation is unlikely to be forthcoming.

FURTHER READING

Beckhard, R. (1969) *Organization Development: Strategies and Models*, Reading, Mass.: Addison-Wesley.

Butler, R. (1991) *Designing Organizations*, London: Routledge.

French, W. and Bell, C. (1978) *Organization Development: Behavioural Science Interventions for Organization Improvement*, New Jersey: Prentice-Hall.

QUESTIONS FOR DISCUSSION

1 Outline the differences between functional, divisional and hybrid organization structures.
2 Why do attempts at organization design so often fail?
3 What do you consider to be the main advantages and disadvantages of a bureaucratic organization?

Chapter 3

Human resource planning

INTRODUCTION

In this chapter we shall look at one of the most important functions of the human resource department, planning (HRP). No organization can expect to work at anything like optimum efficiency without information as to how it uses human resources.

How these uses will need to adapt to ensure that a company's most expensive resource continues to contribute to organizational goals is equally important. Thus HRP both sets the agenda for human resource management and at the same time produces the criteria against which HRM will be judged.

THE PURPOSE OF HUMAN RESOURCE PLANNING

HRP used to be referred to as manpower planning. Currently this title is in decline for two reasons, firstly because of the offence caused to some by the gratuitous assumption that organizations are staffed only by males and secondly because it was felt that the traditional planning processes were often really nothing other than number-crunching activities far removed from the strategic planning activities now seen as more appropriate. For the purposes of this chapter, however, and following Lockwood (1986), the reader should take the two titles of manpower and human resource planning as broadly covering the same area.

It is important that the reader appreciates from the start that there is more to HRP than simply a process of continuous head counts, leading to periodic redundancy and recruitment programmes. We shall take the view here that HRP is an essential and highly sophisticated activity controlled by top management but involving all line and staff managers, not least the human resource professionals. The latter have a highly significant input to make which requires a broad understanding of organizational design and development and a capacity to understand corporate and strategic planning.

Human resource costs are the most significant item in the financial outgoings of most work organizations, whether they are labour-intensive or not. We argue in Chapter 5 that the improvement in the use of human resources is the last remaining and therefore the most significant area in which organizations can gain or regain the competitive advantage. Readers will no doubt be aware of the extent to which firms are currently proposing to shed labour in order to retain this competitive edge. At the time of writing, British Telecom and British Gas come to mind as two companies which plan to shed a significant proportion of their labour force.

It is clear that this process involves more than just the basic task of organizing what are sometimes euphemistically called 'separations' in such a way as to achieve the objective with the minimum of conflict. Many companies have done this only to find within six months that they needed to undertake a recruitment programme to take advantage of improved trading conditions. Both separation and recruitment activities are costly, to say nothing of the impact on morale produced by the coming and going of personnel. There are also training cost implications – both direct and indirect – associated with the throughput of labour.

Others have argued that lost opportunities have been the result of not having the appropriate labour mix at a given time. It is important to remember that HRP is not just about numbers but also about quality and fitness for purpose of the labour force – both managerial and non-managerial. An undersupply may have as grievous a consequence as an oversupply. More commonly, especially in the high-technology sector, specific and crucial niches of undersupply can be catastrophic.

It is therefore important to remember that human resource planning is the activity which ensures that the right number of people of the right kind are in the right place at the right time. It is about quality as well as quantity.

THE PLACE OF HUMAN RESOURCE PLANNING

It is only possible to look meaningfully at HRP in terms of the general planning processes of the work organization. HRP cannot stand alone; neither should it be seen as the sole domain of the human resource department (Craft 1988).

Every organization must engage in some form of corporate or strategic planning. It is fashionable to argue that this is difficult when many changes can occur especially in the environment external to the organization, making planning for more than a few months something of a lottery. Rapid currency changes, changes in the nature of the competition through technological development, to say nothing of political upheavals on an international scale, serve as suitable examples.

Even so, although plans may need to be changed, it is safer to have some plans rather than none. In any case it is unlikely that all the planning activity will have been wasted as a result of any particular internal or external upheaval.

At the very least then we might expect the work organization to have asked itself three major questions:

- What is our function? Why are we here?
- What objectives follow from this?
- Who is going to do what, when and where, so that these objectives can be achieved?

In order for the second and third of these questions to be answered top management will require information from the human resource department. There is little point in developing a strategic plan which has no chance of being acted upon simply because the people with the appropriate skills will not be available.

Similarly, there is little point in preparing for globalization unless the consequent need for restructuring has been thought through and can be implemented in time for overseas units to be staffed and appropriate control mechanisms devised, tested and implemented.

This means that the HR specialists have a crucial role in putting information into the corporate and strategic planning processes. They should know, using dedicated computerized systems, whether enough people with the appropriate skills and experience will be available to start up a new plant; they should know what the age profile of certain groups of employee will be in five years' time, so that top management will be able to assess the feasibility of their proposed plans. They should be able to advise top management as to whether the current organization structure is appropriate for the planned changes. In other words, using their specialized knowledge they should be able to tell top management what is feasible or what needs to be done with regard to human resources in order for their plans to be effectively applied. It should be borne in mind that few if any other groups below the level of top management will have the resources to develop the necessary overview of the organization.

Thus it is important to note that the HR planning process starts with input into the corporate plan. Once the strategic plan with its budget implications has followed from the corporate plan, the HR specialists can begin work on the HR plan itself.

The above paragraph may raise a few eyebrows amongst the accountants. But it is by no means clear that finance-led change programmes have been universally successful; failure is usually because of blissful ignorance of the human resource implications of what has been proposed. The reader may find the discussion on change in Chapter 2 of relevance here.

Figure 3.1 outlines the stages of human resource planning. It shows that the next stage in the process is analytical. The level of demand for the

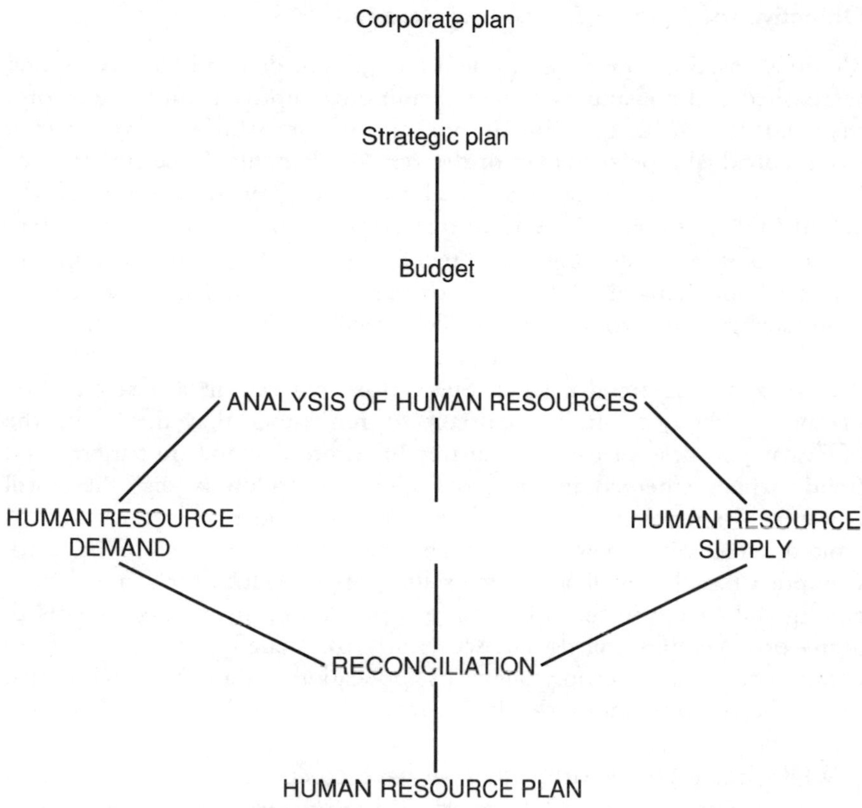

Figure 3.1 The stages of human resource planning

various kinds of labour can now be established. This demand forecasting is not as easy as it might at first appear.

DEMAND FORECASTING

It is important that estimates of labour at all levels take into account any changes in operating procedures which will have an impact on the number and type of personnel required. The positioning of these people will also be an important consideration. At this point it is better if supply considerations are left to one side. The objective of the demand forecast is to produce a detailed description of the people required, with the greatest possible detail as to when, where, with what characteristics and at what cost.

Objective methods of forecasting demand

Methods based on *work study* to define employee demand have been long established and constitute the most traditional approach to demand forecasting. It is possible to define the amount of work which can be expected from individual representatives of the various elements in the labour force by a process of applying established formulas. The dimensions of the labour force can then be described numerically and categorized into types.

Statistical methods fall roughly into two categories: those which extrapolate future labour demand on the basis of past demand and those which use more sophisticated computer modelling facilities. The former historically based systems of forecasting depend on techniques such as regression analysis and ratio trend analysis. Space does not permit a detailed study of these techniques. It is important to remember that they have the potential weakness of basing estimates of future demand on patterns and trends which emerged in the past. The assumption is that these will continue. Extrapolation on the basis of past evidence is obviously of limited value when new activities and new equipment are to be used. Computer-based modelling offers exciting opportunities for demand forecasting and except in the larger, more sophisticated firms it is underused. Many organizations still do not see clearly the benefits that accrue from computerization, preferring to limit its application to those tasks which had earlier been done more slowly by manual or mechanical rather than electronic processes.

Whilst many HR departments now have computerized record systems which can interact with other systems in the organization such as payroll, few see the potential for developing answers to the great 'What if?' questions. It is possible at great speed to discover links between factors in the productive process which had never been thought of and which could have a profound effect on demand forecasting. In the industrial relations area, for example, it is possible to discover what the financial consequences of various proposed settlements might be. This information might be useful in union discussions before the implementation of human resource plans. Is it for example always the case that an increase in production leads to a parallel increase in the labour force? If not, where does the divergence start? Where are the increases in labour and at what relative cost? It might thus be possible to calculate the optimum labour size to achieve the corporate plan.

Subjective methods of forecasting demand

Commonly used are methods of identifying demand based on *managerial judgement*: 'If this is what we have to do, this is what we will need.' It is possible to take a top–down approach or a bottom–up one – beginning the data collection process with top departmental managers and working down to supervisor level or commencing with the supervisors. Essentially the process is the same: one of adding together the separate demands for the various numbers and types of labour into a departmental and later an organizational total. Stainer (1971) notes that although statistical techniques simplify the problem of demand forecasting, they do not replace altogether the need for subjective judgement.

SUPPLY FORECASTING

Equally important is the process of estimating supply from both inside and outside the company. It is obvious that the internal supply of labour does not remain constant. All labour forces have their own peculiar characteristics – age distribution for example, or qualification and skill distribution. As time passes these organizational characteristics change. It is therefore important that the organization knows accurately what the current make-up of the labour force is – managerial, technical, clerical and blue collar. Equally important are the demographic characteristics of the labour force – such as the ratio of males to females, ethnic distribution and so on. Although this kind of information will be necessary for legal purposes, it is apparent that it also has a bearing on future internal and external recruitment policies – especially if the organization is planning expansion in new geographical areas at home or abroad.

No organization exists in a vacuum. There is an interdependent relationship between the firm and the wider social environment in which it operates. This will for instance be reflected in the type and quantity of labour available. So it will be important for the HRM specialist to gain a good picture of the exact nature of the available labour force before any decision to open up a new plant in another part of the country or abroad. Will there be enough labour available with the right skills and at the right time? Will the labour force be prepared to work at the rates of pay which are organizationally acceptable? Will there be an unacceptable level of trade union activity? Are there sufficient housing and educational facilities to cope with the proposed influx of labour into a new area? Will the educational facilities be able to produce sufficient people with the right skills to form a viable pool of labour? Will the area be able to sustain the demands of the new labour force for recreational facilities? All these issues and others must be carefully thought through at an early planning stage, before the finalization of the strategic plan, since it will be too late to raise these issues at the human resource planning stage. Assuming that the answers to the questions are positive, then it should be possible to forecast what the external supply will be and if necessary to consider what steps might be taken to strengthen it by movement of numbers of current employees from one plant to another.

Internal supply forecasting

There are a number of basic statistics which are essential to the HR planning process. Bell (1974) provides a thorough review of the area. The simplest information to collect is a statement as to the total numbers of employees classified by age, length of service, experience and training. Such head counts are simple to execute and indispensable. If done regularly, they will reveal supply-side problems whilst there is still time to solve them. The specialized literature is replete with examples of even the largest firms failing to realize that in the very short term there will be an acute scarcity of a certain type of employee. Equally, others have discovered for example that overwhelmingly large numbers of employees will have retired long before their successors can be trained. Obviously, the categorization will vary according to the needs of the company and with the help of computerized record systems there should be little difficulty in 'pulling out' the required information.

Important to the assessment of supply is the reasonably accurate estimate of employee turnover. The following separation index is useful:

$$\frac{\text{Numbers of employees leaving during the year}}{\text{Average numbers employed during the year}} \times 100$$

As it stands, this formula is not as useful as one might wish. It tells us nothing about the type or grade of employee who is leaving, nor does it tell us how many of the departures were voluntary. It is silent as to the length of service of the leavers. Accordingly it is useful also to calculate an employee stability index:

$$\frac{\text{Numbers of leavers with more than one year's service}}{\text{Number employed one year ago}} \times 100$$

This index enables us to calculate the number of new recruits who leave as opposed to those with longer service. It does not, however, classify the leavers by department and the limitation of one year is rather constraining. If, however, such data were kept over a number of years it would be possible to compare these rates over varying time periods, thus observing wastage trends.

It is obvious from what has been said that these two basic indices can be manipulated and targeted to provide more specific data as to where and to what extent the wastage problems are occurring.

Cohort analysis addresses many of the deficiencies of the methods already mentioned, by analysing the patterns of employee turnover for homogeneous groups of employees, which can be plotted in the same way as a percentage against specified periods of time (see Figure 3.2).

In order to obtain a general picture of survival in the organization the data in Figure 3.2 might be expressed graphically (see Figure 3.3).

Employee Type	*less than 1 year*	*1 to 2 years*	*2 to 4 years*	*4 to 7 years*	*Over 7 years*
Unskilled					
Skilled					
Clerical					
Supervisory					
Managerial					

Figure 3.2 Types of leaver by length of service (cohort analysis)

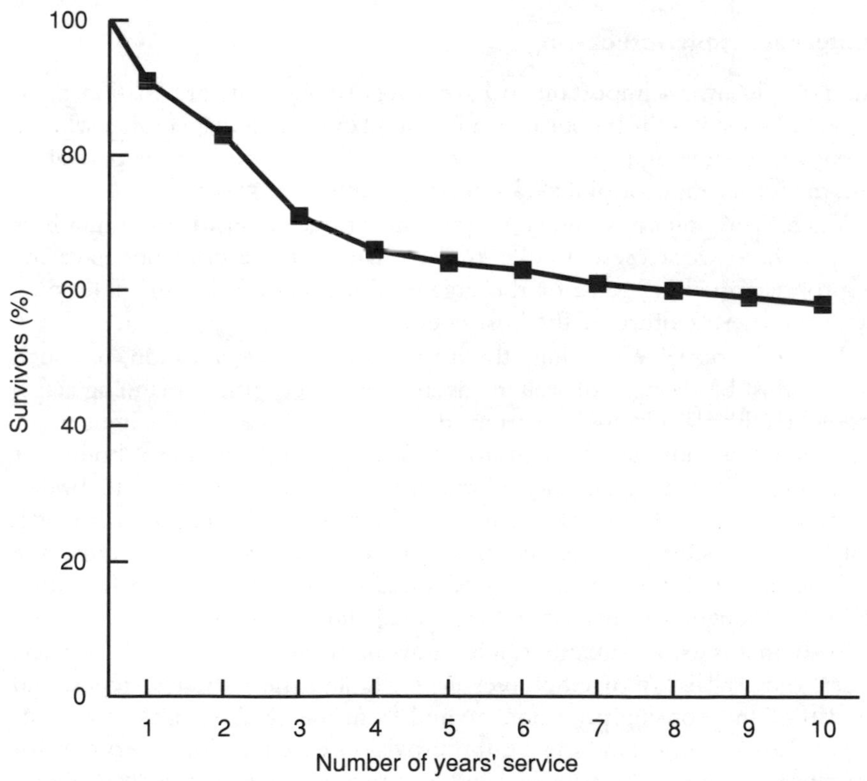

Figure 3.3 Survival rate

Before this section is ended, mention should be made of the need to keep control of the flow as well as the stock of employees. Hitherto we have concentrated on the latter. Readers will be aware of the existence of blockages and shortages in the supply of employees. Perhaps too many people are at the top of their pay scale and whilst experienced enough to gain promotion there is a shortage of suitable vacancies. In other cases the reverse might be true with a more or less chronic shortage of certain types of employee. It would obviously be more efficient if these peaks and troughs in the flow of employees could be better recognized and identified, thus making control through perhaps systematic training or the changing of the number of payment grades and so on more easily achieved. This flow of labour up the hierarchy of the organization is referred to as a Markov Chain, an example of which appears below. A Markov Chain enables management to analyse promotion patterns by looking at past promotion trends. The analysis provides a guide as to the probability of staff moving from one grade to another over any given period of time.

External supply forecasting

Whilst it is always important to have a regular flow of information as to what is happening in the local area of the plant, it is indispensable when a company is thinking of setting up a plant or division, perhaps as part of an internationalization or globalization programme.

There is no point in setting up new plant if there are insufficient numbers of people to work there, or the available labour force does not have the appropriate qualifications, or the organizational culture is out of keeping with the social culture of the host country.

It may be possible to adjust the demands of the organization, but such issues must be thought of well in advance, at the corporate planning stage, not when the plant is due to start production. If for example the indigenous population is not accustomed to working 'normal' western hours, or receiving payment by cheque, or working solidly from Monday to Friday, there are likely to be problems. It might be possible to relocate staff or it might be possible for the managers in the host country to adjust the organizational culture to fit the local social culture. It might on the other hand be thought an unsuitable place to expand operations.

Even in less exotic situations, it is always important to find out local wage rates, the availability of employees generally and the particular types, and transport and housing provisions to and from the likely centres of recruitment. Just as important will be the provision of educational services for employees who may be relocated and for potential sources of skilled labour. Finally, it is worth evaluating the industrial relations climate. A firm with a

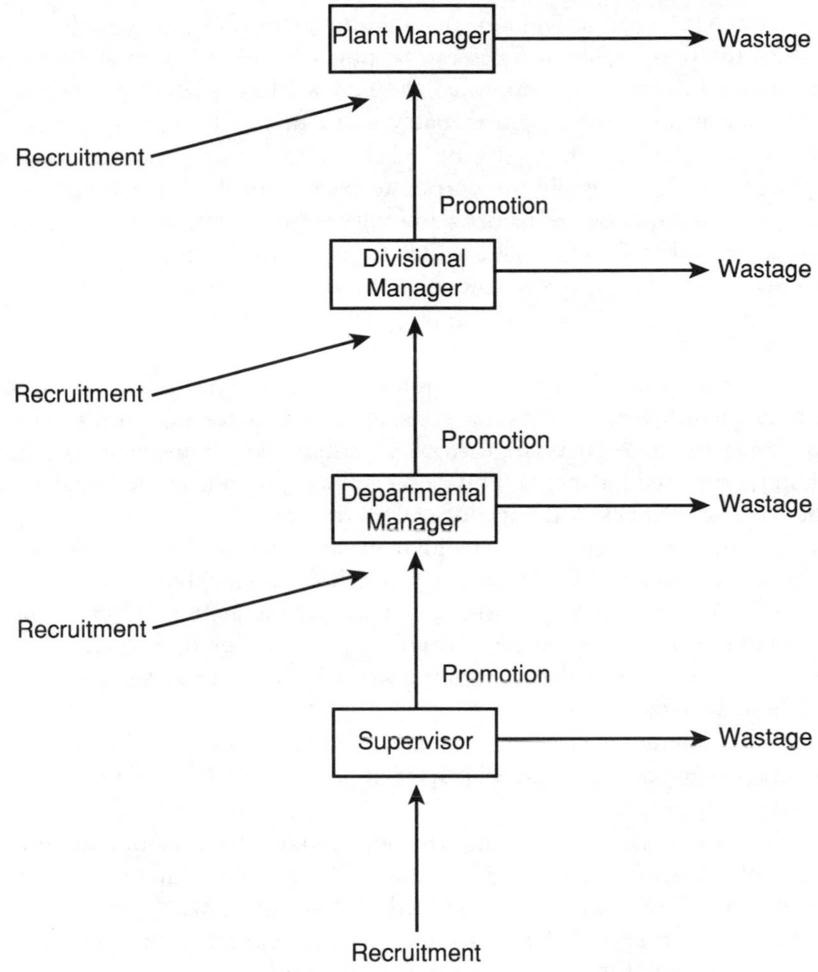

Figure 3.4 A Markov chain

paternalist tradition will wish to avoid a geographical area with a history of robust union–management relationships.

RECONCILIATION

The next stage in the human resource planning activity is to reconcile demand and supply, and identify and adjust any potential shortfalls in the one or the other.

If the supply of labour of any type is less than the demand, then a number of steps are open to the organization. By training and other forms of development it can provide for the identified shortfall, changing the uses to which the present labour force can be put. It is unlikely that all levels of employee will be in short supply, so the new shortages produced through the training programme may reasonably easily be filled.

A further step which might be taken is to reduce the number of employees needed to make the corporate plan work. It might be possible to combine certain operations or even to abandon others without affecting the objectives. Finally, when all else has failed, it will be time to review the objectives and alter the strategic plan in order to meet the corporate objectives.

If it seems that supply will outstrip demand as a result of implementing the corporate plan, then the amount of overmanning will have to be carefully identified and methods considered for reducing staff in these areas. Such methods may range from voluntary early retirement through to compulsory redundancies. This latter step ought not to be considered until possible changes in the use of staff have been assessed. For example strategies such as job sharing, redeployment and retraining may well lead to the necessary reduction in the labour force. If for political or social reasons these means do not make it possible to shed an adequate number of staff, then at this point it would be plausible to reconsider the organizational objectives and to adjust them in such a way as to enable use to be made of the labour surplus.

By now it should be clear that human resource planning is all-embracing. Indeed there have been those who have argued that HRP is in fact human resource management.

It ought to be clear at least that the adjustment of the labour force has clear implications for recruitment, training, role and structural analysis, the introduction of new technology, reward and motivational systems and so on. All these elements of the managerial role are dependent on the size and nature of the work force. At the same time they reflect decisions as to what the organization exists to do and how it proposes to achieve its objectives.

CONCLUSION

We have ended where we began. HRP ought to be both the determinant of the corporate plan and at the same time a reflection of it. HRP is essential to potentially successful long-term planning if for no other reason than that how organizations deploy their work force is the major determinant of success or failure.

No self-respecting human resource plan will, however, simply temper the corporate plan. Once the corporate plan is in place, it becomes the source of human resource management strategy, the yardstick against which priorities are assessed. The success of HR professionals is judged according to how far they have helped the organization to achieve those corporate plans which they were a party to developing.

FURTHER READING

Bell, D. (1989) 'Why Manpower Planning is Back in Vogue', *Personnel Management*, July.
Bramham, J. (1989) *Human Resource Planning*, London: IPM.
Sisson, K. (ed.) (1989) *Personnel Management in Britain*, Oxford: Blackwell.

QUESTIONS FOR DISCUSSION

1 Why is it often said that human resource planning is in effect human resource management?
2 In the forecasting of employee supply, what internal and external factors need to be taken into account?
3 How would you justify the importance of human resource planning to a sceptical managing director of a medium-sized engineering company?

Chapter 4

Dealing with unions

INTRODUCTION

The ambiguity in the title of this chapter is intentional: 'dealing with' can be used in a punitive sense, as in 'I'll deal with you later'; if 'dealing' is emphasized, it can refer to some kind of economic or contractual arrangement, as in 'making a deal with'; and if the emphasis is on the preposition 'with', the phrase can be read as short-hand for a collaborative approach, 'management by consent'. All these interpretations, which reflect tensions between the competing approaches to HRM outlined in Chapter 1, are implicit in this chapter, although the conception of HRM adopted here emphasizes the last two senses rather than the first sense. The different approaches to HRM are most apparent in perspectives on trade unionism, and readers' initial interpretation of the chapter title will provide insight into their own attitudes.

PERSPECTIVES ON TRADE UNIONISM

When workers first began to organize in trade unions in the eighteenth century, their activities were regarded as unlawful and an unwarranted interference in the operation of both market forces and management. The change in attitudes which legitimized trade unionism came gradually over two hundred years. Firstly, as unions became more popular and attracted a wider membership, Parliament repealed the Combination Acts (in 1824) which had made union membership unlawful, acknowledging the political force of the unions before accepting the principle of universal suffrage. Although ten years later six labourers from the village of Tolpuddle in Dorset were convicted of swearing an unlawful oath in connection with trade union membership, the public outcry which followed the sentences of seven years' transportation to Australia demonstrated society's acceptance of the role of unions. Secondly, union leaders were able to demonstrate that they were not dangerous radicals seeking to overthrow the system, but respectable members of Victorian society. Most of these so-called 'top-hatted trade unionists' were skilled artisans who wanted, in addition to the share they were already enjoying in the material rewards of the heyday of British industry and empire, a voice in the processes by which this wealth was being created. A third reason for the acceptance of trade unionism was its spread to other sections of the employed population. From the 1890s, trade union membership increased dramatically as unions for unskilled and semi-skilled workers were formed. The organization of large sections of the working class led to the formation of the Labour Party and the promotion of a more favourable climate for trade unionism to flourish in. Finally, both world wars contributed to an expansion of union membership. Trade unionism took longer to reach white-collar workers, and especially managers, because union membership was seen as symptomatic of disloyalty among these groups and incompatible with career ambitions. From the Second World War trade union membership became more respectable for white-collar workers, professionals and even, by the 1960s, managers.

As trade union membership increased, two competing management perspectives emerged, one rooted in eighteenth-century hostility and the other a result of the accommodation made with organized workers. Fox (1966) contrasted these as 'unitary' and 'pluralist' perspectives. From a unitary perspective, the enterprise is seen as a team having common objectives, where managers manage in the interests of all and any challenge to their authority from trade unionism is seen as illegitimate. For the unitary manager, any opposition from the work force or expression of conflict is a result of agitation, misunderstanding or faulty communications, since the interests of workers and employers are seen as identical. The pluralist manager accepts that there are different interest groups within an enterprise and recognizes the right of workers to independent representation. In adopting a pluralist view, differences are to be resolved, not denied, so it becomes imperative for management to agree mechanisms and procedures for resolving conflict and reaching compromise with trade union representatives.

Writing for the Donovan Commission (see Chapter 11), Fox encouraged the adoption of the more realistic pluralist perspective by management, arguing that where a unitary view is maintained:

> management . . . preserves the pretence of maintaining its prerogatives but nonetheless connives at the extension of unilateral regulation by work groups. Precisely because this extension of informal work-group regulation is not met by management it represents a genuine loss of managerial control. This is the social process by which systematic overtime, overmanning and other diverse manifestations of work-group control have thrived unchecked.
>
> (Fox 1966: 14)

Senior managers needed to face up to the erosion of their authority, acknowledged by front-line managers and supervisors in their granting of informal concessions, and to accept the apparent paradox that formal power sharing was the route to regaining control at the point of production.

Pluralism remained a defining characteristic of the leading institutional approach to British industrial relations, although Fox later rejected it as nothing more than 'enlightened managerialism' (presumably in contrast with the unenlightened managerialism of the unitary approach) and developed a distinctive radical 'materialist' (but not Marxist) analysis. The unitary perspective continued to coexist alongside pluralism, and has enjoyed a revival in the prevailing approach to HRM.

Just as there are competing management perspectives, so different value systems have been identified among work groups (Parkin 1971). When employees adopt a 'dominant' value system, they accept managerial authority without question and make no attempt to oppose management decisions, so probably remain non-union. Often the employment relationship generates grievances and disputes, which motivates workers to organize in a union and on occasions to pursue issues vigorously in opposition to management. The value system underlying this behaviour is described as 'subordinate' because opposition is only sporadic, breaking through the dominant value system when triggered by some perceived provocation. The subordinate value system, or 'factory consciousness', entails only temporary, localized opposition and embodies no coherent view of an alternative order. This limited opposition may be contrasted with a 'radical' value system, or 'class consciousness', which is permanent, generalized and includes an alternative vision. A radical value system is encountered more often in left-wing prescriptions and right-wing scare-mongering than in practice in the consciousness of workers.

The interaction of management and worker perspectives has an important influence on the character of workplace relations. Fox (1974) produced a typology of six patterns of management–employee relations which are combined with Parkin's value systems in Figure 4.1. In the *traditional* situation, the unitary pronouncements of management are accepted by the work force either because they are accompanied by attractive terms and conditions or because the workers' lack of organization is another dimension of their exploitation. The Quaker-owned confectionery companies would provide examples of the first, while a small clothing 'shop' employing ethnic-minority women might correspond more closely with the second.

In the *classical conflict* situation, management cling to the deception of a unitary perspective while the challenge from below of an organized work force erodes effective management control. Some very prolonged stoppages (Roberts-Arundel 1967–8; Fine Tubes 1970–3; Grunwick 1976–7) have arisen where managers were unwilling to moderate, or incapable of

		WORKERS' IDEOLOGY		
		DOMINANT	SUBORDINATE	RADICAL
MANAGEMENT IDEOLOGY	UNITARY	TRADITIONAL PATERNALIST	CLASSICAL CONFLICT	CONTINUOUS CHALLENGE
		STANDARD MODERN		
	PLURALIST	SOPHISTICATED PATERNALIST	SOPHISTICATED MODERN	

Figure 4.1 Patterns of workplace relations

moderating, their unitary views when confronted with the aspirations of workers for effective union organization.

The *sophisticated modern* pattern corresponds with the model Fox was advocating at the time of the Donovan Commission. In this case management accept that workers have a right to independent representation and seek to institutionalize conflict through collective bargaining and compromise.

In the *sophisticated paternalist* case, management's adoption of a pluralist perspective is in advance of the workers' aspirations. Such a situation might arise where a paternalistic employer attempted to encourage joint regulation but the work force maintained a unitary allegiance, believing membership of a union to constitute a vote of no confidence in their employer.

The *standard modern* pattern encompasses all four situations above, recognizing that the behaviour of both management and workers is frequently inconsistent. Typically, managers will voice pluralist views but behave in a unitary fashion, while employees who pose a challenge on specific issues nevertheless endorse the unitary perspective in general.

Finally, in the *continuous challenge* situation, irrespective of management ideology, there is little scope for negotiated compromise because employees have adopted a radical perspective, rejecting the very legitimacy of management. Such circumstances are exceptional and transitory, exemplified by the events of May 1968 in France and Italy.

HRM AND UNIONS

The above typology of workplace relations is as relevant in the 1990s as it was in the 1970s, but the context has altered dramatically. Then, the emphasis was on maintaining high-trust relationships associated with the 'sophisticated modern' pattern of employee relations. Since the 1980s, coincident with the growth of HRM there has been a resurgence of unitary values and Guest (1989b) concludes that HRM is incompatible with pluralist industrial relations. Guest's argument is that the approach of HRM is unitarist and individualistic in contrast with the pluralist, collectivist traditions of industrial relations. Such observations are undeniably true of most current HRM practice, but it would be wrong to conclude that HRM is inevitably and fundamentally unitary and individualist. If this were the case, management indulging in HRM practices would of necessity create a pattern of workplace relations which corresponds with either the traditional or classical conflict models. Moreover, what determines which pattern emerges has less to do with management practices than with workers' aspirations. The traditional (paternalist) pattern can be maintained only until workers become organized and oppose management. It is not certain that any group of workers will organize, but to deny the possibility depends upon accepting the unitarist assumption posited by Guest that there are 'no underlying and inevitable differences of interest between management and workers'. Few people who have ever worked in a subordinate role would agree with such a contention. To reject the notion of an over-riding identity of interest it is not necessary to assume the differences between workers and managers to be those irreconcilable antagonisms of historic proportions central to the writings of Marx. Neither is it necessary to deny an identity of interest at any level: managers and workers alike become unemployed if a company fails, for example. It is, however, inevitable that differences arise as a result of the employment relationship, entailing as it invariably does a frontier of control in the contested terrain of the effort-reward bargain. Managers adhering to unitary values deny the existence of such everyday disputes, an ostrich-like approach which leaves them ill prepared for the challenge of organized workers.

This adherence to unitary values explains why HRM has been prevalent in greenfield sites and enterprises with 'union-free' or anti-union traditions. There is little evidence of the adoption of an integrated HRM approach in unionized UK manufacturing plants, although these have experienced piecemeal HRM initiatives. Guest warns against 'conflating non-unionism with HRM' (1989a: 48), yet this is precisely the effect of declaring that 'management is not practising effective HRM . . . [where] the door is left open for the unions to play a role' (ibid.: 47). Similar sentiments have been expressed by employers whose purpose in applying HRM techniques is 'to wean the workers off trade unionism'. From such a viewpoint the commitment which HRM seeks to foster is seen as problematic for the unions. On the basis of American evidence, Guest acknowledges that 'dual allegiance is possible when a cooperative industrial relations climate exists', but otherwise 'workers may be forced to make a choice'. Employers have been known to encourage such a choice by inviting employees to line up either with their union representative or, if they wished to continue in employment, with their manager. These examples are symptomatic of a unitary, anti-union managerial perspective, which is clearly incompatible with pluralist industrial relations, rather than of HRM as such. The fact that in many cases HRM conforms with this stereotype may be attributed to the current economic and political context because other anti-union activities can be cited which are unrelated to any adoption of HRM techniques. In the last decade key examples would include managerial offensives in British Leyland, British Steel, British Coal, the docks and the newspaper industry.

Pluralist values were in the ascendant for most of the 1970s, and were displaced in some quarters by unitary values in the 1980s as unemployment rose and union power waned. Changes in government reinforced the process but were more symptom than cause; pluralism thrived under Heath's 1974–9 Conservative government, which failed in its attempt to introduce much more modest legal regulation of industrial relations than was introduced in the Thatcher era.

If unitary values are symptomatic of trade unions weakened by an economy in recession, then to the extent that recovery restores union influence there should also be a return to pluralist values. If, on the other hand, HRM does not inevitably entail unitary values, a sophisticated HRM strategist will anticipate change in the balance of power and use these dark ages to establish a high-trust relationship with the employees. The approach to HRM advocated here is compatible with pluralist traditions and builds upon the institutions of collective bargaining rather than seeking to circumvent them. In order to achieve this integration between HRM and collective bargaining, it is necessary to understand trade union objects and methods, and factors influencing patterns of union organization, particularly during the early 1980s.

UNION OBJECTS AND METHODS

The objects of trade unionism are evident from the present legal definition of a trade union as an organization (whether temporary or permanent), consisting of workers, whose principal purpose includes the regulation of relations between workers and employers. A century ago, the Webbs described a trade union as a 'continuous association of wage earners for the purpose of maintaining or improving the conditions of their working lives'. Arguably, both definitions are too narrow, but whichever one adopts it is historically conditioned, reflecting the perspectives and priorities of its period.

Although the objectives of unions are dynamic, a number of themes are so persistent as to warrant their treatment as central purposes:

1 improved terms and conditions of employment;
2 full and secure employment;
3 greater social equality and improved social services;
4 industrial and political democracy;
5 public ownership and control.

This was the order in which the list of trade union objects was submitted as evidence to the Donovan Commission (1965–8) by the TUC, and probably reflects the priorities of the trade unions at that time, even though the TUC stressed that the order was not significant.

The improvement of terms and conditions may preoccupy the unions but higher wages need not be the most important objective. In times of recession, the protection of jobs becomes a priority and focuses attention on alternatives like shorter working time as well as on aspects of economic planning. Improvements in conditions, holidays, the working environment and industrial democracy are normally most attainable during boom periods, while at other times trade unions are forced into a defensive role. As Allen (1966) noted, there is a 'paradox of militancy': militant action is most difficult to organize when it is most necessary and vice versa. More dramatic changes in the distribution of power and wealth in society have been on the trade union agenda since the beginning of the twentieth century but are only pursued sporadically because of the necessity to deal with immediate issues. Union officials face the same difficulties as managers in sacrificing strategic planning to responsive 'fire-fighting'.

These objects are shared by all unions to varying degrees, but the strategies and methods of pursuing them vary with the politics and circumstances of the unions involved. Recent strategies of the new engineering union (AEEU) and the former EETPU (no-strike, single-union deals, pendulum arbitration) arise from the assumption that employer and employee share a common interest in avoiding disputes and raising profits and earnings. At the other extreme, the policies of unions like the NUM and the Furniture, Timber and Allied Trade Union (FTAT) reflect the idea of irreconcilable antagonisms between labour and capital. Most unions, however, employ a range of methods which reflect both opposition and interdependence in the employment relationship.

The old craft unions had depended upon restriction of numbers to secure a monopoly of particular occupations, but collective bargaining is nowadays the primary method through which union objectives are pursued (see Chapter 11). Agreements are made between the parties to determine wages, hours of work and whatever else is discussed. During the 1970s, the bargaining arena was extended to embrace issues like planning that were formerly regarded as sacrosanct areas of managerial prerogative, whereas during the 1980s the scope of collective bargaining was reduced.

Despite the centrality of collective bargaining, other trade union methods take priority over it because without them no serious bargaining is likely to occur. Whatever methods are used to pursue trade union ends, unions need members. Membership recruitment is therefore a fundamental activity of trade unions, and in this respect there is much diversity between different unions. Some unions, like the Union of Shop, Distributive and Allied Workers (USDAW) in the retail sector, are forced to recruit one-third of the total membership annually just to retain current membership, largely because of the high turnover of retail staff. For others, like the print, rail and mining unions, membership was, until the late 1980s, automatic for all those working in the industry. The need to maintain membership, as well as a desire to deter 'freeloaders' (people who obtain benefits of membership, like annual pay increases, without contributing union dues) and potential 'blacklegs' (those who work contrary to a union decision during a stoppage of work), led many unions to establish a 'closed shop', perhaps one of the most contentious aspects of trade unionism.

Under a pre-entry closed shop agreement, newly recruited employees must already be members of a (usually specified) trade union. Under a post-entry closed shop, employees must become members of a particular, or any,

TUC-affiliated trade union within a certain period of taking up employment. In 1989 the *Employment Gazette* estimated that some 800,000 people were covered by pre-entry closed shop arrangements, substantially more than had previously been thought, and the number was expected to increase as legislative restrictions reduced the 1.3 million covered by post-entry closed shops. Later legislative innovations were designed to eradicate the closed shop entirely, although it is too early to estimate the impact of these measures. Similar attempts under the Industrial Relations Act, 1971, had little impact and managements continued to make closed shop (then described as 'agency shop') agreements. Continued legislative efforts suggest that even in the altered economic and political circumstances since 1979, 'compulsory trade unionism' is valued by some employers as part of a strategy for managing human resources. The 2.1 million trade unionists under closed shop arrangements represented 20 per cent of the total membership in 1989. The closed shop is an indicator of extensive unionization, not its cause. Even before legislation imposed ballot requirements, most closed shops usually came into existence only after some 80 per cent of the work force had already voluntarily become members, so less than 4 per cent of all trade unionists could have been 'reluctant members'.

Membership is the first prerequisite but union education follows closely behind, since this enables lay officials to represent their members adequately, and increases rank-and-file involvement. Union education expanded substantially in the 1970s and contracted as quickly in the 1980s when employers resisted paid educational leave. It is insufficient to regard this involvement of membership as nothing more than a means, or method, of trade unionism since participation in the democratic processes of a union is one of the ends of trade unionism. Certain trade union methods are liable to be trivialized by outside observers who regard the methods as outmoded, irrational, or an infringement of individual liberty. Almost all trade union sanctions fall into this category because the pursuit of collective interests frequently collides with the wishes of a minority of individuals (see Chapter 12). Demarcation rules may similarly appear ridiculous out of context, but they developed to protect craftsmen from skill dilution and to reduce competition between groups of workers.

UNION GROWTH AND DECLINE

Figure 4.2 shows that union membership grew from the 1890s but the Depression, which began with the defeat of the miners in 1921 and engineers in 1922, put trade union membership back to such an extent that the 1921 level of union density (union members as a percentage of employed workers) was only recovered in 1971. The steady growth of post-war union membership did not increase union density significantly until 1971 because the labour force was growing at a comparable rate. Manual

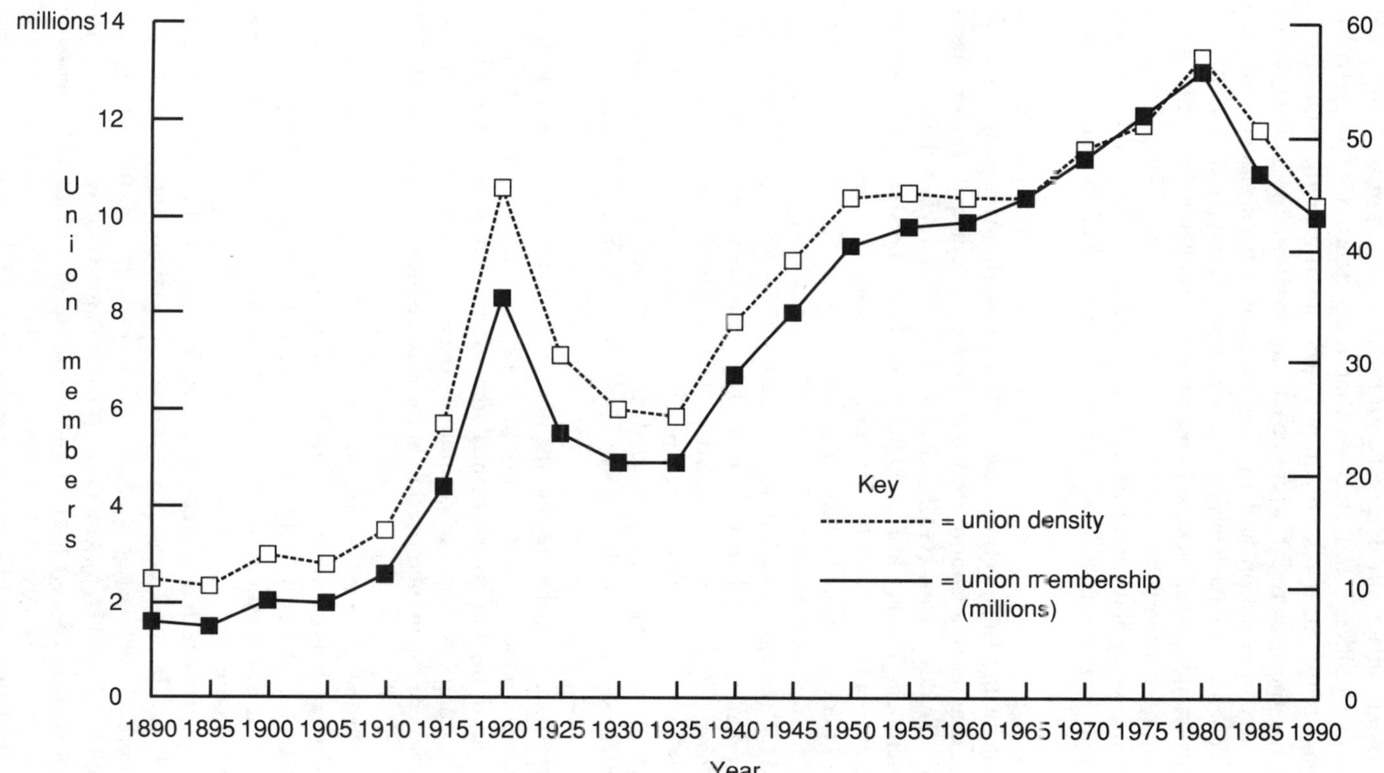

Figure 4.2 Union membership 1890–1990
Source: Department of Employment, *Gazette*.

union membership actually declined with the contraction of well-organized industries like coal, rail and steel so that the extension of white-collar membership is the main reason for post-war union growth. Bain (1970) accounts for the growth of white-collar unionization by the degree of employment concentration and the degree to which employers are prepared to recognize unions. Employer recognition is itself a function of both union density and government action to promote collective bargaining.

There has been a sharp fall in union membership since 1979 as a result of economic recession, industrial restructuring and an unfavourable political climate. The largest union, the Transport and General Workers' Union (TGWU), shrank from two million members to little over one million at the end of the 1980s, despite the amalgamation of several smaller unions. The Amalgamated Engineering Union (AEU, now the Amalgamated Electrical and Engineering Union) and the General, Municipal, Boilermakers and Allied Trades Union (GMB) declined less, but each fell below one million members. The NUM lost 90 per cent of membership between 1984 and 1992: 80 per cent of mining jobs disappeared through restructuring and another 10 per cent of the membership defected to the breakaway Union of Democratic Mineworkers (UDM). Overall, union density fell by between 7.8 and 11.7 percentage points in the period 1979–85, depending on the basis of calculation, or less than in earlier comparable recessions (Kelly 1988). Union membership continued to decline during the second half of the 1980s, while the numbers employed increased (mainly due to an expansion in part-time work); thus density fell further, but the rate of decrease was slower than during the first half of the decade (Waddington 1992).

Factors influencing the decline include long-term changes in industrial structure, economic recession, hostile legislation and employer policies. Well-organized, predominantly manual industries like coal, rail, steel, docks and shipbuilding have been in continuous decline since the Second World War. The loss of union membership in these industries was compensated by organization of expanding manufacturing industries and white-collar workers, particularly in the public sector. Although these processes were underway before the return of Conservative government in 1979, the contraction of heavy industries accelerated during the 1980s, while recession and privatization reversed union growth in manufacturing and the public sector.

Economic activity has increased in service sectors, historically poorly organized, and in small enterprises where ownership fragmentation, dispersed workers and closer relations with management militate against unionization. Moreover, government policies have created a hostile legal environment and reduced both employment and the unions' influence in the public sector. In this context, some employers have adopted a more forceful approach towards unions, in extreme cases using American union-busting techniques, as in the historic 1984–5 coal strike (Winterton and Winterton 1989: 171–82).

For the most part, employers have not sought to dismantle existing collective bargaining arrangements, preferring to restrict the scope of bargaining and decollectivize issues wherever possible (Claydon 1989). In the case of non-union establishments or greenfield sites, however, employers have increasingly resisted unionization and recognition except on their own terms (Smith and Morton 1991). The factors which Bain identified as promoting union growth have therefore operated in reverse to contribute to union decline.

UNION STRUCTURE

In the study of industrial relations, the coverage of unions throughout the economy is referred to as union structure, while the internal composition and administration of trade unions is described as union government. Britain's union structure is the most complex in the world. Although devoid of (explicit) ideological divisions, such as exist in most other European countries, individual unions cross occupational and industrial boundaries in many ways. One consequence is that in a large manufacturing plant during the 1970s it was not uncommon to have more than twelve different unions representing workers. Single-union deals during the 1980s significantly reduced the extent of multi-unionism.

Before these latest changes, as trade union membership grew the number of separate unions diminished, so that by the end of the 1970s the largest twenty unions accounted for something like 90 per cent of the total membership. Mergers are continuing as a response to membership decline and the emergence of five dominant conglomerate unions is likely within a few years. This concentration does little to simplify matters, however, because the structure of constituent unions amalgamating is complex and the rationale for amalgamation owes more to the political compatibility of the leaderships than the industrial compatibility of the memberships.

The classical view of trade unions distinguished three types, to which a fourth was added following the unionization of white-collar and professional groups:

- industrial unions – one union for all workers in an industry, regardless of skill, occupation or location;
- craft unions – organized on the basis of possessing certain skills, developed from craft societies;
- general unions – having no limit to their recruitment interest, which emerged to cater for semiskilled/unskilled workers excluded from crafts;
- occupational unions – recruiting persons following the same white-collar occupation.

The coverage of these different types of unions is shown in Figure 4.3. The traditional typology is inadequate for present-day unions, as most unions will not fit in any particular category. The NUM is defined as an industrial union, but it is not the only union in coal mining (the British Association of Colliery Management, BACM, the National Association of Colliery Overmen, Deputies and Shotfirers, NACODS, and the Association of Professional, Executive, Clerical and Computer Staff, APEX, all have members and, since 1985, the UDM competes for representation of the industrial grades, over which the NUM formerly enjoyed exclusive jurisdiction). Although the Amalgamated Society of Engineers (ASE) could be viewed as a craft union, its successor engineering unions have organized unskilled engineering workers since the First World War. Before the recent merger with the Electricians' Union, the membership base of the AEU defined it as an industrial union in mechanical engineering and a craft union elsewhere. The GMB is typical of the general unions, but it has few craft workers in its ranks and its membership is concentrated in the gas industry (where it is virtually an industrial union), local authorities and Scotland. The membership of Manufacturing, Science, Finance (MSF, formerly the Association of Scientific, Technical and Managerial Staffs, ASTMS) is insufficiently homogeneous to characterize it as an occupational union. In some companies it may be viewed as a union for managerial grades, in others it represents scientific and technical workers, and elsewhere it is effectively a clerical union.

It is generally more useful, following Turner (1962), to consider the degree of openness of a union in terms of recruitment: in open unions

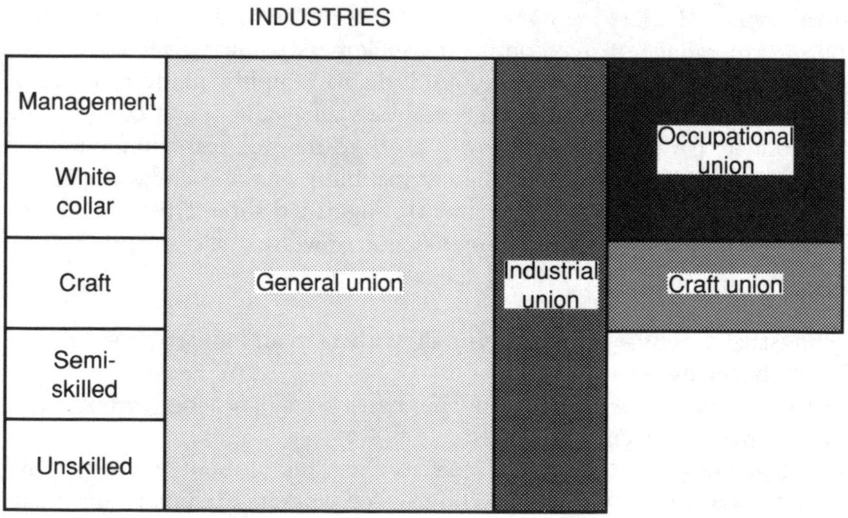

INDUSTRIES

Management
White collar
Craft
Semi-skilled
Unskilled
General union
Industrial union
Occupational union
Craft union

Figure 4.3 Union structure

recruitment is unlimited except by agreement with other unions, whereas closed unions limit recruitment to a particular industry or occupation. Between these polar cases, most unions are open in some areas of recruitment and closed in others. Hughes (1967) noted how some unions grew in the postwar period by increasing membership within existing frontiers, whereas other unions grew by extending the frontiers of recruitment, or by remaining closed and amalgamating with other closed unions.

UNION GOVERNMENT

Trade unions differ markedly in their systems of government but it is possible to provide a general model of the typical organization and

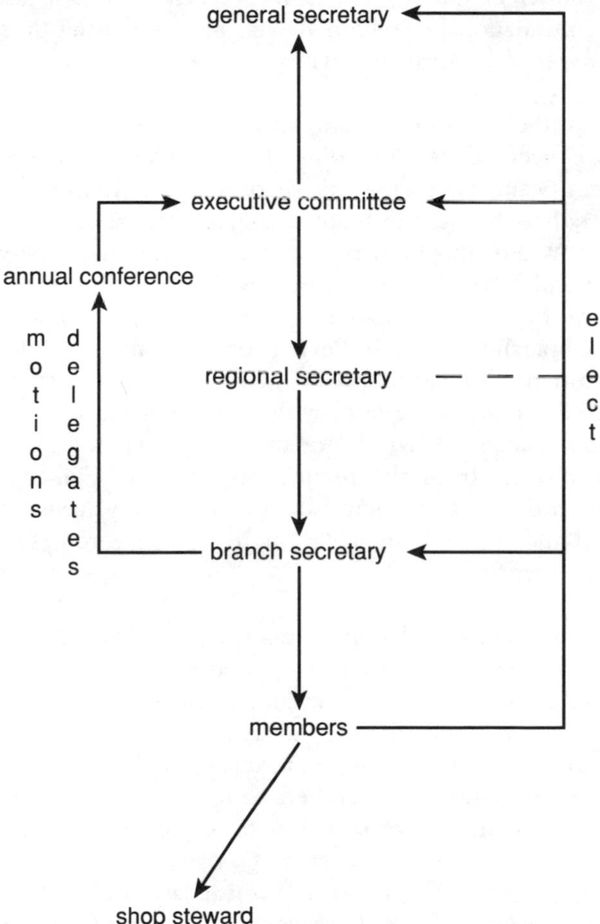

Figure 4.4 Union government

constitution of British unions. Figure 4.4 shows that there are three levels within a typical union: national, regional (or district) and branch levels. The union branch is the point at which members influence the policy of their union; here resolutions are sent forward and representatives elected to the policy-making body, the annual conference. The executive, headed by the two senior officials, general secretary and president, exists to implement and interpret on a day-to-day basis the overall policy established by the annual conference.

The executive and national officials are normally assisted by appointed full-time officers, employees of the union who specialize in research, education, the law, etc. The national organization is mirrored by a regional or district administration, where secretaries, normally elected officials, are often assisted by regional education officers and other appointed specialists, particularly in the larger unions. The branch receives information, advice and assistance from national or regional level, and district full-time officials may become involved in local negotiation at the invitation of branch or workplace officials.

The branch is the most important level of the union so far as the constitution is concerned, but in reality the workplace is where negotiations more often occur. Shop stewards or other lay officials are elected at the workplace rather than at the branch: they are workplace officials, not branch officials. Where the branch is not based on the workplace (the Graphical Print and Media Union has geographic branches) there is more scope for friction between the branch officials and lay officials. The usual result is that the branch becomes irrelevant for negotiations, while retaining its central importance in union policy making. Even where the union branch is centred on the workplace, with a few notable exceptions (like the NUM where branch officials negotiate at pit level) the shop steward organization is distinct from the branch organization. Full-time elected senior shop stewards (or conveners) do not necessarily have any formal authority within the union branch although they may represent all the members of that branch and often members of other unions in the same workplace.

Democracy is a recurrent theme in many discussions of trade union government and several studies have attempted to compare the degree of democracy in different unions. An examination of the formal constitution of union rule books is uninformative, what matters is the way in which unions are governed and administered in practice. The issue is an important one because in order to mobilize members to take collective action against an employer, officials must have power over them: problems arise when this power is not wielded simply to serve the members' interests.

What Michels (1911) first described as the 'iron law of oligarchy' operates in trade unions because of the bureaucracy of experts, the life styles adopted by officials and the apathy of members. The problem becomes most apparent in the 'mature stage' of a union (Lester 1958) when membership growth levels off, decision making becomes centralized and administrators assume leadership positions. It is not simply that union leaders can lose touch with the membership; in their pursuit of goals of stability and security, means become ends in themselves.

Martin (1968) compared the administration of the NUR and the AUEW and found the latter, then under Communist control, was more democratic than the former. In the famous 1962 ballot rigging case in the ETU, however, it was members of the Communist Party, including Frank Chapple (who later became General Secretary and a leading right-winger on the TUC General Council), who were responsible for a breach of the union's constitution in order to maintain control. Clearly the question of democracy versus oligarchy is not determined by the political allegiances of union leaders.

Several factors stand out as being important in relation to union democracy. The first is the election system. A postal ballot is regarded by those seeking union reform as more democratic than the branch block vote because of low branch attendance. Arguably the few activists who attend branch meetings are more qualified to judge but such an elitist view is inconsistent with principles of union democracy. Equally, it is certain that the postal vote is more susceptible to external influences such as the media and to ballot rigging. Postal ballots are also typically associated with a lower poll, on average about 22 per cent (Fatchett 1982) compared with workplace ballots of as much as 90 per cent. The secret workplace ballot meets all the stated objectives of advocates of the postal ballot without the same degree of risk of interference by external influences.

A second factor is the existence of a party system, or organized factions, within the union. There has been a *de facto* party system within the AUEW for years, and something approaching this within the NUM and NUR, with in each case a right-wing Labourist group opposing a Communist and Labour left caucus. In all three unions factions were so effective that the challengers deposed the established leadership. Thus the right gained control of the Engineering Union with Terry Duffy's succession, while the elections of Arthur Scargill by the miners and Jimmy Knapp by the railway workers represented the ascendancy of the left.

Membership apathy facilitates oligarchic control because members' participation is essential to maintain effective opposition. Typically there is little membership participation in branch meetings, although shop stewards and other activists are usually involved. Even so, membership apathy is conditional upon the satisfaction of the instrumental attitudes of rank-and-file members. If the union leadership fails to meet membership aspirations, then the members may leave the union or at least take unofficial action aimed as much at the union leadership as the employer.

Two other factors serve to promote democratic practices within the unions. The decentralization of collective bargaining has weakened the hold of national officials over the conduct of negotiations so that many of the immediate issues affecting members are determined at the level where they can exert most influence. Shop stewards are accountable to their constituents and cannot depend upon protection from full-time union officials. Normative pressures, deriving from members, management, the media and the public, serve to limit the oligarchic tendencies of trade union leaders. Newspaper editors publicize with enthusiasm any transgressions of union leaders (along with politicians and royalty) which come to light, as indeed they should. There is, as Hyman (1971) puts it, a 'prevalence of assumptions that trade unions ought in some sense to operate democratically'. Such assumptions are so pervasive that, despite its obvious hostility towards the unions, there are several arguments in the government's Green Paper (1983) *Democracy in Trade Unions* with which democratic union activists could concur.

THE ROLE OF THE UNION IN THE WORKPLACE

In some of the industrial relations literature, the term shop steward refers only to representatives of manual workers and workplace is used synonymously with workshop. Even before the dramatic industrial restructuring of the 1980s, a significant proportion of union representatives were not manual worker shop stewards, and the majority of employees were no longer in workshops. In this chapter, therefore, workplace refers to any place where people work, whether office, shop, factory or elsewhere, and the term shop steward will be taken to include any lay representative of a trade union or staff association.

There have been two periods during which the number and influence of shop stewards increased in British industry. During the First World War the government's need to secure the cooperation of the ASE in increasing munitions production provided negotiating opportunities for the shopfloor representatives of this old craft union. The second period was associated with the growth of plant bargaining under the tight labour market conditions of the 1960s, which was extensively analysed by the Donovan Commission (1968).

The emergence of shop stewards in British industrial relations has been variously explained as a grass-roots revolt against union bureaucracy, the desire of work groups for local representation, and management's need of employee representatives for decentralized negotiation (Flanders 1964). As recently as the 1960s, the majority of union rule books made no mention of shop stewards although most unions had some form of lay representation at the workplace: further evidence that their origins and power lay in the social organization of work groups rather than the official bureaucracy of the trade union movement.

Since the 1960s shop steward functions have been systematically examined by surveys and plant-level studies undertaken for the Donovan Commission (McCarthy and Parker 1968), the Engineering Employers' Federation (Marsh, Evans and Garcia 1971), the Government Social Survey (Parker 1974, 1975) and Warwick University (Brown 1981).

The Donovan Commission (1968: 29) concluded that the average shop steward was 'more of a lubricant than an irritant'. The majority of managers and trade union members did not regard shop stewards as the initiators of industrial action, although shop stewards viewed themselves as being more militant than their constituents (Parker 1968; McCarthy and Parker 1968: 32).

In spite of the popular image, shop stewards are often reported to be a restraining influence on members, discouraging 'wildcat' strikes. The conflict-prone car plants of the 1960s were characterized by 'unofficial-unofficial strikes', stoppages which were not only in breach of procedure (unconstitutional) and lacking formal union authorization (unofficial), but were also against the advice of local shop stewards. While loyalty to their members may require stewards to support spontaneous action, they must also play according to the rules of the game if stable bargaining relationships are to be maintained with management.

The Warwick workplace survey found shop stewards at 73 per cent of all manufacturing plants and at 97 per cent of large plants with at least 1,000 workers (Brown 1981). Where there are several stewards, there is usually a hierarchy; the likelihood of a senior steward or convener is directly related to the size of the work force and the number of shop stewards (Brown, Ebsworth and Terry 1978).

About 12 per cent of establishments with stewards representing manual workers reported full-time conveners, but they were most common where wages are fixed by single- rather than multi-employer bargaining. Moreover, conveners came into being through managerial initiative (Brown, Ebsworth and Terry 1978) and are clearly associated with larger enterprises (as well as establishments) and the existence of specialist industrial relations management.

In multi-union establishments 29 per cent reported cross-representation, whereby the steward of one union represents, in addition, members of another. In those where shop stewards' meetings are regularly held, 52 per cent reported joint union meetings regularly, and a further 15 per cent occasionally. The forum is typically described as a Joint Shop Stewards' Committee (JSSC). Beyond plant level, combine committees, where stewards from several plants meet to discuss issues of corporate concern and to compare plant-level developments, were reported at 34 per cent of establishments in the case of manual workers, and 44 per cent in the case of white-collar workers.

Surveys suggest that at the peak of shop steward power in manufacturing they often had unilateral control over labour mobility, manning, demarcation and work study, but their control rarely extended to restrictions on output, earnings or overtime working. Shop steward influence declined significantly during the 1980s yet recent workplace surveys still suggest that managers in large unionized workplaces are more likely to be constrained in organizing work than other managers. Clegg (1979: 12–19) argued that shop stewards had most power where they were able to exert some influence over earnings. Given the instrumental attachment to trade unionism of most union members, shop stewards' success in, or enthusiasm for, raising earnings is likely to be the major measure of their effectiveness from the point of view of the rank and file. The ability to raise earnings is largely a function of the structure of collective bargaining (Chapter 11) and the systems of wage payment in operation (Chapter 9).

While surveys provide clues to the issues over which shop stewards are able to exert control, they are uninformative about the processes involved. The plant-level studies by Batstone, Boraston and Frenkel (1977) illustrated the different ways in which shop stewards mobilize and respond to rank-and-file opinion. The work group is the source of shop steward power and influence. Where work groups display solidaristic attitudes, their representatives clearly have more power in dealing with management: contrast the accounts of labour relations at the coal face (Scott *et al.* 1963; Krieger 1984) with those in the clothing industry (Lupton 1963; Edwards and Scullion 1982). Sociological studies suggest a number of other factors, such as technology, which affect work group cohesion and the strategic importance of a work group in the production process.

CONCLUSION

This chapter has examined management perspectives on trade unionism and considered the relationship between these perspectives and different approaches to HRM. It has been argued that an understanding of union objects, methods and organization is necessary to achieve the desired integration between HRM and collective bargaining. The value of working with trade unions has been emphasized as part of a progressive HRM strategy which balances collective interests with the development of individuals.

FURTHER READING

Blyton, P. and Turnbull, P. (1994) *The Dynamics of Employee Relations*, London: Macmillan, Chapter 4.

Gospel, H.F. and Palmer, G. (1993) *British Industrial Relations*, London: Routledge, Chapters 2 and 3.

Jackson, M.P. (1991) *An Introduction to Industrial Relations*, London: Routledge, especially Chapter 3.

Storey, J. and Sisson, K. (1993) *Managing Human Resources and Industrial Relations*, Buckingham: Open University Press, Chapter 9.

QUESTIONS FOR DISCUSSION

1 Is HRM compatible with a pluralist approach to industrial relations?
2 Despite successive legislative attempts to outlaw closed shops, management have often shown a preference for maintaining such membership agreements. Why?
3 'For most members, the shop steward *is* the union.' What are the implications of this for HR strategy in the organized workplace?

Chapter 5

Employee recruitment and selection

INTRODUCTION

As explored in Chapter 1, the development of HRM is a response to the realization that the competitive edge can only be achieved through the efforts of a highly effective and well-motivated staff. The importance of technological excellence has for long been well understood and increasingly provided for.

It logically follows that the recruitment and selection process must be as efficient as possible. It is always expensive and not always easy to rectify mistakes in selection. Often the organization lives with the consequences of poor selection for years ahead. If recruits are not the best available, it follows also that money spent on training is likely to be wasted. Finally, the poor performer has an adverse effect on others, leading to a decline in morale.

So time spent on setting up and monitoring the best possible recruitment and selection procedures is time well spent. The processes deserve the active involvement of all managers. Selection particularly should not be left to the HRM specialist.

In this chapter we shall outline the main stages in the recruitment and selection process.

RECRUITMENT

It is wise to distinguish between 'recruitment' and 'selection'. The former is concerned with the provision of a relevant market from which new employees will be selected. The latter relates to the processes of choosing from that market. Figure 5.1 outlines the most important stages in these related processes.

Even before we can begin the process of identifying potentially employable people, it is important that each and every recruitment bid is linked to and stems from the human resource plan. Only this will ensure that the right people of the right quality and in the right place will be selected. There

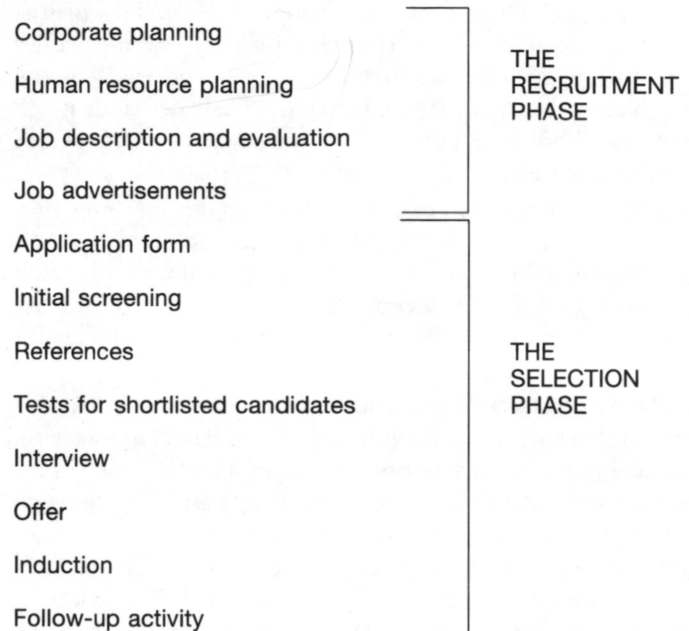

Figure 5.1 Stages in the recruitment and selection process

is clearly no point in taking people on only to have to sever connection with them in six months' time as part of a redundancy programme. Similarly, it would be foolish to recruit people whose skills are not appropriate to future technological developments in the organization.

The human resource plan must itself reflect the corporate strategic plan. The HRP owes its existence to corporate planning and stems from it. Without the existence of the central overall planning process no accurate recruitment targets can be set.

Assuming that the vacancies to be filled have emerged from and are in line with both the corporate plan and the human resource plan, the next stage in the process is to provide a detailed description of the job.

The job description is an essential element in the entire recruitment and selection process. When there exists for most, if not all, jobs in the organization a detailed description of the duties involved and how they relate to other positions, especially with regard to payment, we should be able to form a clear picture of the type of individual we shall be seeking to employ.

There are a number of systems which have been devised to help in the process of matching the individual to the job. One of the most commonly used is the 'seven-point plan' devised by Alec Rodger (1974). This plan is useful throughout the selection and recruitment process. At the earlier stage it encourages orderly thought about the job itself and leads to the listing of the main characteristics of the job, hence the likely demands it will make on the successful jobholder. Figure 5.2 lists the seven points, together with a brief description of each.

With the aid of these headings it is possible to describe the characteristics of the job. With regard to any particular job, for example, item one will require from the successful jobholder different physical characteristics, in a different degree. With regard to item seven, some jobs require more living away from home than others, and mobility is sometimes a crucial element of a job.

The use of the plan ensures that before the recruitment phase gets under way, there is a clear understanding of the job and the demands it makes on the jobholder. Following the job description, it is useful to take the seven-point plan a stage further by developing a person specification, again using the same seven headings. Figure 5.3 provides an example. The reader should note the distinction between the essential and the desirable qualities present in the potential jobholder. It may not always be possible to select an employee with all the qualities one might wish for; but it is important to be clear as to the characteristics on which there can be no compromise.

An equally important consequence of using the plan is the development of job descriptions which enable comparisons between one job and another

The seven-point plan

1 Physical make-up
Health, physique, appearance, bearing, speech

2 Attainments
Type and level of education, occupational training and experience, occupational achievements

3 General intelligence
Level of intellectual capacity

4 Special aptitudes
Mechanical, manual dexterity, verbal, numerical, artistic, musical

5 Interests
Intellectual, practical, constructive, physical, social, artistic

6 Disposition
Acceptability, influence over others, steadiness, dependability, self-reliance

7 Circumstances
Personal goals, mobility

Figure 5.2 The seven-point plan
Source: Rodger (1974)

	Essential	*Desirable*	*How identified*
Physical	100% fitness	—	Comprehensive range of medical tests
Attainments	Specified subjects and grades in GCEs and A levels	Degree or equivalent qualifications	Documentary evidence, amplified by interview
General intelligence	Levels specified in terms of psychometric tests	—	Ability tests of education/intelligence, supplemented by interview data
Special aptitudes	Co-ordination, mechanical comprehension, speed of reaction, handling rapidly changing information	—	Special ability tests of aptitude related to success in flying training
Interests	Aviation and related subjects	World affairs	Documentary evidence, amplified by interview
Disposition	Equable temperament, sociable and co-operative	—	Documentary evidence amplified by interview
Circumstances	Mobility	Initially free from heavy domestic/ family commitments	Documentary evidence, amplified by interview

Figure 5.3 Person specification for military aircrew (based on the seven-point plan)

and thus form the basis of a job evaluation system. It goes without saying that before recruitment gets under way, the organization should have decided upon the relative worth of every post with regard to wage or salary and other non-monetary rewards.

At this point, and not before, it is possible to move on to the next and final stage of recruitment, the advertisement of the job. Decisions will have to be made as to whether to 'trawl' internally for potential recruits or whether, as a policy, to look only outside the organization. There are pros and cons around this decision, but often there is no good reason not to offer the position to those both inside and outside the company. When jobs are scarce, many employees would expect the organization to offer positions to any suitable and competent staff member before 'going outside'. Corporate policy may, on the other hand, regard the influx of new blood as a matter of paramount concern and require the company to recruit from amongst those who could bring in fresh ideas and skills.

Where relevant, it is wise to involve the appropriate trade union in the development of company recruitment policy. Not only is this an area of legitimate union/management concern, but it could prevent disputes about individual cases at a later date.

Job advertising is a skilled activity and the novice would often be well advised to employ the services of a recruitment specialist, if there is no competent internal resource. The advertising medium is an important issue and the wrong choice of newspaper or insertion date can make the difference between a high-quality cost-effective response and a time-wasting and expensive exercise which has to be repeated.

Commonly, positions are advertised in newspapers and specialist journals. It is important in the drafting of copy that:

- there is sufficient detail to allow potential applicants to make an informed decision as to whether they are suited for the position. Details should relate to both the job and the company. It is a mistake to use a box number unless absolutely unavoidable.
- rewards related to the job should be spelt out clearly to prevent time being wasted in processing fruitless applications.
- a favourable image of the company is given. Potentially good employees are often put off by an impression of organizational arrogance. It is worth remembering that even in times of high unemployment the potential employee has choices to make, and good recruits are more likely than others to take a critical position about the employing organization.
- information should be clear as to how to apply for the position; what the later stages of the selection process will be, and the closing date for applications.
- responses should be directed at someone by name, rather than to a department.
- any legal considerations are taken into account. Equal opportunities, race discrimination and general employment legislation set limits on what can be required.

In some cases, particularly when sensitive issues are involved, or when the potential applicants are both few in number and known on an individual basis, it might be advisable to use head hunters. Again care should be taken that these specialists are only used when absolutely necessary. Managers have expressed opinions implying that head hunters are overused and not always as effective as they should be.

SELECTION

Once the potential market has been approached, the recruitment phase has ended and the selection stage has begun. Broadly speaking, selection is the process of eliminating those who are unlikely for objective reasons to perform successfully in the role for which they have applied. This may appear negative, but in reality it is rather easier and more reliable to identify skills and attitudes an applicant does *not* have than it is to identify someone who both possesses these skills at a specific level and is sufficiently motivated to use them.

Following a response to the advertisement, an application form should be sent out. Whether or not the completed form constitutes the basic selection instrument depends entirely on how effective and relevant it is as a data-collecting device. Where a wide range of jobs are to be filled, one application form will not be sufficient. In a large-scale organization one would expect three or more. Difficulties may arise when, for example, a potential chief accountant is asked to give details of shorthand speeds.

It should be remembered that the purpose of the application form is to reduce the numbers of applicants to a manageable short list. Any legal question which helps achieve this could be suitable, but the form should be as short and attractive as possible. The precise instructions given to the applicant will depend upon the uses to which the completed form will be put. For example, French firms commonly ask for completion in the applicant's own handwriting, since a graphological analysis will be used as part of the selection process at this point or later.

It is often appropriate for the HR department to sift through the application forms working on the information contained in the job description. It is unnecessary and unreasonable to expect line managers to evaluate every application, although they should be involved in the decision as to which applicants should constitute the final short list.

References

Whether and when references are worth taking up are moot points. Opinions vary, but there seems a good case for only taking up references from past employers. This is not always possible, for example with recent graduates or school leavers whose college or school record must suffice.

The question remains, however, as to when references should be taken up. If before the final selection procedure takes place, time is likely to be wasted in writing to referees unnecessarily. Sometimes applicants state that they do not wish their present employer to be contacted unless a firm offer of employment is likely to follow the selection procedure. Such wishes should be honoured.

If on the other hand references are not taken up until after the final selection procedure – that is, until an offer is made subject to the receipt of satisfactory references – the question of confidentiality arises. The potential employee who then does not in fact get a firm offer of employment knows why and in all likelihood can guess from whom the offending reference has come. Records kept other than electronically are not subject to the data protection act, so that referees often expect and sometimes stipulate that the reference is provided in confidence.

On balance, it seems easiest if references are taken up for each of the individuals on the short list earlier rather than later, so that the information is available for the final stage of the selection process. Naturally information gained from referees should only be passed on directly to applicants with their prior permission. Where this not to be the case, many referees would give less than comprehensive references or none at all.

In some sensitive cases, or when time is pressing, it may be more appropriate to use the telephone. Referees are often more inclined to be honest in speech than when committing themselves to paper. Where the most senior posts are being filled this method of deriving information about track record is much the most appropriate.

Before leaving this topic, it is as well to remember that the purpose of a reference is to gain as much information as possible as to how the applicants perform at work. Previous performance is the best guide to the future.

Pre-interview selection tests and inventories

Strictly speaking, a test is a system of evaluation which is based on the capacity of an individual to provide objectively right or wrong answers to one or a number of problems. Such tests might measure ability or the relative presence or absence of a characteristic in the candidate compared to the general population or a defined section of it. Intelligence tests and aptitude tests fall into this category and can be sufficiently valid and reliable to give statistically satisfactory statements as to capacity (but not future performance).

On this basis it is claimed that a specific applicant can be said to possess a particular attribute to a greater or lesser extent than any given percentage of a relevant population, say English university postgraduates or financially qualified managers in America.

For a test to be of any predictive value, it must be both valid and reliable. Validity tells us the extent to which a test in fact measures what it purports to measure, and is capable of discriminating between the performance of individuals taking the test. For example, an intelligence test could not be said to be valid if it was more accurate as a test of the applicants' capacity to keep calm in a crisis, or if all those taking the test were to do equally well or badly.

Reliability refers to the extent to which a test is capable of producing the same results no matter how often it is administered. If, for example, the results are affected by other changing variables, including test sophistication, then it is obviously not a wholly reliable indicator.

These statistical processes are not appropriate to the variety of personality questionnaires or inventories which are commonplace and seek information about the characteristics of the applicants and about which there cannot be a right or wrong answer. They are based directly or indirectly on a process of self-report, that is subjects provide information about themselves. This information is then compared against a set of norms or typical responses obtained from groups drawn from a general or specific 'population'.

The uninitiated should therefore be careful to take the necessary advice before using tests in the selection process. They should ensure that any favoured instrument is relevant to the task in hand and not simply something which appears to be both interesting and possessed of a high degree of 'face' or apparent 'commonsense' validity. Unfortunately there are many widely available personality inventories whose fitness for their purpose is simply unproven, or else they are administered by people unable to draw reliable conclusions from the results. It is not uncommon for selectors to lack any clear agreement as to what attributes are significant in the post to be filled and to what degree.

Even when the right test or inventory is used in the most favourable of circumstances, the degree of correlation between performance predictions based on the inventory and future job performance in practice is not much better than random. This should not necessarily be taken as an endemic problem with the test or inventory. It is not possible to take into account all the reasons irrelevant to the capacity of the recruit which will affect eventual job performance. The circumstances in which the job is done may change, or perhaps the individuals with whom the applicant will eventually work may make success difficult to achieve. Or it may be simply that there is no satisfactory definition of what constitutes success, varied responses being obtained from those in contact with the jobholder.

It is unreasonable to measure the predictive performance of tests and inventories against such criteria. At best it might be said of a particular job applicant that there is little to suggest the presence of personal or skill characteristics which are known to be related to poor performance. In other words, tests are more effective as a guide to which applicant not to appoint than which should be appointed.

A constant theme amongst those who comment adversely on personality inventories in particular is that they are 'patent'; that is, subjects can use their intelligence to guess which of a number of responses to give in order to produce the correct profile. This appears to be true of some forced choice inventories. However, it is not always clear to applicants what the 'politically correct' response is, so there is a possibility of either producing the 'wrong' profile or a set of rather obviously random responses. In any event this observation would be less relevant when more indirect and psychoanalytic procedures are in use, for example perception tests in which applicants devise responses to unclear situations.

Increasingly, and in continental Europe in particular, use is made of handwriting analysis as a source of data relating to the inherent personal qualities of a job applicant. Individuals are invited to accompany their application with a 'lettre manuscrite'. This has the advantage of not being 'patent' since it is not possible to control all the characteristics of a writing sample, even if the writer does know what characteristics the sample should exhibit. It is also increasingly argued that the report of a fully trained graphologist is capable of much greater nuance in the emerging profile than that which emerges from the commonly used personality inventories. In Britain merchant banks in particular have found graphological assessment particularly efficacious in the detection of dishonesty and the assessment of emotional stability. Interested readers are directed to the article by Crumbaugh and Stockholm (1977).

It should be remembered, however, that the extent to which a graphological assessment can predict future job performance is no higher than that obtained by the inventories and tests mentioned above (see for example Cox and Tapsell 1991). As with tests and inventories generally, it is most efficient in identifying those who should not be selected.

Most readers will be familiar with many of the other selection methods which are widely practised. Two of the most common are leaderless group activities, designed to assess the leadership potential of job applicants in uncertain situations with no formal power structure. Variants of these processes have been borrowed from the military over the years. Since for a considerable period after the Second World War many personnel positions were filled by those with military backgrounds, this is perhaps not surprising. Outward bound activities, for example, were once popular in the portfolio of selection techniques of many large companies. Administrative difficulties and costs have in recent years led to their replacement by symbolic activities capable of being conducted indoors and more speedily.

For organizations wishing to involve outside specialists in the selection procedure assessment centres have grown in popularity. These are not places but collections of selection activities. Provided those running these activities are familiar with the demands of the job, they offer a professional service which is beyond the capacity of many employing organizations.

In every case, however, before any pre-interview selection procedure is used, it is vital that professional competence is available to draw worthwhile conclusions from the activities and that a rigorous evaluation is carried on to ensure that the methods used are worth the time and effort involved. This feedback must be made available to the selectors, so that the procedure can be adjusted to reflect knowledge as to what are the most effective selection activities in particular cases.

It is not enough to use selection activities to fill time and to give the potential recruit a sense of having been subjected to an exhaustive selection procedure.

The interview

By the time the interview takes place, there should be available a variety of data about each applicant. It may include references, the results of aptitude and intelligence tests, the profiles obtained from personality inventories and the data available from the use of simulation activities. Just as importantly, the necessary data about the job and the demands they make on the jobholder should also be available (the job and person descriptions).

Such data are in themselves no substitute for the interview and cannot replace it. The data can, however, act as another source of information in support of the interview.

Research data collected over many years point conclusively to the fact that the interview is a notoriously unreliable selection method (Mayfield 1964), yet it persists as the most popular selection method. The reasons for this are not hard to find.

Most people (wrongly) imagine themselves to be expert interviewers and are resistant to the need to learn the skills involved. In many cases bad administration militates against a successful interaction. In some cases the techniques employed more or less ensure failure: panel interviews, for example, are by their nature more akin to tribunals and are in general not to be recommended (Torrington and Chapman 1983: 88).

A major problem is that it is difficult both to listen to what is being said and at the same time manage the process of the interview. It is also apparent that human beings are not good collectors of objective information. What the interviewer hears or observes has to be processed and the resulting decision is as much a function of the characteristics of the interviewer as of the interviewee.

None the less, it is difficult to abandon the interview. Firstly, it provides perhaps the only opportunity the candidate has to assess the organization. The employment interview is a two-way process, and applicants will inevitably form views as to whether they wish to work in the organization or not. The interview therefore provides an excellent opportunity for the organization to sell itself to the applicant. This is an important issue which in the past has been undervalued. Many organizations have rather arrogantly assumed that the interviewee is at the disposal of the selectors and is there to help them reach an employment decision. Increasingly companies are becoming more aware of the need to sell themselves to potential employees.

Secondly, it provides the crucially important opportunity for the manager of the potential employee to become involved in the recruitment process. Up to this point it is often unnecessary for the manager to have played more than a relatively minor part. Now, however, at the final stage it is vital that the manager makes the decision as to whether an applicant should be offered employment. Provided that the shortlisting has been done effectively, it is safe for the HRM professional to leave the final decision to the line manager in the knowledge that all of the shortlisted applicants meet the main criteria of suitability.

Finally it might be argued both that there will be information not yet to hand which the interview can locate, and that there are items which have emerged through the medium of other selection techniques which need to be explored with the candidate. Where no selection techniques other than an intelligence test are used, the interview will provide an opportunity to assess the personal and interactive skills of the applicant.

Before exploring the interviewing process in more detail, readers are reminded of the obvious need to take account of the relevant legislation as it affects the selection process. The Equal Pay Act, 1975; the Sex Discrimination Act, 1975; the Race Relations Act, 1976 and the Disabled Persons (Employment) Acts, 1944, 1958 and 1980, are all important in this regard. Readers outside the United Kingdom should check on other national legal requirements which will differ from these provisions.

The skills of interviewing

It is important to bear in mind what purposes are met by the employment interview. This will help develop an appropriate structure for the interview. It meets three basic needs:

- to establish whether the candidate is suitable for the job;
- to provide the candidate with an accurate picture of the job;
- to enable the candidate to gather the information needed to make the best employment decision.

It is clear from these points that the interview must be a two-way process. It will need to be as interactive as possible in order to meet these objectives.

The seven-point plan (see Figure 5.3) has been cited as an orderly job description. It is also designed to be used to ensure that all the necessary information is collected by the interviewer. Whilst it is clearly not a good idea to work through all the elements listed in the plan in the order given, the interviewer should aim to have covered these points one way or another by the time the interview is complete.

By using the seven-point plan as a basis for the interview as well as for the job and person description, it should be possible to compare the information about the job with the information about the applicant so that the best fit between the two can be made. Such a process also helps reduce the danger of concluding a series of interviews with some information about one candidate and not about others. This should help in the process of comparing the merits of a number of applicants.

Whilst the interview is a flawed technique statistically, it can be improved by the adoption of a system such as the seven-point plan or later derivatives based on it. By collecting data of a similar kind from all applicants and by reducing the chances of omitting to collect important information, some, if not all, of the pitfalls of the interview can be avoided.

Interviewing is a skilled process which requires both training and practice. Space does not permit an exhaustive exploration of this area, but the following pointers might prove of value. Try to ensure that:

- there are adequate pre-interview arrangements;
- you follow a system in the interview;
- you retain the information gained;
- you gain the same information from all the candidates;
- you gain and maintain rapport;
- you attempt to measure only what is measurable;
- you provide the candidates with adequate opportunity to find out about the company and the job.

All this is easier said than done. It is helpful if the interview is conducted by more than one person so that a review session can be held during which the interviewers can provide feedback on each other's performance. It is also important that interview decisions are recorded in such a way that follow-up is possible, to see whether and why the employment decisions have been successful or not. There can be no learning without feedback. Effective interviewing should be a continuous learning experience.

Common problems arise in the performance of untrained interviewers, some of which are listed below. Try to avoid:

- jumping from topic to topic;
- engaging in yes/no interrogation;
- talking too much (as a rough guide, the candidate should talk for something like 75 per cent of the time; this will vary of course according to the sophistication of the interviewee);
- making moral judgements and communicating them;
- letting quickly formed superficial overall impressions affect rational thinking;
- dominating the candidate through the development of stress;
- being manipulated by candidates and working to their agenda.

THE ROLE OF THE HUMAN RESOURCE DEPARTMENT

An important aspect of the selection process generally relates to the roles of line manager and personnel specialist. Politically it is important that the

HRM professional is not seen to 'own' the employment decision. If this is felt to be the case, the line manager will lose much of the incentive to make the employment prophecy come true. Indeed there are many instances in which the line manager, not having been involved in the final decision, is committed to making it seem that an incorrect employment decision was taken. 'It's personnel's fault. They will have to get rid of X. What do they expect me to do with the kind of people they send me?' This is an all too common refrain.

Anyway it seems unnatural that a manager should be prepared to assume responsibility for an employee without being involved in the recruitment process. It would constitute an abandonment of the managerial role. It is of course true that not all line managers are skilled in the selection process or are immune from making blunders – particularly with regard to employment law. It is usually useful for a personnel specialist to be present during the interviews to prevent misunderstandings with regard to contractual issues.

CONCLUSION

The personnel professional has a major role to play in the employment process, from ensuring that recruitment is in line with corporate strategy to the monitoring of employment contracts and the auditing of selection processes.

Just as line managers should not relinquish their involvement in staff selection, so professional personnel specialists should not abandon their responsibility for ensuring that there is a coherent recruitment and selection strategy that is well understood and followed. It must be integrated with the needs of the organization and its strategic planning. Adequate training must be available to make the process as effective as possible.

We have argued that effective recruitment and selection are crucial to any coherent human resource strategy. Development, motivation and performance all hinge on the best possible employment decisions. Even the most favourable organizational environment will not encourage effective performance from those unable to achieve.

As we argued at the beginning of the chapter, the improved personal performance of all employees is the basis of enhanced prospects of organizational survival and growth.

FURTHER READING

Rodger, A. (1974) *The Seven Point Plan*, London: National Foundation for Educational Research.

Plumbley, P.R. (1985) *Recruitment and Selection*, London: Institute of Personnel Management (4th edition).

Ungerson, B. (ed.) (1975) *Recruitment Handbook*, Aldershot: Gower Press (2nd edition).

QUESTIONS FOR DISCUSSION

1 Justify the assertion that the final selection decision should be taken by the line or departmental manager, rather than the personnel professional.
2 Given that the interview is a fallible selection method, why does it remain an essential element in the selection process?
3 What major functions does the selection interview fulfil?

Chapter 6

Training and management development

INTRODUCTION

The development of usable skills in employees is one of the most important tasks in which a work organization can engage.

As we have mentioned tirelessly throughout this book, the competitive edge will be maintained by those organizations which use their work force most efficiently. From this it follows that effective training is paramount in the fight for survival and growth. One of the effects of Britain's entry into the single European market is likely to be increased competition for the most able employees, many of them graduates. Graduates in particular expect to be offered post-entry development opportunities.

It is important to ensure, however, that a distinction is made between the quantity and the quality of the training effort. Thoughtless activity which is unrelated to the corporate strategy is not only time- and money-wasting but also in all probability a force for demotivation. Most employees expect the organization to afford opportunities for personal development, and having developed skills and knowledge they expect to be able to use them.

We shall recommend the use of a systematic approach to training and its evaluation. We shall also look at the main training techniques. With regard to management development we shall in addition develop a model for introducing effective MD (management development) efforts. The chapter will conclude with an overview of the way in which employees learn so that expenditure on training and development activities produces the most cost-effective results.

IDENTIFICATION OF TRAINING NEEDS

The most important aspect of the identification stage is organization analysis, which starts with an assessment of the corporate plan. Training has a long history of neglect because it is often seen not to be meeting the needs of line managers. The latter will instinctively know when any particular form of training meets their needs and is worth supporting. It is important then that training is geared to the future development of the organization and is developed in line with human resource planning (see Chapter 3).

Just as important an element in the organization analysis is the assessment of whether training is the appropriate means to achieve a defined need. It is common for managers to identify problems in terms of individual incapacity when in fact there are organizational reasons for the behaviour, which can be alleviated by approaches other than training. Training is not the panacea for all organizational ills. For example, it will not have a great impact on organizational culture, unless it is carried out as part of an organization-wide development programme. Training will have little impact on structural problems such as the presence of a functional structure when a divisional one would be more apt. Training will not in itself cope with problems of poor performance which are related to the reward system in the organization. It might be more apt to replace incremental payment systems with performance-related pay, for example. There is a tendency to view training on the individual level only, without putting it into the context of the organization as a whole. Much money is therefore wasted and the human resource department gains a reputation for an 'ivory tower' posture and for providing training experiences which most managers do not value and try to avoid.

If the identification of training needs has been done effectively, with the involvement of line managers, there should be few instances in which trainees are reluctant to attend a training event or later complain that it was a waste of time. There is always a reason for resistance and it is rarely the result of poor training skills. Failure arises from poor identification of training needs, lack of analysis of whether training is the best response to the organizational problem and non-participation of line managers in the identification process, resulting in their lack of commitment.

One of the factors inhibiting a more positive approach to training amongst some managers has been the problem of measuring results. This will mainly affect those companies which adopt a 'confetti' approach to training and development – hoping that if enough training is carried out, some of it will be of use.

This problem can be reduced by taking a systematic approach to training. Figure 6.1 outlines the required stages. It is essential that all training activities result from the identification of objectives. These may well be identified as part of an appraisal system. There are other means, however, of obtaining the necessary information. Training providers will often find it useful to spend time with departmental managers eliciting from them what they see as the training priorities.

Hopefully line managers will be able to discuss their future human resource requirements; how well they will be able to meet these demands and what skills are likely to be lacking. From this it should be possible to

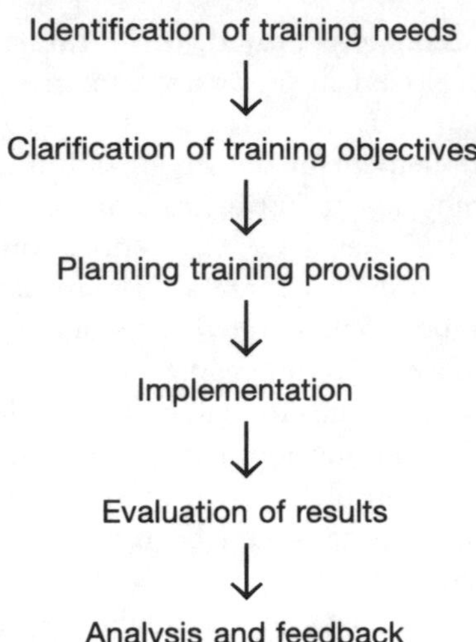

Figure 6.1 The stages in effective training provision

identify shortfalls in available abilities. Managers should be able to identify where lack of skills is currently causing problems. They should be able to provide information which might suggest a training solution. For example, high labour turnover, absenteeism and grievance rates might indicate a need for training in either employees or managers.

Identified training areas can be compared with current training activities and priorities can be developed. The essential point here is that whatever the methods used to collect information, the first step in the provision of systematic training is the identification of objectives, the setting of priorities and the assessment of likely results.

At the individual level, it is important to have available a job specification which spells out the *knowledge, skills* and *attitudes* required to do any particular job. These three elements are important since together they embrace all the aspects of a job.

Knowledge: what jobholders need to know, professional and technical knowledge, knowledge of procedures, knowledge of customers and colleagues with whom they will come into contact; knowledge of objectives.

Skills: what jobholders need to be able to do in order to achieve results at (a) an acceptable and (b) a desirable level; these skills will be more than technical and may include social skills.

Attitudes: jobs vary in the extent and type of behaviour they require; it is important to know what particular characteristics are required – networking abilities for example may be important for a modern-day supervisor.

Once the above information is available, a comparison can be made between what the job requires and what the individual is presently able to offer. The gap between the two is the training arena. Some of these issues will affect most employees and therefore require an OD perspective.

CLARIFICATION OF TRAINING OBJECTIVES

In order to prevent the setting of sloppy and unclear training goals, much interest has been expressed in competency-based training (Boyatsis 1982). This approach to objective setting is *criterion-related*; it is directed at the ability of learners to carry out specific tasks in relation to their present job or a job they will hold in the future. The training goals are expressed in terms of performance outcomes. This is a reaction to training programmes based on little more than the proposition that training is *sui generis* 'a good thing' and thus immune from evaluative efforts in terms of its consequences.

A competency is 'an underlying characteristic of a person which results in effective and/or superior performance in a job'. Boyatsis distinguishes between competencies required for the jobholder to perform adequately and to perform at a superior level. Space does not permit of a detailed account of competencies. Boyatsis (1982) is recommended reading.

Whatever method of clarifying and setting objectives is deployed, the outcomes of the training must be described and must be observable and measurable. Unquantifiable objectives are of little use, turning out to be little more than pious good intentions.

Minimally, there should be a clear statement as to what the trainee will be able to do following the training, in what circumstances and to what measurable extent. There is no good reason why this information should not be given to the trainee before the start of the training activity. There is a good chance that the knowledge will improve the motivation and application of the trainees when they are able to put the various elements of the training into perspective.

The evaluative process is also made easier when clearly stated with precise, objective learning goals.

PLANNING THE PROVISION OF TRAINING

It is important to address the question as to how and where the training should take place. Traditionally training techniques have been classified as belonging to one or other of two groups: 'on the job' or 'off the job'. There are, however, a number of techniques which are suitable for use either in or away from the workplace, that is for which the location is not crucial.

It is worth recalling a general principle of learning theory: the further removed from the workplace, the greater the problem of 'transference'.

This means the all-important carry-over of knowledge from the learning point to the work point. The further the distance, the less likely is the trainee to see the relevance to the work and the more likely is the training to be abstract and too generalized to make for easy practical application.

In particular training removed from the place of application has a tendency to become knowledge-based rather than skills-based. It is simply not possible to develop skills through a process of talking about them. It is also less easy to involve the trainee's line manager in the training process. Training away from the place of work also tends to be more difficult to manage administratively. Generally the most effective and economical training is that which takes place close to the job.

The following training methods are in common use. Readers will be able to decide for themselves into which of the three categories they best fit and which are best suited for different types of learner – non-managers, supervisors or more senior managers.

Action learning. Developed by Revans (1972), groups usually of senior managers come together over a period of time in self-managed small work groups to act as consultants to each other. Each participant will bring to the group a real-life issue to which he or she is committed to finding an answer. So everybody acts as client and consultant. It is important that each group member understands the objectives of the learning method and has the interactive skills necessary to operate in such an environment. It is usual to have an independent process consultant working with these cross-organizational groups. This method is suitable only for managers who have the power to make choices. It is not cheap and can be time-wasting, so that commitment of the members and the availability of a consultant competent in group process is essential. It is true, however, that managers can learn successfully from each other, especially when the learning is problem-centred and under their own control.

Appraisal. One of the most cost-effective methods of management development, appraisal is something which all managers should be both providing for their subordinates and receiving from their own manager. Through the process of reviewing the manager's performance – a process which should be led by the appraisee – counselling will identify successes, review progress and allow for the mutual exploration of alternative, more effective work behaviours. The feedback which the manager will receive and the process of setting objectives and quantifiable targets for the next review period are excellent problem-centred and individualized forms of development.

Assignments. Used often at the end of a training programme, they are useful as a source of feedback as to what has been learned and also to reinforce the learning. They can of course be used in other circumstances, particularly to broaden the experience of trainees. They too need to be planned, so that in sum they improve the competence of the learner in a definable and coherent manner.

Case study. Commonly used in managerial training, on MBA university programmes and the like. Managers can learn by looking at real events and drawing from them principles which they can apply in their own work. Whether advantages accrue depends on the management of the session by the trainer. Since little is at stake, the thinking can be careless and limited to the case rather than aimed at possible applications in a variety of situations.

Coaching. A series of informal meetings between manager and learner following an agenda relevant to the learner's needs, it includes simple techniques such as asking questions, delegation and the setting of projects and assignments. Care must be taken in avoiding fall-off in commitment and the loss of learning objectives.

Computer-based learning. This opens up a new horizon for trainers. Programmed learning provides for interaction between the material and the learner which is economical of time yet offers the opportunity for instant feedback, which reinforces learning. Interactive video allows for different solutions to problems to be tested and for sequential decision taking based on the data provided on screen. The interaction involved prevents the dangers of passive learning and allows for some control of the learning process by the learner. Where learners are widely dispersed and trainers are in short supply, the combined use of computer and video has much to commend it.

Demonstration. Sometimes referred to as 'sitting next to Nellie', this is the archetypal 'on the job' training. The learner is shown what to do, then attempts the activity. This training has the advantage of being problem-centred, and the feedback is immediate. The potential disadvantage is that much depends on the skills and knowledge of the demonstrator. Poor working practices can easily be passed on since the control of the quality of the training is limited.

Do-it-yourself learning. This does not mean simply allowing learners sufficient space and time to manage their own learning. It requires management by the trainer. Learning objectives have to be set, briefing the learner as to where the necessary information might be found and broadly what information is required. The monitoring of performance is an essential element in maintaining commitment and assessing what has been learned.

Instruction. As the name suggests, this is perhaps the most traditional form of learning. It is not without value, however, if well done. It requires clarity of objectives, good explanation and description, and ample time for practice. There needs also to be a mechanism for follow-up to ensure that learning has taken place.

Job rotation. In this well-established method of learning, again, it is important that trainees are not moved around to fill gaps for reasons of administrative convenience, but that their experiences are planned and monitored. Experience for its own sake has only limited learning potential. It is important that the sum total of the experiences leads to a definable goal and each part is relevant to its achievement.

Lecture. Not the most effective of learning methods, though more effective for those who enjoy the mental process of abstract conceptualization, it is more suited to some subject areas than others. It tends to be a passive experience and as such the learners' attention span is usually much shorter than the lecture. Care should be taken that visual aids are used, that question and answer sessions break up the monotony of one-way communication, and that the learners understand the practical implications of what they have learned.

Team development. One of the most significant skills of successful managers has been shown to be the capacity to build and maintain effective working teams, usually of around five to seven people. Group dynamics training has three purposes: to improve the effectiveness of working groups; to allow individuals to learn how they operate in groups and with what effect; and to develop the interactive skills of managers. The degree of structure in such groups varies, as does the length. Typically, however, the individuals in the group learn by attempting to achieve tasks and then analysing their performance and planning to improve. The services of a skilled trainer are essential to encourage the groups to work at a sufficient level of intensity to allow for the giving and receiving of personal feedback and to encourage the group members to learn from their experiences.

THE EVALUATION OF TRAINING

There can be no learning without feedback. This is as true for training and development efforts as anything else. It is essential that training programmes are evaluated and the necessary changes made on the basis of the feedback received. Having said that, it is not always easy to obtain useful feedback, and learner and trainer often collude in preventing the emergence of information as to the efficacy of training efforts either because it is too difficult or because one or more parties fears the consequences of a negative report. The most thorough analysis of evaluation has been provided by Hamblin (1974). He describes feedback as happening at one or more of five levels:

Reactions (Level One). At the end of the training experience learners are asked their opinions of the event. This information is usually collected by questionnaire. Participants have little to gain by saying the event was anything other than a success and the trainer is similarly placed. The resulting information is of limited use. It tells the organization little about the impact of the training in the workplace.

Learning (Level Two). The data are a little more pointed. As a result of comparing the performance of a trainee before and after a course by means of a test of some kind, it is possible to measure in a quantifiable way the extent to which learning has taken place. It still does not tell us whether any of the learning will be applied, however.

Job behaviour (Level Three). In many ways this is the most useful and practical level at which to collect information. What is measured here is the extent to which there has been any change in behaviour after the training as compared with before. This implies that information has been collected beforehand from the bosses of participants. The views of the participants and their colleagues at work should also be collected. But this is not as easy as it seems. There may be a multitude of reasons why the behaviour of a trainee has not changed on return to the workplace, only one of which might be the inadequacy of the training itself. Limited opportunity to put new ideas into practice, changes in role, and unrelated rewards are further possible reasons. None the less it might be argued that for whatever reason, the training was not successful and that further review will be necessary.

This level of evaluation is very important and is also feasible. It is disappointing to learn that the most common types of evaluation are of the Level One and Two types. The reasons are often bound up with the initial lack of involvement of line managers in the planning stages and the lack of effort made in carrying out a needs analysis. Such problems lead to a reluctance on the part of trainers to collect the necessary data.

Not infrequently, in the writer's experience, there is no incentive for trainers to collect any information beyond the reactions level, since managers are sufficiently impressed with favourable throughput statistics at the training centre, with 'bums on seats'.

Organization (Level Four). This level of evaluation is more complex, but its value if carried out is none the less important. Here the focus of intention is on whether the training, however effective, is relevant to the departmental goals of the organization, bringing improvements in output, quality or morale for example. Frequently, training takes place which is quite out of line with the needs of the operating units and therefore fails.

It was common in the 1960s to undertake what was called sensitivity training through the medium of 'T groups'. Fortunately much of the training had minimal impact on the workplace and the participants became discouraged. Had it had more impact there would have been a rather awkward clash between the managerial styles of newly returned participants and the dominant style of the work group.

It is important then that the training takes into account the strategic plans for the group from which the trainees are drawn and that it is consonant with the culture. If it is not, it will surely fail to have an impact. The information required for this level of analysis does not come easily to hand. It requires a good deal of pre-course discussion with the participants and their boss, to ensure that the training will not be either irrelevant to the department or likely to be rejected. It is worth noting again that training is not the most effective way to bring about culture change, though it may have a part to play in an integrated approach to it.

Ultimate value (Level Five). Here the issue is: how has the organization as a whole benefited from the training? Has it helped it to survive, will it help it to develop in the directions planned? Is the trainee now able to contribute more to the goal of increased profitability? What is good for the individual might not necessarily be good for the organization. At this level the training staff need to be in close contact with top management. Issues such as strategic planning are involved. It is difficult to find methods by which the training outcomes can be directly related to these organizational goals, even supposing them to exist. There are many variables other than the presence of a number of well-trained staff which have an impact on organizational health and development. It is rare then that training evaluation takes place at this level in practice.

There seems no reason, however, why more effort should not go into the improvement of feedback particularly at Level Three and also at Level Four.

MANAGING MANAGEMENT DEVELOPMENT

So far in this chapter we have concentrated on training. All of what has been said applies equally to managers and non-managers. There are some issues, however, which are particularly pertinent to the development of managers. It is essential to target accurately management development activities and to interpret the term to mean any planned activity designed to enable managers to operate more effectively in the achievement of organizational goals.

The term training implies too narrow a view of these planned activities. It suggests that training is about sending enough people on courses for attendance targets to be met and trainers to appear credible at performance review time.

The emergence of MD plans must take place as part of the corporate planning process. That in the past this link has been far from clear is an important reason for the low interest in training and development generally on the part of pragmatic line managers who have historically been unwilling to allocate the necessary financial resources and to endow trainers with the power to develop and carry through development plans of any significance.

The days are over when professional trainers could 'potter' with pet projects without the active involvement of line managers and without financial targets against which their efforts could be evaluated. It is all part of the process of integration which, we argued in Chapter 1, is an

Table 6.1 Types of management development activity

STYLE		FOCUS *Individual*	*Group*	*Organization*
STYLE	*Prescriptive*	e.g. General management courses, qualification courses, some forms of appraisal	e.g. Some forms of team building, project-based learning, some forms of management by objectives	e.g. Some forms of management by objectives, some forms of organization development
STYLE	*Consultative*	e.g. Counselling, coaching, needs analysis, career planning, specified experience, task-related courses	e.g. Analysis of problems, identification of needs, role negotiation, action learning, some forms of team building	e.g. Organization analysis and feedback

important distinguishing feature of human resource management as opposed to personnel management.

Frequently, management development has wide implications for the organization as a whole. When sufficient numbers of managers are developed in the same way, MD can become a form of organization development.

The focus of management development

Few organizations share the same structure. Equally, few operate in an environment which is identical. Accordingly, organizations develop their own culture and preferred ways of operating in order to respond to the circumstances they face.

There is then, no one right recipe for management development. It will vary from organization to organization. Even within the one organization, different departments have different problems and require different development activities and strategies. It is wise to adopt a contingency approach and to ensure that sufficient analytical work has been undertaken before an action plan is developed. We can say, however, that in general management development can be aimed at one or more of three levels as described in Table 6.1.

It is commonly felt by managers that management development has for its purpose individual behaviour change. This change can be brought about through a process of providing the manager with new skills, attitudes or knowledge. It is true that the outcome of all training is behaviour change and it is also true that there will be a body of knowledge and skills that any manager will need to carry out a specific job. In such cases, identifying what this knowledge is and then arranging for the individual manager to obtain it is an appropriate form of management development. This focus on the individual is by far the most common.

What is often overlooked, however, is that behavioural change such as better performance or improved attitude to the job can often be achieved more effectively by changing the immediate environment in which the individual works – the development of the work group. Managers sometimes perform less well than they might, not through any shortcoming in inclination or capacity but because there are constraints surrounding the role which either encourage the observed undesirable behaviour or prevent the adoption of any other behaviour.

Take for example a manager who is reluctant to delegate responsibility to others, even reluctant to fill vacancies, because immediate subordinates are seen as a threat. One approach might be to encourage the manager to confront the 'real' personal reasons for the behaviour. Another approach, and almost certainly more effective, would be to look at the manager's role and see whether it is big enough to engage all his or her abilities. If for example managers feel that there is not sufficient work of the right quality to keep them occupied, then they will not feel inclined to surround themselves by immediate others who will see their role for what it is and may even diminish it further. In this case the group should be the focus for change and the redefining of roles becomes an important issue.

In this example the behaviour is a symptom of a problem and not the problem itself. A major reason for the ineffectiveness of much development is that it addresses symptoms. It is always worth analysing whether the target for change is the individual manager or the circumstances in which the manager operates.

Change should also be seen in an organizational context; the third focus level displayed in Table 6.1. The writer has worked in organizations where there has been a major need for greater risk taking amongst managers, greater willingness to assume ownership of problems. Instead, behaviour of quite a different type has predominated: buck passing, 'head below the parapet' routine, following behaviour which neither stretched the individuals concerned nor achieved much in the way of corporate objectives.

Such situations are not unfamiliar. They are rarely the result of poor selection. Rather they reflect an inadequate culture – the preferred ways of managing. These cultural elements are themselves a reflection of the reward system. Managers tend only to practise rewardable behaviour, so 'what you reward is what you get'. If the organization both declares a need for dynamic, risk-taking managers but at the same time operates a reward system that promotes people and enhances their salary on the basis of incremental scales, seniority and 'no recorded fault', the behaviour that will result will be the behaviour which is rewarded – risk-averse behaviour.

Where there is dissonance between what the organization says it wants (the espoused theory) and what it rewards (the practice), invariably it will encourage the latter.

Where such conditions exist, what is required is an organization-wide assessment of the elements in the culture which require changing, followed by an effective change programme. Focusing attention on individual managers – no matter how many of them – will not bring about the required change. In this case the organization itself should be the focus of change. Individual behaviour will change in its turn once the root problem has been addressed.

So we have seen that there are three levels of management development activity focusing on individual behaviour: values and attitudes of managers in groups and finally organization structure.

The style of management development

The second dimension in Table 6.1 is the method by which change in individual behaviour is introduced. It can be prescriptive or consultative.

Examples will come readily to the mind of the reader of attempts to bring about changed behaviour in a prescriptive manner with resulting resistance and failure. In recent years many organizations have introduced appraisal systems. It is not uncommon for the need for them to be felt by personnel staff rather than the appraisees or indeed the appraisers. Little or no consultation may take place with those at the receiving end. The result is a lack of commitment. However sophisticated the appraisal scheme, little will be achieved if those involved lack the commitment to make it work. As a result many schemes have been abandoned.

Any system of management development which is introduced without taking into account the expressed needs of the user may be said to be prescriptive. There are occasions when this approach is appropriate. It can be argued that new starters require an induction programme, or that aspiring managers in professional departments will need to undertake training to gain qualifications. In such cases, it is suitable for the line managers of such employees in conjunction with the human resource department to define training needs and arrange for their provision.

Where, however, new ideas are being introduced, or the active involvement of those being developed is crucial yet uncertain, then prescriptive approaches are unlikely to be effective.

In such cases the consultative approach may have more to offer. Appraisal, career planning, job rotation and mentoring require the active involvement of the trainee. Who knows the trainee's needs best – the trainee or the boss? Each will have information unknown to the other. Effective training requires the pooling of this knowledge to ensure that the most appropriate training opportunities are offered and used.

In the heady days of the 1960s there was a great deal of money available in large companies for management and organization development. There is a celebrated account of a major company which planned to alter its management style to fit the changing demands of an increasingly well-educated work force. Top management arranged for all managers to attend an expensive 'off the job' training programme during which they would learn about the new participative management style. Although many managers had doubts as to the efficacy of the plan and first line managers feared for the safety of their jobs, the company introduced the development plan by way of notice boards informing managers when and where to report for the training. Needless to say, there was a groundswell of revolt, particularly from supervisors who threatened to strike. Top management decided not only to withdraw the training events but to abandon the entire change programme. In this particular company, the possibility of change – any change – had been put back many years. Truly, the medium is the message.

It is important therefore to ensure that proposed change at whichever of the three levels explored previously in this chapter is well based on data obtained by means of organization analysis and diagnosis. Equally important is the need to think carefully about the method of introducing the change. It is not always appropriate to introduce change on a consultative basis. Where the commitment and active involvement of the learners are paramount, however, the obvious option is to involve them in the design of the development experience.

How managers learn

Learning involves the commitment of both learner and trainer. Students will need to adopt a flexible style and trainers must be prepared to vary training methods to suit the learning approaches of the trainee.

Kolb *et al.* (1984) have argued that learning involves four processes:

The beginning point of the learning process is some form of *practical experience* – perhaps an awareness of being successful in a task. It is possible to take this experience and make *reflective observations* about it (what did the individual do or not do?).

If learning is to be effective it is important that the learner then moves on to the stage of *abstract conceptualization.* In order to prevent the likelihood of a repetitive and time-wasting process of repeating the two earlier stages, the learner needs to develop generalizations as to what happened in situations which have some shared characteristics.

Finally, the learning process is complete when these generalizations are put into practice in new situations, a process of *active experimentation.* This allows for the reinforcement of the learning or encourages a recycling of the learning process, beginning again with the gathering of data.

Let us take an example of a child learning to ride a bicycle. It is likely that early attempts will result in falling off the machine (practical experience). Hopefully the child will reflect on these mishaps and observe what happens if things are done differently – riding faster or slower, using a different part of the foot on the pedals and so on (observation and reflection). With persistence, periods on the bicycle will exceed in length those on the ground. The child will be able to form abstract concepts based on these separate experiences – for example, understanding that reducing speed when cornering reduces the risk of falling. Should the child so wish, this learning can be reinforced by experimentations – some successful, others not. The necessary behaviours associated with cycle riding will become second nature. This later process is one of adding to the stock of experience and completes the learning cycle.

Effective learning therefore allows of both an inductive and deductive mental process. Inductive learning is the result of experiencing an event and drawing a conclusion from it. Deductive learning comes about through the process of applying a general theory to a particular situation. Both deductive and inductive processes are vital elements in learning and are mutually dependent. All of the four stages in the 'cycle' are important and take place to a greater or lesser extent every time we learn something. Our learning ability is hampered therefore if we are inclined to use some of the four dependent processes more than others.

Honey and Mumford (1986) have added an alternative description to the four stages in the learning cycle, as is shown in Figure 6.2. The alternatives (in brackets) are behavioural and can be broadened into a description of the characteristic work behaviours of individual managers. Both Kolb and Honey and Mumford have developed personality inventories which enable managers to define which of the four stages in the learning cycle they tend to rely on and as a result what personal characteristics they display as managers as well as what learning environments are most appropriate for them.

Thought must be given not only to defining what the manager needs to learn but how this learning process will take place. Managers for instance do not necessarily take well to the participative experiential training methods which many trainers seek to deploy. The more the time, place and method of training take account of the needs of the learner, the more effective will be the learning process.

CONCLUSION

A period of economic recession is a fruitful time in which to invest in change. Unfortunately, as the experience of the United Kingdom, amongst other countries, suggests, there is every likelihood that insufficient

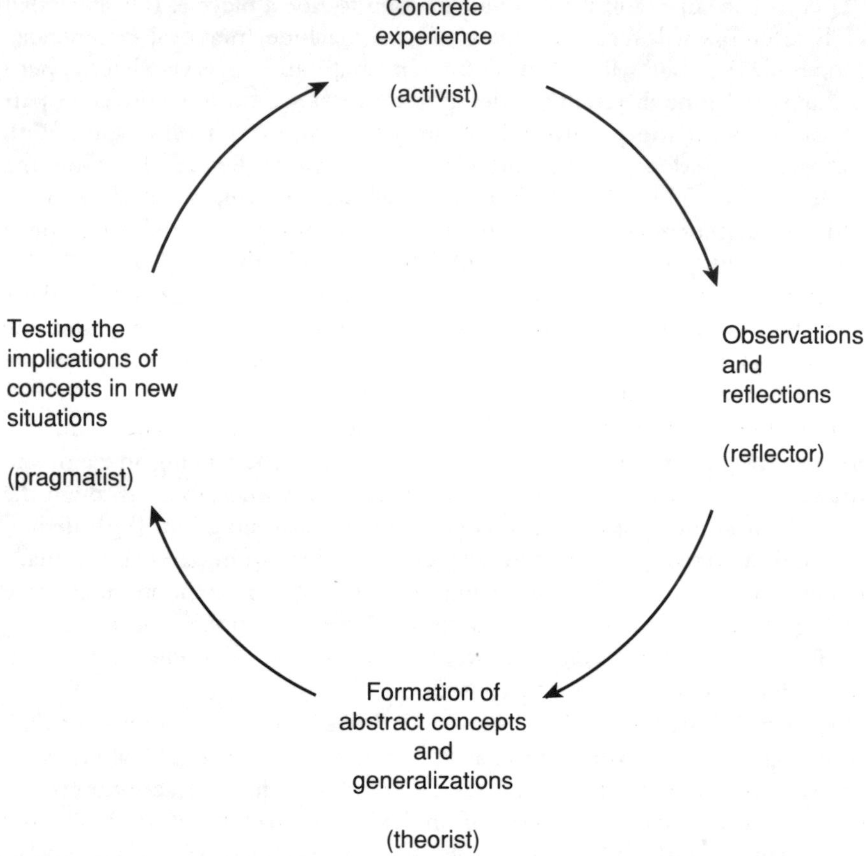

Figure 6.2 The learning cycle

resources will be available and the economic upturn will once more be accompanied by a chronic shortage of skilled labour.

Part of the reluctance to train and develop staff at all levels stems from a feeling that the training process is unpleasant and generally irrelevant. It is therefore thought as well to leave it to peripheral managerial groups such as professional trainers.

We have argued that training will only assume its rightful importance when it becomes valued by managers. This sense of value will depend on the provision of training and development experiences which are based on the mutual respect of learner and trainer.

Goals must be set with the maximum of learner involvement and training overall must respond and be related to the perceived problems of the learner. This will require in practice the individualization of training and the involvement of the learner in the planning process.

Most adults are themselves a learning resource and their experience and enthusiasm should be used in the implementation of training and development plans. Such processes will ensure a degree of activity which, as we have seen, is important in gaining commitment. Their involvement in the evaluation stage is important for the same reasons.

Token attempts at evaluation which are developed and controlled by the trainer are likely to continue to produce a poor basis for the planning of future training. Evaluation holds the key to the wider acceptance of the need to develop staff. At the moment when it becomes clear that there is a favourable 'bottom line' consequence of training expenditure, the problem of under-financing will disappear.

FURTHER READING

Burgoyne, J. and Stuart, R. (1978) 'Management Development Programmes: Underlying Assumptions about Learning', in J. Burgoyne and R. Stuart (eds) *Management Development: Context and Strategies*, London: Gower Press.

Molander, C.F. (1986) *Management Development: Key Concepts for Managers and Trainers*, Bromley: Chartwell Bratt.

Walters, B. (1983) 'Designing and Resourcing Training', in D. Guest and T. Kenny (eds) *A Textbook of Techniques and Strategies in Personnel Management*, London: Institute of Personnel Management.

QUESTIONS FOR DISCUSSION

1 Describe the main characteristics of a systematic approach to training.
2 What learning principles should be taken into account in the planning of management development?
3 Why is evaluation so important in training and development? What in your view are the most effective methods of evaluation?

Chapter 7

Equal opportunity

INTRODUCTION

This chapter explores equal opportunities (EO) issues in the HRM context. While most people would support abstract ideas of fairness, the application of equal opportunities principles may be problematic in practice. Our own preferences and prejudices may operate unconsciously to disadvantage certain employees or job applicants, and the institutional arrangements which are made for recruitment, selection, training, supervision or promotion may have a similar effect. Aside from intentional discrimination, such as advertising a vacancy for a man only, there are four ways in which unfair discrimination can occur. Discrimination may arise from unequal treatment, whereby a different set of standards is applied to a particular group, for example if an English language test were given only to job candidates from an ethnic minority. Even where the same standards are applied, these may disadvantage a particular group and so represent the unequal effect of formally equal treatment. For example, a minimum height requirement for a post, applied equally across gender, could exclude a higher proportion of women than men and would need to be justified as a qualification for a job. Thirdly, practices such as word-of-mouth recruitment may perpetuate disadvantage arising from past discrimination which has maintained a work force from a dominant ethnic group. Finally, discrimination may take the form of retaliation against other employees who seek to oppose established discriminatory practices or speak out about sexual harassment.

At this point the reader should, perhaps, pause and question whether they genuinely believe in equality and fairness as principles in employment. The arguments in favour of equal opportunities reduce to the moral and the technical. The moral argument is straightforward: all people have a right to be treated equally irrespective of gender, ethnic origin, colour, religion or sexual orientation. This principle does not preclude unequal treatment on the basis of job-related criteria: clearly if there are fifty applicants for one job, forty-nine will be disappointed. Similarly, employees who are persistently late or absent may be treated differently as a result of their behaviour, but disciplinary action (see Chapter 12) must be consistently applied in a non-discriminatory way.

The technical argument is that discriminatory practices introduce human resource inefficiencies. If a person discriminates against particular applicants, using criteria which are not job-related, they may be denying the enterprise an opportunity of recruiting the best candidate simply on the basis of gender, ethnic origin or some other job-irrelevant characteristic. Moreover, discrimination and other unfair practices can have a negative impact upon morale. If, for example, female employees perceive that the fast track for career progression is only available to men, they will understandably become resentful and either seek career advancement with a different employer or become resigned to a no-prospects job and contribute accordingly.

Although these moral and technical arguments are largely self-evident, discriminatory practices are so ingrained in human behaviour that governments in most industrialized countries have found it necessary to legislate. Equal opportunities legislation is designed to constrain the behaviour of the minority of individuals who consciously intend to discriminate unfairly and of the majority who accept the abstract principles but who nevertheless unconsciously discriminate. The moral and technical arguments are therefore supplemented by legal compulsion: certain discriminatory practices in employment are unlawful. Clearly, therefore, anyone involved in managing human resources must address equal opportunities.

The remainder of this chapter examines the basis of gender and ethnic inequalities in society and considers various means for developing equal opportunities. In exploring the roots of inequalities we are better able to understand our own attitudes and those of others. Legislation and human resource practices are considered as complementary mechanisms to promote EO.

THE BASIS OF INEQUALITY

Women and workers from ethnic minorities both occupy a disadvantaged position in the labour market and often suffer from discrimination. They are concentrated disproportionately in work that is unskilled and low paid, and, in the case of workers from ethnic minorities, have a higher rate of unemployment than average. These problems need to be viewed in the context of the social structure and distribution of income in Britain at large; as general living standards improve, these workers become less disadvantaged, but when the economy is in recession inequality increases and the position of the disadvantaged worsens. Marx and Engels referred to the workers who comprised this bottom stratum as the 'lumpen proletariat' and noted that the Irish and Jewish immigrants formed a substantial proportion of them in nineteenth-century Britain (although they were silent on the subordination of women). Where the majority of members of the lumpen proletariat derive from distinctive ethnic backgrounds, this has been variously described as the 'marginal working class' or 'underclass'.

The underclass, subordinate to, and socially segregated from, the indigenous working class, is maintained with the cooperation of the dominant ethnic groups within the working class. Thus indigenous (white, Christian) workers in France, Germany and Spain are insulated to a degree from fluctuations in demand for labour by the temporary employment of migrant workers from Algeria, Turkey and Morocco (Castles and Kosack 1973). Even in the USA, where there is no *Gastarbeiter* system of temporary alien labour, the underclass has been shown to comprise the 'ethnic poor', Puerto Ricans and Mexicans who work in low-wage, non-unionized service industries and have high rates of chronic unemployment. Similarly, in Britain, black workers who were attracted to this country from the Commonwealth during times of labour shortages in the 1950s and 1960s were typically employed in jobs where low pay and poor conditions made it difficult to retain indigenous labour. Such workers were often disadvantaged in terms of language, culture and work experience, and while the state was ready to utilize such labour, inadequate provision was made for housing, education and social services. With the rise in unemployment during the 1970s, inner-city problems were exacerbated and black youths experienced discrimination in addition to existing disadvantages (Smith 1974, 1976).

It is characteristic for the underclass itself to be divided along ethnic lines. Inevitably, one group becomes established as the predominant underclass until circumstances cause an influx of another group. Thus Irish immigrants to England formed the underclass in London from the 1860s, but from about 1875 they were joined by Jews fleeing Polish pogroms and Tsarist persecution. Just as the indigenous workers had complained that the Irish undercut their wages and were difficult to organize, so the Irish accused Jews of undercutting them in the labour market. Similarly, when Asian workers entered Britain in the 1970s, they were initially in competition with the Afro-Caribbean workers who were already established as the new underclass. Rimmer (1972) documents the development of ethnic work groups in foundries, where industrial conflict was complicated by racial tensions between different groups of black workers.

The notion of a 'dual labour market' helps to explain the concentration of women in particular occupations. Most women are confined to the secondary sector of boring jobs with no prospects and rarely enter the primary sector of well-paid secure jobs with career prospects. Thus men overwhelmingly predominate in top jobs such as doctors, managers and barristers, whereas nurses, secretaries and cleaners are predominantly female. Women are also held to form part of a 'reserve army of labour', brought into employment when required by employers and repelled in response to economic or technological changes. Thus women were drawn into munitions work during the two world wars only and form the bulk of seasonal workers in food processing and agriculture.

Neither the dual labour market nor the reserve army theory explains the root cause of women's subordination (indeed both concepts can equally be applied to subordinate ethnic groups). Sociologists point to gender roles within the family or household and their associated ideological underpinning. In the patriarchal society the primary duties of women, bound to wage-earning men by a cash nexus, are to sustain the wage labourer and to reproduce him. These duties entail the provision of meals, the maintenance of the household and the rearing, as well as the bearing, of children. Thus women are isolated in their domestic role outside the social relations of production. When women enter employment it is overwhelmingly in occupations which mirror their household role: teaching (especially primary, nursery), nursing, hotel and catering, secretarial, cleaning, food processing and clothing. Women's wage labour becomes an extension of women's domestic labour. Homeworkers, the vast majority of whom are women, and many from ethnic minorities, are largely denied access both to legal protection and representation by trade unions.

Both with women workers and ethnic minorities, the low unionization of the underclass should be seen as part of their exploitation. Not only is the underclass exploited in terms of relative rewards, but also in terms of disposition to become unionized. The objective condition of the underclass is maintained as a result of the propagation of an ideology condoning that position by society at large, and by the failure of the trade unions adequately to represent the interests of the underclass either because this has little prospect of adequate returns, or for fear of alienating their majority membership.

The very concept of 'race' is confusing because it may refer to ethnic or national origins, colour or, in some cases, religion. Nevertheless, it is possible to identify racism as a belief that certain ethnic groups are somehow 'inferior' to others. Racism is probably endemic to all societies, but causes particular distress in the employment field during times of economic recession. The dominant group, typically white Anglo-Saxon Protestants within the British and American contexts, expresses its prejudice towards groups which it considers to be inferior in the employment area by refusing to accept 'coloured' (or Jewish, Irish or whatever) supervisors, avoiding jobs in which the underclass is predominant, and expecting to earn more than members of the underclass, even for performing the same job.

Racism is a serious problem in society at large (see Dummett 1973), and the trade union and labour movement has not escaped the problem. Black workers have joined trade unions and in some, like the rail and the health service unions, there has been no evidence of any antagonism from white workers. However, there have been isolated problems where work forces are racially divided in terms of skills. In the Mansfield Hosiery dispute of 1972, white skilled workers closed ranks against Asians in order to preserve higher wages, status and job security. Full-time union officials allowed themselves to be pressured by the white membership into reinforcing this divisive tendency, so the credibility of the union was eroded among black members. There have even been odd cases of individual union members with right-wing connections attempting to operate within the movement. As a result, some trade unions introduced rules making membership of racist or Fascist organizations incompatible with membership of the union. Such moves, however well-intentioned, opened the way for broader exclusions or expulsions of 'extremists' (which could ultimately result in excluding Communists and other left groups which have campaigned against racism), and to legislation restricting 'unreasonable exclusion' from union membership.

LEGISLATION TO DETER DISCRIMINATION

While laws improving employment security were extended during the 1970s, legislation was simultaneously introduced to promote equality and prevent discrimination at work on the basis of gender or race. The first statute was the Equal Pay Act, 1970 (EqPA), which was followed by the Sex Discrimination Act, 1975 (SDA), on which the Race Relations Act, 1976 (RRA), was modelled.

Equal pay

The principle of 'equal remuneration for men and women for work of equal value' derives from Convention 100 of the International Labour Office and has been an aim of the Trades Union Congress since 1888. The EqPA 1970, which came into force at the end of 1975 and was amended by the SDA, provided for men and women in certain circumstances to receive the same terms and conditions in their contracts, collective agreements and pay structures. The Act is worded in the female throughout, but its provisions apply equally to men.

The right to equal pay occurs in three situations: where a woman is employed on like work with a man in the same employment (s.1.4 EqPA); where the work is rated as equivalent with that of a man in the same employment (s.1.5 EqPA); and where a discriminatory pay structure or collective agreement exists (s.3 EqPA).

In the first case, 'like work' means that the work is the same or of a broadly similar nature, where differences are not of practical importance. This second part has been held to relate to what is actually done, rather than what a job description contains, so even a major contractual difference may be ignored if seldom invoked. The second case of work rated as equivalent is aimed at removing the loophole of 'like work', whereby an employer could pay men more for work which would be rated (in job evaluation terms) as lower than the work of women simply because the two sexes are segregated occupationally.

Where an individual complains to a tribunal under s.1 EqPA that a term of her contract is less favourable than that of a man in the same employment, she must therefore show that the work is the same or of a broadly similar nature, or rated as equivalent, and that the differences are not of practical importance. The employer must then demonstrate either that the complainant is not doing similar work, or that the variation is due to a 'genuine material difference' between the cases compared (s.1.3 EqPA).

There are several genuine material differences, other than gender, which an employer may use as a defence. It has been held that an employer may legally offer different terms and conditions in different locations, even if these are staffed by different sexes (since the difference can be attributed to local labour market conditions). A different rate of pay for men and women can also be defended where an employer can demonstrate that a genuine grading system not designed to conceal discrimination is being operated. Historical anomalies are also defensible where regrading has left certain men who were in the former grade receiving a higher rate than those now entering the job. In such cases these men preserve their pay through 'red-circling', but the employer must show that this applies regardless of gender, and did not arise in any way because of past discrimination.

The third aspect of the EqPA is collective, relating to discriminatory pay structures or agreements, and enables trade unions, employers or the Department of Employment to submit a claim to the Central Arbitration Court (s.3 EqPA). Claims can be made to the CAC to remove discrimination by extending any provision to workers of one gender which currently is applied to those of the other, or to raise women to the lowest male rate.

The issue of equal pay for work of equal value has become increasingly important since the mid-1980s. Plumer (1992) analysed recent tribunal cases and found that there was significant variation in terms of the choice of factors to be taken into account when comparing jobs, the scoring system used, the weighting given to scores on each factor to produce an overall measure of two jobs, and the interpretation of 'equality'. In some cases, jobs rated from between 79 and 98 per cent of the value of a comparator job were defined as not equal, while in other cases jobs scoring 79 per cent of the comparator were defined as equal.

Sex discrimination

The SDA renders unlawful certain discrimination on the grounds of sex or, in the employment field, marital status (s.3 SDA). The provisions are worded in the terms of discrimination against women but apply equally to men (s.2 SDA). The SDA introduced the important concepts of direct and indirect discrimination. Direct discrimination occurs where a man discriminates against a woman on the grounds of her sex or treats her less favourably than he treats a man (s.1.1.a SDA). Indirect discrimination arises where a person applies to a woman a requirement or condition which is applied equally to a man but:

(i) which is such that the proportion of women who can comply with it is considerably smaller than the proportion of men;
(ii) which cannot be shown to be justifiable irrespective of the sex of the person to whom it is applied;
(iii) which is to her detriment because she cannot comply with it (s.1.1.b SDA).

The SDA makes discrimination unlawful in a number of fields, but we are concerned with the area of employment, covered by Part II of the Act. The SDA makes it unlawful for an employer to discriminate against a woman in recruitment:

(a) in the arrangements he makes for the purpose of determining who should be offered that employment; or
(b) in the terms on which he offers her that employment; or
(c) by refusing or deliberately omitting to offer her that employment (s.6.1 SDA).

It is also unlawful for an employer to discriminate against a woman:

(a) in the way he affords her access or opportunities for promotion, transfer or training; or
(b) by dismissing her (s.6.2 SDA).

Similarly, it is unlawful for a trade union to discriminate against a woman:

(a) in the terms on which it is prepared to admit her to membership; or
(b) by refusing . . . her application for membership (s.12 SDA).

Also, it is unlawful for qualifying bodies (s.13 SDA), vocational training bodies (s.14 SDA) and employment agencies (s.15 SDA) to discriminate on the grounds of gender.

Exceptions to the unlawfulness of sex discrimination exist where 'being a man is a genuine occupational qualification for a job'. Major cases are:

(a) reasons of physiology (excluding strength) or authenticity (e.g. male models);
(b) grounds of decency (e.g. lavatory attendants);
(c) the job is living-in and separate accommodation cannot be made for the sexes;

(d) the job must be held by a man because it is in an all-male prison or hospital;
(e) the job provides personal services which can most effectively be provided by a man;
(f) there are restrictions imposed by laws regulating the employment of women (e.g. with respect to health and safety) (s.7.2 SDA).

The SDA (s.53) established the Equal Opportunities Commission (EOC) to work towards eliminating sex discrimination and to promote equal opportunities between men and women, as well as to review the working of the SDA and the EqPA. The SDA is enforced through industrial tribunals and the burden of proof rests on the claimant (s.63 SDA), which reduces the power of the legislation, but this has been overcome to some extent by the ruling of the Employment Appeal Tribunal that where a difference of treatment is established by comparison between a male and a female, a prima facie case of discrimination is raised.

Racial discrimination

The RRA, which replaced the 1965 and 1968 Acts, makes it unlawful to discriminate on racial grounds in similar circumstances to those in which sex discrimination is unlawful. 'Racial' grounds under the Act refers to colour, race, nationality, or ethnic or national origins (s.3 RRA), but not religion. The Act is modelled on the SDA and thereby covers both direct discrimination, where a person is treated less favourably on racial grounds (s.1.1.a RRA), and indirect discrimination, where treatment is formally equal but has a discriminatory effect (s.1.1.b RRA).

In the employment field, as with the SDA, the RRA makes discrimination by employers unlawful in recruitment (s.4.1 RRA) and terms of employment and promotion (s.4.2 RRA). It is unlawful for trade unions to discriminate against a person on racial grounds in terms of admittance to membership (s.11 RRA), as it is for qualifying bodies (s.12 RRA), vocational training bodies (s.13 RRA) and employment agencies (s.14 RRA).

Exceptions to racial discrimination again exist where 'being of a particular racial group is a genuine occupational qualification for a job', the major instances being:

(a) authenticity in the entertainment field;
(b) authenticity in photographic modelling;
(c) authenticity in places where food or drink is provided;
(d) the job involves the provision of services for welfare of a racial group and can be most effectively provided by a person of that racial group.

The RRA (s.43) established the Commission for Racial Equality (CRE), now known as the Community Relations Council (CRC), to work towards eliminating racial discrimination, to promote equality of opportunity and good relations between persons of different racial groups, and to review the working of the Act. Complainants must bring their case, within three months of the action complained of, to the attention of an industrial tribunal (s.54 RRA), which is empowered to award compensation which may include elements for trouble, inconvenience and hurt feelings.

EQUAL OPPORTUNITY AND HUMAN RESOURCE PRACTICES

While legislation may limit the worst excesses of discriminatory practices in employment, the CRE and its successor the CRC recognized that most advance is likely to be made through the practices of management and unions committed to promoting equality of opportunity, so they encouraged employers to adopt EO policies. Over the past decade many employers have publicized their EO policies in all job advertisements, demonstrating at least an awareness of demographic changes which may cause recruitment difficulties in the future, and, in most cases, a genuine commitment to increase opportunities for women and members of ethnic minorities.

For an EO policy to be more than simply a pious statement of intent (or in the worst case cynical image building), employers should allocate overall responsibility for the policy to a senior member of management; agree the policy with the relevant representatives of employees; make the policy known to all existing employees and applicants; provide training to support the initiative; and develop procedures and practices in line with the EO policy.

An affirmative action plan is essential to put equal opportunities principles into practice within an enterprise, and this must include both the formal systems of organization and the informal systems relating to the attitudes and behaviour of individuals. An EO programme must begin with a survey of existing employees and an audit of HRM policies and procedures. The employee survey is designed to identify where women and ethnic minorities are under-represented or concentrated. The age structure, patterns of turnover and career progression to date of these groups should be compared with a reference (white, male) group.

An audit of the formal HRM policies and procedures is necessary to identify practices which may operate to disadvantage women or minority groups. Any HRM procedures identified which appear to be discriminatory, or to have that effect, must be altered to promote EO. Once a gender and ethnic survey of existing employees has been completed, EO objectives can be established and incorporated into the human resource plan (see Chapter 3) developed to meet the organization's future labour requirements. Affirmative action impinges on all HR activities. For example, in recruitment (see

Chapter 5), employers promoting an EO policy should use women and minority-group members as role models in job advertisements, as selectors and interviewers, and on recruitment drives to schools and universities. The EO policy must be continually reaffirmed in all publicity and, while an affirmative action programme takes time to become effective, without it there is no return on a 'passive' commitment to EO.

Similarly, training procedures (see Chapter 6) should be designed so that women and minority groups are not disadvantaged either in their access to training or the way in which it is organized. It is unlawful to restrict access to training according to gender or ethnic origin, but this may be an unintended effect of arrangements for determining who should attend training sessions, or simply the timing or location of the training. Women may be less likely to put themselves forward for training which involves periods of absence away from home, while employees drawn from ethnic minorities may have special dietary requirements which will need to be accommodated. Training programmes may have an adverse impact on women or ethnic minorities where male-oriented activities are involved or where the command of English required to follow the training is significantly greater than will be required to perform the job. An affirmative action plan will consider ways of promoting the participation of women and minorities in training, and the law allows for positive discrimination to provide training designed to remedy the under-representation of these groups in certain positions.

Every aspect of formal HRM procedures must similarly be scrutinized as part of the affirmative action to promote EO. Thus performance appraisal systems (see Chapter 8) need to be culture-free and to be operated in such a way that women and minority workers are able to derive the same developmental benefits as other employees. Women should ideally be appraised by women, and the fact that there is often not a sufficiently senior woman in an enterprise to perform the task is further evidence of their under-representation in management positions. At the very least, appraisal training should include a consideration of how gender and cultural differences affect the appraisal process.

Non-discriminatory pay structures are a legal requirement, but some forms of payment may unintentionally disadvantage women and minority groups. The problems of performance-related pay (see Chapter 9) in particular are analogous to those of appraisal, where the subjective element of performance review may be influenced by subconscious sexism and racism. The observation of a recent study (Thompson 1994) that 'attractive' people are given significantly better ratings under performance-related pay must be a cause for concern.

Although the law also prohibits unfair selection for redundancy on the grounds of gender or ethnic origin, redundancy procedures may nevertheless disadvantage these groups, and would need to be modified under an affirmative action programme to promote EO. The traditional 'last in, first out' agreements, for example, are formally non-discriminatory at the level of individuals, but discriminate against groups which exhibit a higher labour turnover, such as women and ethnic minority workers. If the organization is committed to EO, then the reasons for the higher turnover of these groups must be recognized and length of service not made the primary determinant of who is selected for redundancy. Indeed, in the case of women selected for redundancy from a mixed-gender work force, there would arguably be a case of unfair dismissal (or unfair selection for redundancy) if the 'last in, first out' principle is applied. If it could be demonstrated that the proportion of women who could comply with a particular length of service requirement was lower than in a similar group of men because some women leave the work force temporarily when their families are young, the 'last in, first out' principle could constitute indirect discrimination.

The audit of formal HRM policies and procedures should identify where change is necessary to promote EO practices. Since the strategy for change will need to engage both the formal and the informal systems, it is important to identify how changes to one may affect the other. The primary requirement for changing the informal system to promote EO is that those affected and likely to play a part in the change process should be convinced that a problem exists and that there is a need for change. The employee survey may increase awareness of the issues and demonstrate the extent to which a problem of under-representation exists, but there is always the temptation to explain away such findings in terms of women or minority workers not applying for the posts, not having the required experience or qualifications, or simply having different career expectations. The audit of HRM procedures then becomes important in convincing individuals that the problem also has something to do with the policies and procedures of the organization.

Even once senior management are convinced of the need for change to promote EO, there are limitations to what can be achieved through formal systems. Managers and supervisors may be trained to understand how direct and indirect discrimination operates in an organization and introduced to new procedures developed as part of affirmative action, but the informal system needs to support changes in behaviour, and this may need a change in attitudes. Using organizational development tools (see Chapter 2), interventions in the informal system can be used to articulate a need for formal changes to the policies and procedures. More often, however, the informal system undermines the effectiveness of both legislation and a company's formal EO policies.

There are several reasons why so little progress has been made towards the goals of EO. The white male (and we could add without exaggeration Anglo-Saxon Protestant) predominates in positions of power in British society, so most of those best placed to promote change have no personal experience of discrimination and disadvantage. The EO policies in an organization may conflict with, and are frequently subordinate to, other organizational goals. Values which could be described as sexist and racist are an inherent part of socialization, which influences the attitudes of individuals and their behaviour in the informal system.

Given these difficulties, Wainwright (1981) offered an alternative strategy comprising eight stages designed to promote attitudes and behaviour conducive to the maintenance of effective EO practices:

1 identify the group to be responsible for the development and how employees are to be kept informed of its progress;
2 discuss problems revealed by the employee survey and HRM audit;
3 review formal systems and recommend changes;
4 explore existing attitudes and identify needs for attitudinal changes;
5 establish training to tackle issues of cultural bias or stereotyping;
6 once one area, such as recruitment, has been addressed, change a small number of group members to broaden involvement;
7 use achievements to date to illustrate the role of EO practices in the organization's future;
8 take positive steps, such as special training provision, to increase the participation of women or minorities.

All of the above suggestions could be initiated unilaterally by management without reference to employee representatives, and indeed this would be inevitable where employees were unorganized. However, where some form of employee representation exists, the approach adopted in this book (see Chapter 4) would recommend that representatives are involved in the change process. During the late 1970s, the TUC recommended the insertion of an EO clause in the collective agreements negotiated by affiliated trade unions. Such a clause commits the parties to developing 'positive policies to promote equal opportunity in employment regardless of workers' sex, marital status, creed, colour, race or ethnic origins' (McMullen 1978: 117). Some agreements broadened the concept of equality of opportunity to include religion and sexual orientation. The EO clause is rather like the company EO policies it was designed to promote: it represents nothing more than a starting point and a statement of intent, so has to be policed and administered to become meaningful.

Similarly, the commitment to EO within a trade union must be measured in terms of the practices of lay and full-time officials, and the arrangements made within the organization to promote the active involvement of women and minorities. Trade union policies have not been immune from racism and sexism in the past. Many of the craft unions especially had restrictions on membership for women, and even in female-majority unions only a small proportion of full-time officials are women. Nevertheless, the trade union movement as a whole is nowadays far more enlightened and has done much to promote EO in employment.

Clearly, the application of any statement or agreement, as with the enforcement of the law, depends largely upon the willingness of employers and trade unionists to pursue equality of opportunity in earnest.

CONCLUSIONS

This chapter has traced the origins of inequality in society and shown how discrimination can result from attitudes and behaviour which are irrational but condoned to such an extent that we are all, unconsciously, socialized into adopting stereotypes and negative images of people different from ourselves.

Legislation to combat discrimination on the basis of gender or ethnic origin deters the most blatant unequal treatment, and the inclusion of both direct and indirect discrimination requires individuals to consider their actions carefully in order to avoid unconscious discrimination. Nevertheless, a fundamental change of attitudes is required to move beyond mere acquiescence with legal requirements towards behaviour which actively supports the promotion of a fairer society.

An integrated human resources strategy can make a major contribution to promoting EO, but this requires commitment to the principles throughout the organization. A positive action programme is designed not only to remedy deficiencies in the formal system's policies and procedures, but also to promote change in the informal system and to create an organizational culture in which individual attitudes and behaviour support the development of a work environment free from discrimination, inequality and unfairness.

FURTHER READING

Braham, P., Rhodes, E. and Pearn, M. (eds) (1981) *Discrimination and Disadvantage in Employment*, London: Harper & Row.

Castles, S., and Kosack, G. (1983) *Immigrant Workers and Class Structure in Western Europe*, Oxford: Oxford University Press.

Dummett, A. (1973) *A Portrait of English Racism*, London: Penguin.

Equal Opportunities Commission (1978) *Guidance on Equal Opportunity Policies and Practices in Employment*, Manchester: EOC.

McMullen, J. (1978) *Rights at Work*, London: Pluto, 1978.

Rimmer, M. (1972) *Race and Industrial Conflict*, London: Heinemann.

Smith, D.J. (1974) 'Racial Disadvantage in Employment', *Political and Economic Planning*, Vol. XL, 544, reprinted and enlarged 1976.

QUESTIONS FOR DISCUSSION

1 'The promotion of equal opportunity is less of a priority for most enterprises than the maintenance of competitive advantage.' Discuss.
2 Is legislation an effective mechanism for eliminating discriminatory practices in employment?
3 If developing a positive action programme as part of a human resource strategy, would you begin with the formal or informal system? Why?

Chapter 8

Performance appraisal

INTRODUCTION

Performance appraisal is fundamental to the entire process of human resource management. In Chapter 1, it was argued that the development of HRM as opposed to personnel management involved a culture change. Important elements in that change include greater concern for the development and motivation of individual employees. Carried out effectively, performance appraisal is the dominant process for achieving these objectives.

This chapter will seek to examine performance appraisal, a concept around which there is still much confusion; to outline the philosophy which underpins worthwhile systems; and to examine the key managerial skills and processes involved.

APPRAISAL IN CONTEXT

There are at least three possible uses for appraisal: it can be used as a technique for reviewing current performance; it is often used to aid the process of managerial succession planning; finally it is sometimes seen as an important part of a wage payment system. Braddick and Smith (n.d.) list overt and covert needs which the various parties involved in an appraisal scheme might have. These are reproduced in Figure 8.1.

Many problems have arisen precisely because too much is asked of an appraisal system. It is difficult to see how, for example, the three possible objectives can usefully be combined in the one activity. Different relationships are required of the manager and jobholder in each case, and they cannot be combined effectively.

This is not to argue the absence of a link between appraisal and pay, but rather to propose that discussions about pay should be separated from review of current performance. The former discussion inevitably involves an element of negotiation and competition which are alien to a proper review of performance. The latter requires an open supportive approach to

PARTY / PURPOSES	APPRAISER	APPRAISEE	TOP MANAGEMENT	PERSONNEL
POSSIBLE OVERT	Performance improvement Identify potential Validate previous training Establish training needs Update job definition Relate individual performance to company objectives Salary administration Improve mutual understanding Set targets/objectives Indicate needed changes in organization Get appraisee's feelings about boss, his or her job, the company	Feedback on personal effectiveness Personal future with the company Resolve problems Establish training needs Communicate with boss Question the system/ organization	Identify future potential Audit for succession planning Promotion of participation/ motivation Improve individual/ organization productivity Identify organization strengths and weaknesses Reveal training needs Reveal individual aspirations Reinforce organizational objectives Provide feedback to staff on performance	Analysis of training and developmental needs Manpower/succession planning Salary administration
POSSIBLE COVERT	Strengthen manager's position Get away with the interview without disrupting relationships 'Knobble the unruly', e.g. control deviation Induce changes in behaviour beneficial to department/system Get information about problems otherwise unspoken Placate impatience etc.	Ingratiate with reciprocal confidences Confirmation of acceptability Minimize stress Demonstrate 'equality' with boss Negotiate special favours/rewards or relationship with boss Reassurance	Show evidence of concern for people Indicator of morale Check on attitudes to and effectiveness of top management Reinforcement of organization values As a symbol of equity and 'justice'	Monitor effectiveness of appraisal system Aid recruitment 'To be seen to be doing something' Reinforce personnel values and norms Documentation for legal aspects of discipline/dismissal Give power to personnel department

Figure 8.1 Purposes of the parties to the appraisal process
Source: Braddick and Smith (n.d.)

common problems, and is concerned with how the jobholder can improve performance in the present job.

Naturally there will be a degree of evaluation in any appraisal – implicit if not explicit. It is important, however, that any such evaluation is used in the process of allocating rewards only as a different exercise and at a different time.

So far as this chapter is concerned, therefore, the term 'appraisal' should be seen as a purely developmental activity and not as part of a pay review.

Performance appraisal and management development

It is now generally agreed that it is not possible to produce a list of common factors which motivate any individual employee. Vroom (1964) and others have argued convincingly that motivation comes about through a psychological process in which the individual feels that personal needs have been satisfied. But there is no consensus as to these needs. For some they will include the need to achieve, and to have autonomy and responsibility. For others, however, security, a steady income and continuity of employment are the main rewards which work has to offer. Without doubt expectations of work change as we progress through the life cycle; at one time prospects for rapid promotion may be important. At another, the main reward comes from the experience of steady, regular employment with an assured if not spectacular income.

It is of vital importance that the employee's manager is familiar with the forces which motivate all those individuals for whom there exists a direct reporting relationship. A major managerial responsibility is to provide, so far as is feasible, the circumstances and the environment in which staff feel encouraged to operate most effectively. Day-to-day informal contact is not sufficient to provide the manager with the knowledge of employees on which to build a needs-based approach to staff motivation. Regular and intensive face-to-face discussions are required.

Equally important is the role of performance appraisal in releasing the potential of the employee. Basic to personal skill development is access to feedback, or knowledge of results. The employee's immediate manager is the individual most appropriate to provide the necessary information through the process of performance review.

Without feedback, there can be no learning. The basis for anything other than random behaviour is a knowledge of the gap between intended and actual results. Anyone who has for example attempted to master computer-based keyboard skills will know that it is only when sufficient errors appear on the monitor screen in the way of feedback that appropriate corrective steps are taken to improve performance. Detailed study of the monitor allows problem identification and this is the first step in the process of changing action patterns to those more suitable to the desired outcome.

Managers do well then to ensure that they and their employees have access to information as to performance and that this information is available in a palatable form to both employee and manager. Managers should take the opportunity provided by the appraisal process to test their assumptions as to how effectively they are managing and how procedures and systems are actually working. Those in the best position to know are the people who work for them.

Effective training provision ought to be dependent on appraisal activity. Critics of training processes in the United Kingdom and elsewhere have argued that much time and money are wasted on providing training that is perceived by the learners as irrelevant, distantly removed from their real needs and provided without their involvement in its planning. The result is a low rate of training activity generally. This ought to be a matter of national concern, since the provision of training is an essential element in organizational success.

Trainees often report that they were 'sent' on training programmes when much of the content was irrelevant and the teaching methods were not appropriate, and that they hope to avoid training in the future. Basic to this 'training-averse' orientation is the lack of involvement by the learners in the identification of training needs and the limited degree to which much training is needs-related.

Effective appraisal has the power to be the major source of information relating to the development needs of employees. Since it reflects the outcomes of mutual exploration of employee strengths and weaknesses, it has the potential to be of high quality and to sustain the commitment of the learner.

The good performance review is the most powerful opportunity for self initiated and self-appropriated learning to take place. It is the most effective and cost-effective form of management development. It is effective because it is problem-based and individualized. It is cost-effective because it is relevant to the learner and provided in the immediate context of the job.

It is appropriate to conclude this section with a résumé of the findings from an Institute of Personal Management report on current attitudes of managers to appraisal generally:

- most employees want to know what their manager expects of them in their job and how well they are thought to be performing;
- most managers would benefit from hearing and discussing the views of their subordinate staff about working problems and the possibility of job improvement;
- most employees would like to have opportunities for discussing their career ambitions with their manager;
- effective decisions about the content and use of training courses and

other forms of training require the identification of individual employee training needs;
- whilst these needs can to some extent be met by informal means, a more systematic approach can ensure a consistently higher level of benefit;
- within a staff development scheme, benefits should accrue to both manager and employee: the *manager* should gain from improvement in work performance and in the achievement of training plans which are directly relevant to the needs of the organization; the *employee* should benefit from the creation of a more constructive working relationship with management, from more job satisfaction and from assistance in furthering career ambitions.

Performance appraisal and organization culture

It is important to remember that any potentially effective form of appraisal must be in sympathy with the culture of the organization. No appraisal system will of itself change the culture; rather it will be a reflection of it. It is vital then that an appraisal system is only introduced after careful thought as to whether it is appropriate and with the active support of top management. Examples abound of the best-intentioned schemes being introduced in unfavourable circumstances. The results are invariably unfortunate. In some cases the appraisal scheme has been withdrawn after a short time. In other cases, the scheme itself has been distorted to fit the organizational culture. For example, there has been a strong tendency for organizations run on broadly bureaucratic lines to favour appraisal systems which are largely concerned with the completion of pre-printed forms. Details have been collected about employees through the medium of managerial reports and often based on assessment of personality. In some cases known to the writer these assessments have not been seen by the appraisee. In many cases, much more effort is spent in the completion of the forms than in producing relevant developmental plans for the unfortunate employee. There should be little surprise when such schemes are held in ridicule, since they are largely seen as time-wasting or, worse perhaps, as punitive.

It is almost certainly the case that in some organizations the least harmful course of action would be to shelve any serious attempt to introduce appraisal until the managerial climate had undergone significant change. That said, the prevailing trend for organizations to take more seriously the retention and development of the human resource, especially at managerial level, suggests that the future for well-thought-out schemes is generally favourable.

THE PERFORMANCE APPRAISAL PROCESS

Some appraisal systems, as well as attempting to achieve mutually exclusive objectives, as was noted earlier (p. 109), can deteriorate into nit-picking, win/lose relationships in which the manager attempts to impose requirements for improved performance onto unwilling employees who do their best to resist.

This traditional form of an active manager relating to a passive employee requires 'turning on its head' if a more productive relationship is to develop. The initiative must be transferred in part to the employee, especially in the early stages of the appraisal. For this to occur, the meeting must be planned well in advance. Assuming the normal annual review, at least two weeks' notice should be given. During that period, both manager and jobholder should prepare for the appraisal.

Job holders should be encouraged to consider, amongst other things, the following:

- what they consider their job to involve;
- the main tasks dealt with during the year;
- how they feel about their performance;
- problems and difficulties which have arisen;
- experience gained and lessons learned;
- requirements which jobholders have of their manager to help further achievements in their present job;
- assessment of training and other developmental needs.

The *manager* should consider:

- the responsibilities of the jobholder;
- the data available pointing to the quality of the jobholder's performance;
- indicators of the jobholder's level of motivation;
- the extent to which previously agreed targets have been met;
- indicators of performance gained from discussion with other managers who come into contact with the jobholder;
- indicators of performance gained from reviewing data obtained from the jobholder's clients;
- any changes which may take place and which are germane to the jobholder.

Something like two hours should be set aside for uninterrupted discussion. A venue other than the manager's office is preferable if the telephone cannot be subdued. The setting should be as free of status symbols as possible: for example, the manager should avoid sitting behind a large desk; a comfortable arrangement which encourages free communication is preferable.

Unless there is knowledge of what the jobholder has done and is doing, it is unlikely that the manager will be able to talk other than in generalities or to form views as to what has gone well or not so well, thus making the setting of relevant objectives difficult to achieve.

It is this pre-meeting activity which transforms the traditional approach to performance appraisal by emphasizing the importance of the jobholder's self-appraisal. The manager responds to the view of the appraisee, rather than the reverse.

At the same time, the effect of the manager's obvious grasp of what the jobholder has been doing and accurate knowledge of good and less satisfactory activities makes for a more realistic interaction. Where possible the manager should be able to support generalized feelings about the jobholder's performance by specific instances.

The manager's role is not a passive one. Managers will need to listen carefully, ask questions which elicit further information and lead the jobholder to explore issues which have been glossed over or forgotten. The meeting will not always be amicable or easily managed. It has the potential to be a learning experience for both manager and jobholder, provided the manager is able to exercise the basic skills required.

THE COMPETENCIES OF PERFORMANCE APPRAISAL

Whether the objectives discussed above are achieved will depend largely on the interpersonal skills or competencies of the manager. At least five types of different behaviour may at one time or another be required of the manager in the appraisal. They are listed below in the order in which they are likely to be required. It should be remembered that not all of these behaviours will be relevant to every appraisal. The manager must have them available as part of the repertoire and be sensitive and flexible enough to use them as the situation warrants.

Reflection. This is the obvious stance for a manager to begin an appraisal. The manager listens carefully, and demonstrates this by periodic restatements of what has been heard. As with a mirror, the information is repeated with the minimum of distortion and evaluation.

Consultation. As a result of the reflective process, the jobholder begins to relax and feels encouraged to express personal feelings and concerns. The manager may be able to help the jobholder look at problems from a different perspective.

These two managerial skills are the stock in trade of any manager acting as consultant. Consultants help others identify real problems as distinct from symptoms of problems. They help others in identifying options and in deciding for themselves what future action is required. The more time is spent in analysing the extent and nature of problems, the clearer will become possible solutions.

It is important that the jobholders feel free to think about and raise issues which relate to problems beyond themselves, for example departmental structure. Such discussions will naturally provide a source of learning for managers themselves. Performance appraisal is a two-way process.

Prescription. After the stage of problem exploration, the discussion can become more solution-centred. It may be possible for the manager to suggest ways to improve or change work patterns. For prescription to be effective, it is important that the jobholder understands and is committed to the views being expressed. Plans for change are more likely to become reality if they stem at least in part from the jobholder.

Negotiation. There normally comes a point when the interests of the manager and the jobholder cease to coincide. 'Trading off' may be a suitable and realistic way forward: 'If I do this for you, will you do that for me?'

When both parties have recognized problems and seen the possibility of solution, this approach provides a way forward without either manager or jobholder feeling exploited.

Direction. Despite the best efforts of the manager, from time to time there will be jobholders who are loath to part from accustomed ways of behaving and feel that they have a vested interest in the status quo. In such cases and only when it is clear that movement will not take place by other methods, the manager will be justified in becoming directive. It might be that the manager has a better grasp of the issues involved and knows this to be the case; or perhaps the manager is under pressure to bring about change from other quarters and there is little room for choice.

Direction is appropriate when despite every effort, the manager has been unable to motivate the jobholder by any other method. This is not the behaviour of choice.

Two of the above behaviours are problem-centred, and three solution-centred. The more the appraisal centres upon the problem-centred styles, the more the relationship will be characterized by mutual respect and the greater will be the amount of rational thought. In reality appraisals will have within them a mix of these styles, any of which may be appropriate at any given point.

As the meeting moves on, the manager will want to introduce information relating to the jobholder's performance. The following five points are worth bearing in mind:

- persistently negative criticism has a negative impact on the achievement of goals;
- persistently positive criticism affects behaviour very little one way or another;
- generalized criticism of any sort is not as helpful as specific criticism.
- participation in goal setting helps to increase commitment;
- performance improves most when specific goals are established.

PERFORMANCE OBJECTIVES

The next stage of the performance appraisal process should be the setting of agreed performance targets for the following review period, usually twelve months.

It should be obvious by now that it is important that these are set by a process of mutual agreement. Targets which are arrived at through a process of competitive bargaining, which is likely if an annual increment is at stake, will lead to the jobholder pressing for easily attainable targets. The manager, sensing an opportunity to get value for money, may equally well press for targets which are unlikely to be achieved in practice. This point is pursued in greater depth by Molander (1986).

Wherever possible, the targets should be limited to perhaps five or six achievable goals, even though the jobholder might be enthusiastic enough to agree to more.

Generally it is important that the targets are quantifiable and expressed in precise terms so that it is possible to measure performance at a later date. There is little point in allowing vague promises to pass for targets. They need to be precise as to what is to be undertaken, when, how and by whom. If they can be quantified and the quantification agreed to, there seems no obvious reason why this should not be done.

The appraisal process should not rule out the setting of objectives which are not quantifiable, however, or many worthwhile objectives would then not be pursued. For example, it might be of great importance that a jobholder works on improving relationships with specified others. It will not be easy to measure any change that might occur; but the objective should not be dropped on that account.

Some readers may be reminded of Management By Objectives – an almost messianic movement of the 1960s which was based on the belief that until mutually dependent targets were set for all levels of the organization, much effort would go to waste. It is difficult to argue with this basic proposition, but difficulties were encountered since many organizations were reluctant to set objectives at the highest level. Corporate planning was neither well understood nor implemented, thus rendering unlikely the logical progression of targets from top to bottom of the organization. Needless to say, the doubtful benefits of 'mission statements' had at that time yet to be explored.

It seems much more practical to implement the basically logical ideas behind MBO at a more manageable level. The author would argue that the appropriate place for target setting is within the context of performance appraisal.

It is important then that the feedback and objective-setting stages of the appraisal are followed by development planning. It is likely that the jobholder will wish for training opportunities and perhaps changes in role, even perhaps a change in job. It is important that the manager is as open as possible at this stage. It is not good practice for the manager to raise the expectations of the jobholder when there is little or no hope of them being fulfilled.

It is equally important that the jobholder is made aware of the activities which need to be developed to increase chances of advancement and knows that all reasonable help in this direction will be available. Performance appraisal has deserved a poor reputation in those organizations where promises are made, for example with regard to training opportunities which are not in fact available. Often they have not been pressed for hard enough by the manager on behalf of the jobholder. Similarly, promises to sort out acknowledged difficulties in material supply, work-flow patterns or intergroup relationships which are not fulfilled lead to justified cynicism.

We have concentrated on what might be called 'blank form appraisal', characterized by the absence of pre-printed documentation. Once the objectives of the jobholder for the next review period have been agreed and development needs identified, the agreed items should be noted. Also worthy of note is any action that the manager might have agreed to undertake and which is germane to the jobholder.

There seems no good reason for this form to leave the custody of the two involved. Schemes in the past have become bogged down in a paper chase with quite unnecessary copies of a standardized form wending their way up, down and across the organization.

Group-based performance appraisal

Offe (1976) observes that the size and complexity, together with the increased hierarchical and functional differentiation, of work organizations have led to more complex systems of internal control. Where managers are unable to judge whether the technical requirements of the task have been fulfilled, as a result of what is called 'task discontinuity', they are forced to rely on factors in the performance of the jobholder other than technical competence. Behavioural and attitudinal criteria are thus increasing in importance. Although these criteria may be seen as 'peripheral' by some, they are likely to remain. The increasing differentiation between manager and subordinate encourages a changing focus of control.

For these reasons it is probable that in future years we shall see a revival of interest in group performance appraisal rather than the individually oriented systems discussed up to this point and which occupy the attention of most current writers.

The author has for long argued that since managers spend something approaching 75 per cent of their time working in groups, increasingly multifunctional in nature, the setting of individual targets is counterproductive (Gill and Molander 1970). It leads to increased competition when team work is more appropriate. Just as importantly, it leads to a lack of knowledge of what others are trying to achieve and makes mutually beneficial cooperation difficult.

Assuming that the manager has developed the group targets, it is almost certainly more effective for these to be shared with the group and for the group itself to play a major role in the allocation of tasks amongst its members. This does of course mean that the identification of individual responsibility and performance will be more difficult to assess – a difficulty for the human resource management purist.

Paradoxically, however, the same purists would place great emphasis on total quality management. Deming (1986), one of the pioneers of TQM, was a great advocate of the view that quality can be best achieved through the increased participation of employees in the decision-making process.

TRAINING FOR PERFORMANCE APPRAISAL

It is essential that some form of training takes place for all those who are to be involved in performance appraisal. Mackay and Torrington (1986) observe that 30 per cent of manual employees, 62 per cent of clerical and secretarial and 70 per cent of supervisory staff, as well as the vast majority of managers, are liable to some form of appraisal system. This means that any training scheme is going to be costly. Finance will play a major part in the decision as to whether sufficient training takes place.

From experience the author suggests that a period of three days is the minimum useful period. The training period should cover three stages.

Stage One. A review of why the scheme is to be introduced and how: a discussion of the importance of self-appraisal by the jobholder, and the relationship between performance review and motivation; outline of the preparation the manager will need to make before beginning – timing, location and so on; information the manager should collect in advance – data from the previous review period and other performance indicators and information available to the manager.

Stage Two. Increased self-awareness for the manager; what motivates him or her? Here management style profiles and personality type indicators will be useful. A working knowledge of transactional analysis will be helpful, not only for providing feedback, but also as a mechanism for helping the manager analyse the processes going on in the performance appraisal. The basics of effective counselling and coaching as they relate to performance appraisal are important. There are a number of training films which can be used to reinforce this training.

Stage Three. Practice: this is a most important element in any training programme. Managers might work in trios using specially prepared role play material, each acting as manager, jobholder and observer. It is important that the observer monitors the behaviour of the manager and is responsible for providing feedback.

Peer group feedback is usually more acceptable and often sharper because it comes from another line manager who will have a good grasp of routine problems and time pressures. The manager should be encouraged to review performance during the practices. Two practices for the manager as consultant is the minimum.

Training should also be provided for jobholders. They need to know the proposed nature of the scheme. They also should practise being both appraiser and appraisee so that they have a feel for the relationship from both angles. They too need to know what preparation they should undertake prior to the appraisal.

CONCLUSION

By no means all schemes follow the recommendations of this chapter. What we have sought to do is to suggest the type of scheme which has the best chance of success in the long term. The battlefield of management is littered with the carcasses of dead appraisal systems. Untimely death is frequently due to lack of thought as to the most appropriate system for the organization culture, too many mutually exclusive objectives of the system, lack of consultation at the acceptance stage, leading to misunderstandings as to motives, inadequate training for both manager and jobholder and, most commonly of all, systems which place too much importance on the completion of forms. A common cause of failure has been the preference for personality assessment, often inaccurate and always unhelpful, rather than a system anchored to the actual observable behaviour of the jobholder.

It is possible to avoid these pitfalls as has been described in this chapter. If the organization is successful, it will be able to exploit the most cost-effective and practical method of staff development.

FURTHER READING

Fletcher, C. and Williams, R. (1985) *Performance Appraisal and Career Development*, London: Hutchinson.

Randell, G., Packard, P. and Slater, J. (1984) *Staff Appraisal – A First Step to Effective Leadership*, London: Institute of Personnel Management.

Torrington, D. and Weightman, J. (1989) *The Appraisal Interview*, Manchester: UMIST.

QUESTIONS FOR DISCUSSION

1 'Staff appraisal is one of the cheapest and most effective forms of management development.' On what grounds might this view be argued?
2 What are the major defects of traditional assessment-based appraisal systems?
3 What ought to be the characteristics of a worthwhile set of performance objectives?

Chapter 9

Payment

INTRODUCTION

Pay is a necessary though not in itself a sufficient element in the motivation of employees. Accordingly the development and maintenance of a fair and equitable wage and salary system is one of the most important tasks of human resource managers and an important measure of their competence.

In this chapter we shall look at the various methods of wage and salary payment and identify likely developments in this area. A major focus for this chapter will be an assessment of performance-related pay.

OBJECTIVES OF WAGE PAYMENT SYSTEMS

The overall objectives of a pay system are in essence 'the manipulation and control of the relationship between performance and reward'. More precisely, there are said to be four major objectives of a payment system:

- the maintenance of a satisfactory level of output at an economic price;
- the maintenance of a competitive system in comparison with those in other relevant organizations;
- the development of a just and equitable system which ensures the maintenance of differentials based on the relative value to the organization of various jobs. This will involve the use of job evaluation;
- the encouragement of modification and change in work processes and structures by being adaptable to changing needs, so that labour can be used in the most effective way.

Reward systems must be planned and their performance monitored. As discussed in Chapter 1 HRM places great emphasis on the value of the individual and the need to use his or her abilities. Although currently something like 80 per cent of wage settlements are arrived at collectively, we may expect HRM-oriented organizations to see pay as part of an overall package of rewards which needs tailoring to the needs of the individual.

Certainly financial rewards should not be seen as a sufficient element in a reward package. Money is an extrinsic factor, external to a job. It is not an element of the job itself. As Herzberg (1968) has pointed out, the role of money – especially when allocated on a collective basis – has the potential to be a great dissatisfier. In itself it is insufficient to motivate employees on a permanent basis. The possession of a felt fair wage or salary is the essential precondition in the quest for high levels of motivation. It is the start of the motivation process, not its finish.

It is important therefore to see pay as only a part of any reward package. Since individuals find different rewards satisfying, there needs to be an element of individualism in the design of rewards and preferably an emphasis on recipient involvement in the design of the package.

TYPES OF WAGE PAYMENT SYSTEMS

We shall briefly consider five major methods of wage payment: time rates, payment by results, measured day work, group and plant-wide incentive schemes and 'staff status' schemes.

Time rates. A basic rate per hour or day is paid for time worked. Performance and productivity levels are not considered. There is no incentive element built into the calculation of the wage rate. Underlying these basic systems is the belief that the pay system should encourage harmonious relationships between employee and management, and that the task of motivation rests with management and not with the pay system. This method of wage payment is the most common in the UK.

Management is attracted to time rate systems because they enable a greater degree of employee flexibility to be maintained, since employees can be moved from job to job without the need to consider the wage implications for individuals. In addition much of the conflict entailed in piecework systems is avoided. It might be added that time rates leave the problem of motivating the work force with management rather than delegating it to the pay system.

Payment by results (or piecework). Following the Second World War, one of the many problems facing the stability of production and threatening stable industrial relations was piecework. It was seen as a mixed blessing and had decayed in several important ways. In the 1970s it began to be abandoned and replaced by other schemes such as measured day work and productivity agreements. The former sought to establish a much more controlled stable and fixed relationship between pay and output. The latter was designed to establish a relationship between pay and broader organizational change.

Generally in a piecework system an individual's pay is made up of a base rate for the job with a variable payment related to output in addition. Normally the measurement criterion is quantity rather than quality. A bonus is paid when a standard output is exceeded. Though once popular, there is evidence that this payment method is losing ground. The argument for this method of payment is that it produces a direct relationship between effort and pay. Effort is rewarded speedily and directly, which enhances the motivational effects on the employee.

There are said to be many difficulties with this method of payment, not least that as technology becomes more sophisticated more jobs are machine-controlled and the element of choice as to how hard to work has been reduced for many employees. Brown (1962) successfully raised the case against piecework many years ago. Others in later years have reinforced the same arguments (Whyte 1972; Lupton and Bowey 1975). Major difficulties often arise because:

- piecework gives rise to much unrest, haggling and feelings of frustration amongst both employees and managers. Rarely do employees fully understand how their total weekly wage has been arrived at. This gives rise to suspicion of managerial malpractice;
- although much emphasis is placed on the need for work study, it is generally understood that the timing for many jobs is too slack, thus giving rise to easily earned overpayment and encouraging wage drift;
- quality is liable to suffer in the push for quantity;
- the system encourages inflexibility of labour: it is difficult to move employees from job to job without raising problems of lost earnings;
- indirect workers not immediately involved in the production process cannot be rewarded in the same way for increased output, which causes dissatisfaction;
- the responsibility for motivation tends to pass from the hands of management into those of the employees who can decide how hard and for how long they work.

Given these difficulties, it is hardly surprising that the method has lost popularity. None the less, as Torrington and Hall (1991) report, in 1988 over a third of male manual employees and over 16 per cent of non-manual males were in receipt of incentive payments.

It would be difficult to understand the persistence of this form of payment in the light of the arguments against it, were it not that it offers management an easy way out of problems on a short-term basis by adjusting the bonus. In addition there is the added charm of encouraging employees to feel that they have some significant control over their conditions of work. Finally managers and others are wedded to the proposition that incentive systems must work because common sense suggests so. Despite much evidence to the contrary, the search continues for Bunyan's 'delectable mountains'. Unlike many managers, however, Mr Christian 'awoke and beheld it was a dream'.

Measured Day Work. Very common in the 1960s and 1970s, MDW was seen as an improvement on the flat rate and piecework payment systems. A rate for the job is calculated by work study methods as with piecework. In addition an incentive element is built in to the payment before work commences. If the expected production level is not reached, the employee is liable to be moved to another job, or the wage rate adjusted. The advantages of MDW include the following: management remains in control of production; the employee receives an expected income at an enhanced level; there is much less room for haggling in what is a relatively easily understood payment system. On the other hand, others have noted that the incentive is not so powerful since it is buried in the 'normal' pay. This method of payment has, however, proved popular amongst motor manufacturers in particular.

Group and plant-wide incentive schemes. Employees share in a bonus which is linked to output level and paid to employees on a regular basis. Unlike piecework, these schemes are designed to encourage group collaboration at a variety of organization levels. Normally there is regular contact between management and employee as to the working of the scheme to ensure its general acceptability. Profit-sharing plans fall into this category. The difficulty with these plans, especially at company level, is that the link between personal effort and reward is too remote both in terms of time and in terms of readily understood connection. Many other intervening variables will come between the effort of, say, an individual employee in a stock room and the overall performance of the company. Sudden changes in economic trading conditions and political upheavals readily come to mind as examples.

Staff status schemes. These are designed to lessen the divide between wage and salary payment systems and usually are elements in a harmonization plan. Lupton and Bowey (1975) report that during the 1960s and 1970s more than a quarter of a million employees moved to a salary scheme. Such harmonization attempts usually involve levelling of differences between blue- and white-collar workers with regard to a wide range of issues including pensions, holiday entitlement and hours of work, as well as method of payment (*Industrial Relations Review and Report 1989*).

There are clearly many advantages for the employer, not least the greater control of wage drift through the elimination of historic and contentious bonus payments; administrative costs are saved and there might be an improvement in loyalty levels of employees. On the other hand, the organization will be involved in higher costs as people move on to staff status and management will have less opportunity for flexibility to accommodate crises as the possibility of overtime working disappears. Notwithstanding these arguments, in many minds there are strong ethical reasons for harmonization and it is a move supported by the European Community.

TYPES OF SALARY PAYMENT

Traditionally, salaried employees are paid by the month and basic earnings tend to increase with length of service. Rarely is salary related to output.

The basic payment is on a time rate basis paid monthly in the form of one-twelfth of the annual payment. The annual payment is normally negotiated personally on appointment. It may be further supplemented by additional payment on a performance review basis, together with profit sharing, cost of living allowances, fringe benefits and, most commonly, incremental payments based on predetermined scale.

Employment is terminated with longer notice than for the wage earner. Salary earners are generally seen as a group with expectations of advance, based on performance, experience, qualifications, age, or a combination of these factors. Typically payment increases throughout the employment period of the individual.

These traditional differences between the two groups of employees, based on little more rational than historically relevant social class and status differences, are beginning to become less significant through the trade union pressure for harmonization. Equal pay and other non-discriminatory legislation has also led to greater compatibility not only between racial and sexual groupings but also between salaried and hourly paid sectors of the labour force.

Flat rate systems. A single rate is paid for the job, as for some wage earners. It implies little change in performance and no reward for merit.

Age scale systems. This system of stepped payments made on the birthday of the employee usually ceases when he or she reaches 21. The state of the labour market will be taken into account when fixing the various rates of pay.

Incremental payment systems. The most common method of paying salaried employees, a salary range is set up for a particular job with minimum and maximum points. Within this range graded steps will be added. Normally the employee is appointed at or near the bottom of a particular scale dependent on qualifications. An annual increase in salary is achieved by moving up the incremental scale normally one step at a time. Whilst this system is easy to understand and is appealing to bureaucracies because it avoids individual bargaining and introduces a high degree of predictability, it does not identify and reward high achievement and accordingly encourages mediocre performance.

Flexible incremental scales. These avoid some of these problems to a certain extent by allowing for increments to be awarded in units of more than one, or indeed for no increment to be paid at all.

Merit rating systems. A bonus based on merit is paid over and above the earned increment. This system implies some form of review by means of which the capacity of the employee is rated in relation to a predetermined level of bonus.

As Fowler (1988) has pointed out, merit-based schemes assess performance in terms of behavioural traits rather than in terms of the achievement of specific objectives. As such, it is explored here separately from individual performance review.

As early as 1950 factor-based merit rating was popular – a system by which the worth of an individual was established by rating performance against an average of ten 'factors' often linked to personality traits. Other companies relied on the simpler approach of attempting an overall personality classification based on a five-point grading system. From the mid-1980s things began to change, with greater emphasis on performance-related assessment and more sophisticated appraisal systems.

Profit-sharing systems. The payment of an additional bonus based on profit earned by the group or the company is not uncommon. The bonus can be paid in shares or cash. Financial legislation allows corporate tax relief for profit-related schemes of this kind.

Commission and bonus payments. Especially common amongst sales personnel, additional performance-related payments in the form of commission can be made, related directly to increased sales volume and so on. As with wage payment systems an additional payment may also be made to salaried employees, in the form of a Christmas bonus for example.

Cafeteria payment systems. These are relatively novel developments which relate reward to something more than cash and allow for an increased level of flexibility in the allocation of rewards. It is clear that the needs of employees vary according to the life cycle. At some points there are likely to be mortgages and school fees to be paid, so cash is the most important form of reward for work. Older managers on the other hand may feel that they would prefer to receive a lower level of cash payment, the difference being made up by enhanced pension provision or perhaps longer paid holidays or a company car.

For the employee these systems have obvious advantages. But once again they threaten collective bargaining and hence traditional adversarial methods of salary negotiation. It is possible also that they limit the freedom of employees to move from one organization to another since they will not always be able to take the reward package with them.

From the employer's point of view, however, such payment systems fit well with HRM principles of individualization, allowing for a greater degree of interaction between employee and employer without the involvement of collective interests.

PERFORMANCE-RELATED PAY

Brady and Wright (1990) have argued that 'performance pay is one of the most dynamic issues in human resource management and arguably the most topical component of reward policy today'. As with incentive pay, performance pay can broadly be defined as 'the link between financial reward and individual, group or organization performance' (Armstrong and Murliss 1991).

The difference between performance-related pay (PRP) and incentive payment is that the former rewards performance whilst the latter is supposed to stimulate it. Incentives are for the blue-collar worker, whilst PRP is for the managerial elite. It would appear that the reward culture has escaped the shop floor.

PRP rewards the managerial deserving – those who have contributed to the success of the organization. The emphasis now is on individual performance and merit rather than on individual bonus. Incentive schemes are designed to prevent management being 'ripped off' by calculating manual employees who themselves exert control over the wages budget.

In important respects then, incentive payment systems and PRP are essentially similar in structure but differ in their motivational basis. As PRP had declined under one guise it reappeared in the 1980s under another as part of a general revival of interest in pay systems.

The Tory government and the CBI are in favour of payment systems which focus on the performance and needs of individuals. The National Health Service is also said to be committed to the view that performance levels should be linked to levels of reward.

Cannell and Long (1991) report that over two-thirds of private sector firms and over one-third of public sector organizations have some form of individual performance review scheme. On the other hand it should be remembered that in something like two-thirds of all organizations time is still the basis of at least some of their salary calculations. Generally in practice it seems that performance-related pay increasingly means individual performance review.

Three types of performance pay system are common:

- individual merit and performance-related systems based on appraisal or assessment of the individual using various indicators and leading to a payment integrated into the base salary;
- bonuses in the form of separated payments to the individual related to output as measured in units of production; piecework fits into this category;
- bonuses geared to the performance of the group, section, department or organization, again not integrated into the base pay but paid on a collective basis.

Performance-related pay fits well with the underlying philosophy of human resource management as outlined in Chapter 1. In particular HRM:

- is committed to improving individual employee attitudes to work;
- is committed to the task of differentiating between good and poor performers – rewarding the former and weeding out the latter;
- is committed to the pursuit of effective salary administration through a process of targeting salary expenditure;
- is committed to salary flexibility, thus allowing change in payment to be made to suit the changing needs of recruitment;
- is committed to a policy of individualization rather than collective salary distribution; the increasingly pragmatic acceptance of variable payments for the same job by unions has accelerated this process;
- is committed to integrating elements of the HRM programme, for example using payment systems as part of the process of developing organization structure. Commonly this means the development of flatter structures with wider spans of control.

In the eyes of a committed HRM professional there seems little to cavil at in these points. Equally most readers will agree with the notion that more should be paid to those who make more effort. Practical difficulties can arise, however, which make the application of the theory difficult to achieve without the danger of unintended consequences arising which may defeat the overall purpose of IPR (individual performance review) systems – the procurement of the most cost-effective and efficient labour force. The following section will examine some of the major problems which arise with IPR in practice.

PERFORMANCE-RELATED PAY: UNINTENDED CONSEQUENCES

1 Managers have pointed to the likely lack of objectivity in IPR. There is evidence to suggest that managers are not immune from conscious or subconscious favouritism. Paperwork and training do not always prevent effectively irrational decision-making processes. It is difficult for any manager to be in possession of all the relevant information and for even the available data to be weighed objectively.
2 Whilst it is relatively easy to set objectives it is easier to measure action rather than effectiveness.
3 There is little evidence that IPR motivates the bulk of employees – by definition the middle-range performers – in an organization. Interest seems to be geared to encouraging the already high achievers rather than stimulating the poor or mediocre managers.
4 The evidence that motivation is improved over the long term is not yet clear even for the high performers. Senior managers themselves are

sceptical of any such link. Few theories of motivation posit such a one-to-one connection between money and effort. Human needs are too variable for simplistic approaches to motivation theory.

5 Even when there is likely to be a link between performance and pay, it is likely that the link between performance and contribution to organization effectiveness will be less clear cut. The appraisee will focus on those aspects of the job which produce visible and quantifiable results closest to the achievement targets of the appraiser.
6 Managers are aware of the increased emphasis on team work. Increased technological complexity makes it vital. It is arguable that the IPR process militates against the development of team work as individuals strive to appear more effective relative to their colleagues in the struggle for favourable notice.
7 Unless all employees are subject to the same IPR system, it is likely that many will find themselves being urged to work harder in the interests of the few obtaining their targets. Whilst this altruism may be evident in some cases, it is not a force which should be relied upon. Many IPR systems fail because they are limited to a small number of the most senior managers.
8 There is evidence that IPR systems are inflationary. The annual awards to poor performers have been shown to be as high as, if not higher than, the general run of increases in other organizations not operating IPR systems.

This section will conclude with three examples of the difficulties which may arise with IPR.

The case of the variable budget

Manager X spends £1,200,000. Her budget is, alas, only £1,000,000. Her performance lacks sparkle.

Manager X spends £1,200,000 and her budget is £1,250,000. Her performance is promising.

Consultant advice: Renegotiate the budget.

A problem of time-keeping

Manager Y discovers that he must frequently reimburse passengers for the late arrival of a rail service – as per Customer Charter.

Consultant advice: Identify how late on average the service is and, rather than spend time and money on finding out what the problem is, why not reschedule it to arrive half a minute after its normal late arrival? Then the service will persistently arrive ahead of schedule.

Keeping the bed warm

The average hospital stay for a patient on a particular ward in a northern hospital is discovered to be twice as long as the national average, according to the annual statistics.

> Consultant advice: Send the patients home before the expiry of the average length of stay and then readmit them later the same day or soon after. This way, as shown by the statistics, bed occupancy and throughput seem to have increased at no extra cost.

The above examples are drawn from newspaper accounts of actual events. They point clearly enough to the problems of IPR.

It is important before moving on to the last section of this chapter that the reader recognize that there is nothing illogical in attempting to relate performance to reward. The point being made here is that it is difficult to achieve this goal unless great care is taken and the organization is sensitive to the unintended consequences of what is apparently logical behaviour.

LIKELY FUTURE TRENDS

In view of the difficulties described with the various forms of wage and salary payment, it is likely that in future we shall see much flatter organizations with fewer levels from top to bottom in product-based organization structures (see Chapter 2). Such structures complement current emphasis on total quality management and customer satisfaction.

These structures also allow broad band payment systems in which managers have far more room for manoeuvre once incremental steps are removed and wage and salary increases over a much larger monetary span are at the discretion of the manager. Flexibility in the use of labour is likely to be achieved and realistic career paths followed without the frequent need for employees to push for regrading as the only way to circumvent their salary ceiling.

The foregoing discussion in this chapter should alert the reader to the possibility of setting team or group targets rather than those which are individually based. This may be accompanied by group rather than individual appraisal. Not only can indirect workers then share in a merit system, but equally importantly the pressure on individuals to shine relative to their peers will be less acute, which will encourage the development of team rather than individual working.

It will also reduce the amount of interpersonal conflict in groups – often a reflection of the individual pursuit of goals which are not complementary and which set individual against individual as each strives to meet personal targets.

HRM AND PAY

It is hoped that by now the reader is aware of the necessarily close connection between pay systems and the wider organization culture. Pay cannot be seen as a discrete issue with little or no implications elsewhere.

Payment methods both reflect and have an impact upon the organization culture.

Accordingly what is a good payment system for one organization or part of it will not be suitable for another. As White (1985) has pointed out, for example, upon the corporate strategy of the organization will depend its recruitment and retention policy: which type of employee is key to the success of the company? What does this mean for differential payment and general conditions of service, including training and development opportunities?

Again, if a company is planning to develop a global presence in the market place, what does that mean for the organization structure? Can it any longer be controlled from the centre? If not, then what type of structure will be most appropriate? Assuming the setting up of quasi-independent national groupings, then pay systems will develop to take into account the culture of the host countries and the particular characteristics of the national labour forces.

If a company opts to introduce total quality systems it will be logical to assess the payment system to ensure that it rewards behaviour which leads to customer satisfaction rather than the maximization of short-term profit. Tiernan (1988) summarizes Deming's view (1988) that work standards which prescribe arbitrary numerical quotas and targets should be eliminated and replaced 'with helpful leadership'. Deming also argued that barriers between departments must be broken down.

> People in different areas such as research, design, sales, administration and production must work in teams to tackle problems that may be encountered. . . . The effect of evaluation by performance, merit rating, or annual review of performance is devastating – team work is destroyed, and rivalry is nurtured. Performance ratings build fear, and leave people bitter, despondent and beaten. They also encourage mobility of management. Systems of management are in place in the Western world that must be blasted out, for survival. New construction must be commenced. Patchwork will not suffice.
>
> (Tiernan 1988)

At a more prosaic level it is clear that pay systems and levels can be used as part of human resource planning with the aim of increasing the number of employees in those areas which are likely to develop and not discouraging departures in those areas in decline.

CONCLUSION

In this chapter we have looked at prevalent wage and salary payment systems with particular emphasis on merit- and performance-related payment systems generally. We have argued that their increasing popularity is not an unmixed blessing. The mechanisms for applying what so clearly seem to be at first sight commonsense principles of payment – that individual achievement should be related to reward – are not yet free of unwanted consequences which frequently outweigh their benefits.

All too often in the past administration of payment appears to have had a life of its own as a discrete activity with its own jealously guarded skills of measurement and evaluation, and not necessarily in accord with the long-term interests of the organization.

If a cardinal principle of human resource management is to be recognized – the importance of integrating managerial effort – then attention to the direct and indirect effects of various payment systems must be well understood so that they are tailored to contribute to strategic planning.

Concentration on quality is increasingly a characteristic of most strategic planning. It is an important element in human resource management as employee effort is directed towards organization survival and development. There is no area more important in the push for quality than high levels of employee motivation. Such levels will not be achieved even minimally unless the reward system makes its contribution.

Time enough to explore the modish mechanisms of total quality management when these matters have been addressed.

FURTHER READING

Armstrong, M. and Murliss, H. (1991) *Reward Management*, London: Kogan Page.

Fowler, A. (1988) 'New Directions in Performance Pay', *Personnel Management*, November.

Tiernan, T. (1988) 'The Man Who Taught the Japanese About Quality Management', *Works Management*, May.

QUESTIONS FOR DISCUSSION

1 Describe the major unintended consequences of individual performance review schemes (IPR).
2 Why is pay such an important element in strategic human resource management?
3 What in your view should be the objectives of a payment system?

Chapter 10

Quality of working life

INTRODUCTION

The purpose of this chapter is to review factors affecting the commitment of employees to organizational goals and to explore ways of raising and maintaining such commitment. The title reflects more than an instrumental concern with securing worker compliance and gaining productivity improvements. In keeping with the approach to managing human resources developed in this book, it is argued that the most effective way of sustaining employee commitment is to provide an environment in which the quality of working life (QWL) meets individuals' needs and aspirations. To identify what is entailed requires an understanding of theories of motivation, measures of job satisfaction and ways of designing jobs to satisfy human needs. Every manager needs to address the issues developed in this chapter in order to build the commitment of their staff and improve their own effectiveness. The strategy outlined here takes the theory further and argues that empowerment and the establishment of high-trust relationships are critical factors in developing and retaining a highly motivated work force to meet the future needs of the organization.

THEORIES OF MOTIVATION

Motivation is a generic term describing the willingness of employees to expend effort and exhibit desired patterns of work behaviour in terms of levels of performance and commitment to the enterprise. Motivation theory is therefore concerned with factors influencing attitudes conducive to desired behaviour, rather than with structural conditions and management organization, which may be viewed as necessary, but not sufficient, to motivate individuals. Motivational theories are conventionally classed into content theories and process theories. Each will be considered in turn.

Content theories of motivation

Content theories consider factors 'driving' behaviour within a person. Probably the best-known of these is Maslow's (1943), according to which individuals have five sets of needs that may be arranged in a hierarchy. Motivation is held to arise from striving to satisfy these needs and only when the lower-level needs are satisfied are individuals motivated by striving to satisfy higher needs. At the base of the hierarchy are physiological needs, such as food and water, followed by security needs, such as safety and the absence of threats. At the third level, Maslow describes affiliation needs, for friendship, love and belonging, which motivate people once their physiological and security needs have been met. After affiliation needs are satisfied, individuals are motivated by esteem needs, personal feelings of achievement, recognition and respect. At the apex of the hierarchy are self-actualization needs, where individuals who have satisfied all lower needs are in the process of developing their own stature. Pinder (1984) has summarized research suggesting that senior managers are more able to satisfy esteem and self-actualization needs, while employees with little job control, such as in motor vehicle assembly plants, experience no opportunity to pursue higher-level needs. Critics of Maslow's theory cite the general paucity of empirical supporting evidence, and the qualifications and exceptions noted in his original work (Wright 1989). Certainly Maslow's approach may be considered to be unduly complex and, despite the logical appeal of the hierarchy, the relationship between the different levels is inadequately specified.

Herzberg's (1959) motivation theory had at least as much impact as Maslow's, and differed in distinguishing two sets of factors: motivators, the presence of which was held to produce job satisfaction; and hygiene factors, the absence of which would cause job dissatisfaction. Unlike Maslow's hierarchy, where an individual's motivation depends upon the level of needs above those already satisfied, Herzberg's theory presents a simple dichotomy: fail to meet hygiene needs and people are demotivated, develop motivators and people will become motivated. Among the hygiene factors were remuneration, interpersonal relations, working conditions and supervision. Motivators included opportunities for personal achievement, recognition, responsibility and individual advancement and growth. According to Herzberg, therefore, once hygiene factors had been adequately addressed (avoiding job dissatisfaction) the route to increased job satisfaction is through providing motivators. Despite the success of job enrichment strategies (see below), there is little support for the notion that factors influencing job satisfaction fall into the simple dichotomy suggested by Herzberg.

Alderfer's (1972) ERG (existence, relatedness, growth) theory offers an approach which represents an advance on both Maslow and Herzberg, incorporating the concepts of a hierarchy of needs and needs frustration as well as fulfilment. At the base of Alderfer's hierarchy are existence needs (a combination of Maslow's first two categories and most of Herzberg's hygiene factors); at the next level are relatedness needs (interpersonal relationships paralleled by Maslow's affiliation needs); while at the apex are growth needs (provided by opportunities for personal development analogous to Maslow's top two categories and Herzberg's motivators). ERG theory suggests that the satisfaction of one set of needs (such as existence needs) leads the individual to focus on the next higher level (relatedness in this case). Equally, however, the frustration of a set of needs (such as growth needs) leads to a concern with the next lower level of needs (relatedness in this case).

There is sufficient common ground among the content theories to generalize and suggest that, given adequate remuneration, job security and working conditions, employee motivation and job satisfaction may be advanced by addressing three sets of needs: affiliation, power and achievement (Hellriegel *et al.* 1992: 219). These needs will be met, respectively, by structuring work to allow meaningful social interaction, by empowering individuals and work groups, and by providing opportunities for personal development and advancement. The content theories of motivation provide a useful starting point, allowing managers to identify work-related factors conducive to employee motivation, but they neglect to take into account the personal factors which influence individual behaviour. To understand these behavioural aspects, process theories of motivation must be considered.

Process theories of motivation

Whereas need theories of motivation focus on instinctive behaviour, process theories are more concerned with cognitive behaviour. The most influential and comprehensive process approach is known as expectancy theory, which considers the whole work environment. According to Vroom (1964), individuals are motivated to work when they anticipate achieving what they expect from their jobs. As rational beings, employees balance these rewards against the effort required to attain them, and act accordingly, making decisions about accepting employment and about how hard they will work. The immediate results of behaviour associated with a job, such as productivity, absenteeism, quality, are termed first-level outcomes, while the rewards that these may in turn produce, such as promotion, pay increases, job security, are termed second-level outcomes. As well as these positive incentives, negative outcomes such as demotion, boredom and fatigue are considered. People are concerned to avoid negative outcomes as well as to receive positive outcomes, and expectancy theory emphasizes that the value of incentives differs between people: for some, money is valued most highly, while for others recognition or self-esteem may be more important.

In the expectancy model, an individual expends effort producing performance to secure incentives (and avoid negative incentives). Whether the outcomes achieved satisfy individual needs is a measure of the value of the incentives (to a particular individual). The balance of incentive achieved to effort expended, or effort-incentive expectations, will influence the degree to which an individual is motivated to perform. Clearly if employees believe the target level of performance is beyond their reach, or if the incentive outcomes are inadequate, they will not be motivated. Also, it must be remembered that in addition to effort, a variety of other factors influence job performance.

Like expectancy theory, equity theory is concerned with the balance of inputs and outcomes, effort and reward. According to Adams (1963), the major factor is how fairly an individual believes he or she has been treated in comparison with others. The individual therefore makes calculations on which behaviour is based, not in absolute terms, but in relation to others. Individuals weigh inputs and outcomes according to their own perceptions of a situation and perform an exercise rather like job evaluation to compare their own outcome-input ratio with the perceived ratio for others. Where, having compared these ratios, an individual feels properly rewarded (in terms of pay and other outcomes) in relation to others, equity exists. Where the perceived ratios of outcomes to inputs are dissimilar, then inequity exists.

Inequity causes tension in an individual and within a group. To reduce the tension individuals may adjust inputs. Thus, a person who feels underpaid (and undervalued) in comparison with another whose perceived contribution is lower than it should be for the outcomes received may be demotivated and reduce inputs. Conversely, the overpaid worker may increase output to balance the ratio with other workers. Alternatively, inequities can be removed by altering outcomes; individuals may, for example, claim parity of earnings with their comparator group. Thirdly, individuals may adjust their perceptions, distorting their views of their own or others' inputs or outcomes to achieve mentally the equity which is unattainable in reality. People can make a similar adjustment by altering their reference group or by moving to another job.

Other ideas concerning employee motivation are related to process theories. The concept of goal setting is important as a process of specifying the desired outcomes to which individuals should work. The model of goal setting and performance developed by Locke and Latham (1990) begins with the challenges provided for the individual. Goals should be challenging but not unattainable, and clear so that individuals know what is expected of them. The second aspect of goal setting concerns a range of moderators, factors influencing the relationship between goals and performance such as ability, goal commitment, task complexity and feedback. Thirdly, goal setting involves mediators, such as direction of attention, effort and persistence, which affect performance. High task performance is associated with challenging goals in the presence of moderators and mediator mechanisms. Rewards for high performance may be external (including all elements of the remuneration package, see Chapter 9) or internal (a sense of achievement and pride in attaining goals). According to Locke and Latham, job satisfaction is increased through goal attainment, so some compromise on goal difficulty may be necessary to optimize both performance and satisfaction.

Reinforcement is another concept relevant to process models of motivation. Managers aiming to motivate employees must be able to influence and control the consequences of their behaviour, using four methods of reinforcement. To promote desired behaviour, positive and negative reinforcement is employed. Positive reinforcement rewards good performance, while negative reinforcement threatens the loss of something desirable. Thus the employee who performs adequately avoids unpleasant outcomes and the high performer experiences pleasant outcomes. Undesirable behaviour is addressed by two other types of reinforcers. Extinction is a form of conditioning which involves withholding positive reinforcement to discourage undesirable behaviour. Its inadvertent use can also discourage desirable behaviour, which should be acknowledged and reinforced regularly or subordinates will feel 'taken for granted'. Punishment is another method for following up with unpleasant consequences poor performance or unacceptable behaviour. Although effective in stopping the behaviour in question, punishment invariably causes anger and resentment. Such problems are minimized by depersonalizing punishment through a disciplinary procedure (see Chapter 12).

Having reviewed the elements of theories of motivation, it is appropriate to consider how QWL can be measured. Management must be able to assess the job satisfaction of employees in order to identify QWL problems and to monitor the effectiveness of motivation strategies.

MEASURES OF QWL

The strategic function of HRM is to maximize profits and QWL by managing people more effectively. The principle that effective HRM strategies contribute to increased profits and improved QWL is, however, easier to enunciate in theory than it is to demonstrate in practice. While profits are affected by the success or otherwise of managing human resources, there are many other variables involved and it is difficult to disentangle separate effects. Some initiatives to raise QWL may be followed by increased profits, but this does not prove causality. Profits may have increased because the external environment has altered: the global market may have increased or market share may have increased because a major competitor is encountering difficulties. If every conceivable variable except the HRM initiative has remained constant, then it is easier to demonstrate the bottom-line impact of strategies to raise QWL, but in practice the situation is seldom as straightforward. Also, to assess outcomes against initiatives without examining the intervening processes would be to ignore the obvious fact that all management strategies, whether QWL programme, broader HRM initiatives or corporate strategies in general, follow a tortuous route through any organization. What is eventually implemented may be a mutated form of the original plan or following its mediation through different managerial interests and its renegotiation with the work force.

If the evaluation of QWL initiatives in terms of profitability is problematic, fortunately other measures exist which are more valid for monitoring job satisfaction. For convenience, these can be grouped under three headings: output measures; employee attitudes; and individual withdrawal. Each will be considered in turn.

Output measures

The most widely used output measure is productivity, which usually means labour productivity. The importance of labour productivity to industrial success is self-evident. Britain's competitive advantage as an industrial nation declined from the late nineteenth century as a result of the higher productivity growth in American and German manufacturing industries, while in the last few decades Japan has been in the ascendant for similar reasons.

Productivity may be defined and measured in terms of the return on factor inputs: labour productivity as output per person hour or capital productivity as the value of production per unit of capital investment. Clearly HRM strategies are designed to influence labour productivity but it is important to recognize that capital investment can have a more dramatic effect on output per person hour than is likely to result from QWL initiatives, and that labour productivity trends can only be attributed to QWL effects when capital inputs such as technology and quality of raw materials are constant. In practice, therefore, both labour and capital productivity measures should be examined together.

The productivity of individual workers is most easily assessed where there is least task discretion: usually the output of blue-collar factory workers can be measured in production units per hour, whereas for white-collar and managerial employees tasks may be more open-ended and less amenable to straightforward measurement. Even where relatively unambiguous output measures can be devised, it is necessary to identify contingencies. For example, falling labour productivity among production workers in a biscuit factory may be a result of problems with machine down-time, which in turn could either reflect inadequate investment in replacement machinery or some productivity problem of maintenance workers.

Diverse measures are appropriate for different groups of employees: in marketing both sales performance and market penetration may be relevant, while in maintenance, total down-time and average down-time may be informative. Qualitative measures of labour productivity are at least as important as quantitative ones and most forms of productivity-based remuneration (such as payment by results and performance-related pay) acknowledge this by only rewarding work performed to an acceptable standard. Quality may be monitored by negative measures such as the percentage of defects in production, customer complaints or other deviations from operating parameters.

Monitoring output in the ways considered above offers the closest approximation to bottom-line measures of QWL or job satisfaction. Moreover, such monitoring is normally routinely undertaken for operational purposes, so no additional effort is required. The main disadvantage is that output is subject to a wide range of influences in addition to worker motivation. Output measures are therefore most useful as an early warning system, alerting management of job performance problems, whether in terms of work rates or quality. In such circumstances there is a need for further investigation of QWL issues using the other measures considered below.

Employee attitudes

Employees' experience of satisfaction at work (or lack of it) is a product of their individual attitudes or orientations to work and the work context itself. While there is much that management can do through the design of jobs (see below) and by maintaining a healthy work environment (see Chapter 13), improving QWL also demands an understanding of employee views and attitudes. Employee attitudes can be investigated directly (primary measurement) or indirectly (secondary or inferential measurement) as a means of assessing QWL and job satisfaction.

The most direct way of examining job satisfaction is through an attitude survey of employees. This form of primary measurement was popular during the human relations era of personnel management and is enjoying a revival in some American companies. Using surveys it is possible to monitor job satisfaction trends, compare departments or sites, and identify specific issues with which management need to deal in order to improve QWL. An attitude survey should not only be organized in response to a perceived problem, but should be part of a process whereby management regularly solicits the views of employees on a wide range of issues and facilitates extensive consultation when proposing changes.

Unlike an opinion survey, which records what people say, an attitude survey is designed to discover attitudes on which employee beliefs and actions are based. What people say is generally an unreliable guide to what they do, so attitudes do not correspond exactly with opinions. A variety of survey methods can be adopted, including semi-structured interviews with individuals and groups, but most commonly a self-report questionnaire is adopted. Whatever method is used, the survey should be anonymous, as employees may otherwise be reluctant to express views openly. If independent consultants are used to undertake interviews, workers may still fear being identified to management. Paradoxically, using consultants may also lead employees to feel that management are not really interested, otherwise they would ask the questions themselves. The main disadvantage of the questionnaire approach is the inability to explore issues in depth and to pose both unprompted and prompted questions in the way that an interviewer can. An anonymous questionnaire may also elicit a few mischievous responses but this is only serious where opposition to the survey is being organized within the work force, a situation symptomatic of management failure to build a high-trust relationship.

Objections from management to the use of an attitude survey take several forms. It may be seen as a sign of weakness, in much the same way that negotiating with unions appears to the unitary manager (see Chapter 4), but the pluralist manager would argue that being able to organize an attitude survey (or negotiate with the unions) is a sign of strength or confidence. If we accept that authoritarianism is outmoded and inefficient, the management by consent which must take its place requires intimate knowledge of employee attitudes. Some managers would argue that an attitude survey is unnecessary because they know their workers' views, a posture which may be mirrored in the attitudes of union representatives. For all their sincerity, neither is likely to be correct, as daily misunderstandings demonstrate; both can be persuaded that if the survey proves them correct, this will vindicate their existing practices whereas if not, then the issues need to be addressed. Sensitivity by both managers and union representatives over being 'circumvented' can best be dealt with by involving them in the questionnaire design and gaining their support for its objectives.

The survey can provide vital information on specific grievances which can then be dealt with earlier, and can inform HRM policy so it is formulated to match employee aspirations. The survey can also be a vital safety valve, relieving tension before it is openly expressed as conflict and letting employees know that management are concerned with QWL. There is much empirical evidence that simply organizing an attitude survey raises morale among employees, although it should never be done for this purpose alone. Employee expectations are also likely to be raised when a questionnaire is completed, so management must be committed to acting on the findings.

A long list of statistics can be monitored as indirect measures of employee attitudes and QWL. Employee health records may highlight patterns of illness, identifying times or areas where illness is concentrated (see Chapter 13). Statistics on grievances taken through procedure are also relevant, especially if classified according to the nature of complaints. The permanent resolution of persistent problems must be a first priority of a QWL programme. Disciplinary cases can be monitored in the same way, so that when individual chronic cases are excluded more general problems can be identified behind a 'discipline problem' in a particular department. The reasons for disputes can also be usefully analysed, although care needs to be taken in uncovering latent as well as manifest issues. Like health records, these measures of conflict should have been recorded and monitored already as part of a procedure for dealing with such issues (see Chapter 12), so their use in a QWL audit need require no significant additional resources.

All of these secondary measures of QWL may be considered to be inferential because of the complexity of causes, motives and meanings of social action. Ill health, especially, can be caused by factors outside the work context, such as inadequate diet, while a high incidence of disputes could reflect bargaining opportunities in the labour market rather than any QWL deficiency. The measures should be seen as complementary, reflecting different responses to a possible common root cause of low QWL. Thus individuals may respond to a QWL problem in an internalized way, 'bottling up' resentment and becoming ill; in a constructional way by complaining under a grievance procedure; through defiance, resulting in disciplinary action; or by protest, leading to disputes. Since individuals may adopt different responses to the same situation, the measures need to be considered in parallel. Also, since these are inferential measures, other causes should be explored alongside QWL issues. The measures of individual withdrawal considered below are secondary methods of assessing job satisfaction, and are arguably also inferential. However, their accuracy and reliability for monitoring QWL have long been established and they are therefore accorded special validity as distinct measures.

Individual withdrawal

Employees experiencing low job satisfaction are thought to seek ways of withdrawing from the work situation because it is unpleasant. Withdrawal may take the form of work avoidance, measured as absenteeism, or job avoidance, measured as quit rate or labour turnover. Levels of absenteeism and labour turnover both reflect and influence the morale of employees.

Where either becomes excessive, the human resource plan can be frustrated and operations paralysed, but even 'routine' or 'acceptable' levels of absence and turnover impose significant costs on an enterprise and therefore need to be monitored and controlled. From a business viewpoint, absenteeism is any failure of an employee to report for or remain at work as scheduled, regardless of reason. Scheduled absences, such as holidays and compassionate leave, are budgeted for and represent part of the remuneration package. Unscheduled absence, whether due to sickness or withdrawal from work, is more disruptive because it is unexpected (although a prudent HRP analyses recent absence trends) and because it has an impact on labour productivity and costs. In the UK, the cost of non-attendance at work was estimated to be running at £5 billion per year in 1987. In the USA, for General Motors alone, absence was costing $1 billion in 1984.

Absence rates are normally calculated as a percentage of worker shifts lost:

$$\frac{\text{worker-shifts absent} \times 100}{\text{worker-shifts possible}} = \text{absence rate}$$

The average annual duration of absence per person may also be calculated:

$$\frac{\text{worker-days absence per year} \times 100}{\text{total workforce}} = \text{average duration}$$

In addition, it is useful to measure the frequency of absence in terms of absences lasting one day or less, representing voluntary withdrawal, and the number of separate periods of absence lasting more than one day or shift. The proportion of workers present throughout a one-year period who had no absences is a measure of how widespread absenteeism is among the non-transient work force. The rate of days lost is most easily calculated but least useful because it is heavily influenced by a few long spells of absence. Absence as a form of conscious withdrawal can be assessed by the 'blue Monday' index, which contrasts absence rates on Mondays (the highest) with Fridays (the lowest). Absence peaks are also found during the summer months and particularly around statutory holidays and annual factory shut-downs.

International comparison (with the usual caveats about accuracy, reliability and variations in official definitions) suggests that absenteeism is considerably higher in the UK and USA, and lower in Japan, than the average for western industrialized countries. In the UK, the rate of one-day absences in clothing factories is typically four times the average for manufacturing industry as a whole. Absenteeism, particularly one-day absence, is generally higher among women workers, and especially younger females, but gender is only one factor. Variations in absence rates between workers of the same sex and occupation, but in different workplaces, are explicable in terms of variations in work organization, particularly in relation to the degree of collective control workers have over their work situation (Edwards and Scullion 1982).

A survey by the CBI (1987) found absenteeism was highest among full-time manual employees and lowest among full-time white-collar workers. Nevertheless, absence was more likely to be concentrated amongst certain individuals in the case of manual workers than with white-collar staff. The most common causes of absenteeism reported for manual workers were 'poor motivation', 'family responsibilities' and 'unauthorized extension of holidays', while for white-collar staff, the reasons given were 'family responsibilities', 'work-related stress' and 'poor motivation'. It is important to recognize that these were the views of management, not the workers involved, whose motives and meanings may well have been quite different. The major factors believed by managers to have reduced absenteeism were 'improved monitoring and control', 'fear of redundancy' and 'peer group pressure' for both manual and white-collar workers.

The most effective solutions to absenteeism involve a combination of strategies to bring long-term improvements in QWL (see below), combined with effective procedures for monitoring and control. Such procedures should include: self-certification and reporting; provision for legitimate absence; discipline of unjustified absentees; and supervisor training in counselling.

Labour turnover is a natural characteristic of employment, as workers retire or leave for family reasons and replacements are recruited. Some employees leave for career development and such transfer of skills and experience benefits the enterprise. However, like absenteeism, high turnover is thought to indicate low morale or job dissatisfaction. The effect of high labour turnover can include disturbance of the working group, feelings of insecurity (creating more impetus for others to leave), resentment of new workers and a crisis for supervision with the influx of inexperienced workers. Labour turnover is costly to the enterprise in terms of advertising vacancies; recruitment, selection and training of recruits; substandard work; overtime working; and lost production. The conventional methods of calculating indices of annual turnover and labour stability have already been outlined (see Chapter 3) and need not be repeated here. In examining turnover as a measure of job (dis)satisfaction, more sophisticated approaches may be used to establish relationships between the propensity to leave and such factors as job, department, grade, age and length of service. Different statistical models are available based on assumptions of lognormal, exponential and Weibull survival functions. The analysis of turnover must be supplemented with information about why employees leave. Separations fall into three categories: voluntary, involuntary (e.g. dismissal) and unavoidable (e.g. maternity). The exit interview provides an opportunity to establish the underlying reasons as well as the overt stated reasons why a person is leaving. Exit interviews should not be used to try to persuade an individual to stay, and must be private, confidential and sympathetic.

It is important to recognize that turnover rates vary considerably between different industries. In UK clothing, quit rates of over 25 per cent per annum are commonplace, whereas in other industries 10 per cent is more usual. While high turnover is not unusual among female manual workers, in clothing the phenomenon also extends to male workers, and women clothing workers have higher quit rates than women in electrical engineering. Other factors, such as the generally lower earnings in clothing than in engineering, are also important. High turnover does not necessarily indicate serious worker discontent; it may simply be that opportunities are felt to be better elsewhere. Turnover varies with length of service, so it is not uncommon for greenfield sites to experience high quit rates initially. Among the reasons for quitting, pay is invariably the most important, followed by the nature of the work and job insecurity.

The control of labour turnover is most positively viewed as management of retention: the maintenance of a work environment compatible with employees' values which reinforces their reasons for staying. Several of the measures designed to control absenteeism are relevant, with the addition of the exit interview as a major part of monitoring.

JOB DESIGN

Job design refers to the specification of tasks which constitute a job description and the allocation of work within that framework. Motivational theories would suggest that optimum job design seeks to utilize fully the skills and competencies of individual employees, while devolving maximum responsibility to provide opportunities for decision-making and personal development. Invariably the extent to which jobs can be designed along these lines is constrained by the nature of productive processes, but managers should strive towards these principles in designing technological systems and associated work organization in order to raise QWL.

A variety of job design strategies may be distinguished according to their degree of complexity and the impact which they have upon the nature of work. Firstly, there are forms of job enrichment which seek to build into jobs those aspects which are associated with job satisfaction and employee motivation. Secondly, there is the socio-technic systems approach, which seeks to find optimum social and technical solutions in the design of jobs. More radical approaches to job design are centred on enskilling, where employees are encouraged to increase their level and range of skills, and empowerment, where employees are involved in managerial decision making and the autonomy of individuals or work groups is developed. Each of these approaches is considered below.

Job enrichment

Almost since industrialization began, a dominant feature of work has been its organization along lines which are generally described as 'Tayloristic'. Although F.W. Taylor (1911) offered the first codification of scientific management, its basic principles, derived from Adam Smith (1776), had been adopted much earlier (Babbage 1833; Ure 1835). Taylorist work organization is characterized by an extreme division of labour with the majority of workers requiring few skills and having little discretion in the performance of tightly prescribed tasks. The approach which attributes primacy to economic needs as the basis of human motivation is the foundation of modern work measurement in which task elements are subdivided and rationalized. Braverman (1974) described the process as involving three stages: the division of labour; the separation of conception from execution; and an increase in management control over the labour process. According to Braverman's analysis, the negative effects of this degradation and dehumanization of work are seen in widespread job dissatisfaction and the reactions of alienated labour to boring jobs. Job enrichment can be seen as an attempt to ameliorate these negative effects of Taylorized work.

The least sophisticated way of tackling the problem is through job rotation, where workers exchange stations in order to reintroduce an element of task variety without altering the basic division or the intensity of work. This solution might be adopted in situations where capital commitments constrain major changes in work organization, such as a mass production assembly line.

The degradation of work under Taylorism is exacerbated by technological changes whereby increasingly complex task elements become incorporated into machinery (or software) and the work is deskilled. At the same time, such changes offer an opportunity to restructure work organization through job enlargement. Job enlargement may take two forms: horizontal or vertical. In the former case, the worker is allocated a wider range of tasks, reducing the overall division of labour (and perhaps intensifying work). Advocates of job enlargement like Davis never claimed that more of the same dehumanizing tasks in a job would lead to increased satisfaction. Rather, they were 'recommending the addition of different tasks – those leading to closure, self-regulation and autonomy and resulting in fundamentally different relationships of the job holder to the work process' (Davis 1971). Herzberg (1968) described vertical job enlargement as a process of job enrichment whereby scope for achievement, recognition, responsibility and advancement is designed into work. The empirical evidence that job enrichment is associated with job satisfaction and improvements in work performance is substantial (Campion and McLelland 1991).

Hackman and Oldham (1980) developed a job characteristics enrichment model which focuses on increasing the skill variety, task identity, task significance, autonomy and feedback in a job. The model relates these core job characteristics to critical psychological states which in turn have personal and work outcomes: motivation, quality, satisfaction and commitment.

Nevertheless, the scope for job enrichment is often limited by the technological configuration of work. For this reason, researchers at the Tavistock Institute of Human Relations developed the socio-technic systems approach to optimize both social and technical systems.

Socio-technic systems

The socio-technic systems approach seeks to match the design of the social system of actors and the design of the technical system within which they operate in order to optimize the total system. The development of an open socio-technic systems model of industrial organization may be regarded as the major theoretical contribution of the Tavistock Institute of Human Relations, while their major empirical contribution concerned the analysis of social behaviour and functioning of industrial work groups. These contributions were nowhere more evident than in the coal-mining studies, which differed methodologically from most other Tavistock work in emphasizing research rather than consultancy and in adopting a comparative rather than case study approach.

The Tavistock studies represented a departure from focus on the human relations climate to a consideration of technology as a major factor influencing industrial behaviour. While some writers who emphasized technology were guilty of technological determinism, this was never the case with the Tavistock analyses because technology was always seen as influencing behaviour only through its effect on work organization. Moreover, the Tavistock studies made two distinctive innovations in the debate on the relationship between technology and social structure. The first was in challenging the classical view that task specialization was necessary for industrial efficiency, two decades before Braverman (1974) produced his critique of Taylorist work organization. The second was in demonstrating the choice of alternative forms of work organization which were available for a given technology, making possible the optimization of social and technical systems. As Trist (1968: 354) noted, 'the studies in the British coal industry . . . provided the first detailed empirical evidence of the superiority of certain forms of work organization over others for the same technological tasks.'

A recent review of technological developments at the coalface has demonstrated both the complex interrelationship between the dimensions of technology and work organization, and the impact of the wider context of the labour process, especially in relation to the balance of power between labour and management (Winterton 1994). In particular, the move to longwall mining greatly facilitated mechanization because coal cutters could be used more efficiently than was formerly possible. With mechanized mining the changes in the material technical base and technique of production were significant, but changes in work organization had greater impact upon face workers. The miners' weakened bargaining position following their defeat in the 1926 lockout and the depressed state of the industry between the wars enabled the employers to intensify work and impose new forms of work organization to the detriment of miners' health.

After nationalization, coal was needed to fuel postwar reconstruction, the miners' bargaining power was restored and they reacted to the work situation with absenteeism and unofficial stoppages. It was in this altered context of coal demand outstripping supply and apparently intractable labour relations problems that the National Coal Board considered alternative forms of work organization to alleviate the social dislocations of the 'three shifts' mechanized system. The Tavistock researchers were therefore afforded a unique opportunity to undertake action research to develop a more human-centred organization of work at the coalface.

Experimental forms of work organization derived from the single place tradition were described as 'composite longwall working' and made the whole of the shift team's skills available. Composite work groups were shown to experience greater job satisfaction and better social health, as well as being more productive. The effectiveness of composite longwall working was never extensively assessed in other areas because the development of power loading transformed face work and made the experiments appear irrelevant. While the substantive recommendations of Trist and colleagues became redundant, the principles they identified were relevant to subsequent technological changes.

Power loading brought associated changes in the technique of production and work organization which restored some of the miners' control over the pace of work. Although the industry suffered decline from the late 1950s and management sought further ways of exerting control through increased coalface supervision, miners retained much of their control at the point of production. Then the first oil shock of 1973 restored the miners' power in the labour market. The incentive schemes introduced in 1977 with the aim of re-establishing indirect supervision were tailored to computer-based work monitoring developed as part of an automation programme. The material technical base and technique of production are not fundamentally different from power loading, while changes in work organization stem from the strategies of control developed by management since the late 1970s but only implemented in the aftermath of the miners' defeat in the 1984–5 strike.

The development of automated mining could be described as a textbook example of the use of systems engineering, but in defining the system the human interface was inappropriately specified. Human factors were only considered in a Taylorist sense of designing new technology to reduce dependence on workers' skills and increase management control. Wider socio-technic considerations were ignored, yet from the Tavistock experiments the negative social effects of work intensification and deskilling could have been predicted. These negative social effects, manifest in low morale and continued production delays, are the result of using technology as a weapon against the work force. Even at the time of writing the human factors assessment of the new technologies by British Coal has not extended beyond an ergonomic study of control room operations. It is ironic that socio-technic action research has ultimately had so little influence in the industry which provided the setting for one of its most widely acclaimed examples.

Enskilling

The limitations to the Taylorist approach to job design have long been recognized in Japan. Writing in 1979, Konsuke Matsushita, a leading Japanese industrialist, stated provocatively:

> We are going to win and the industrial West is going to lose out: there is nothing much you can do about it, because the reasons for your failure are within yourselves. Your firms are built on the Taylor model: even worse: so are your heads. With your bosses doing the thinking while the workers wield the screwdrivers, you're convinced deep down that this is the right way to run a business. For you, the essence of management is getting the ideas out of the heads of the bosses into the hands of labour. We are beyond the Taylor model: business, we know, is now so complex and difficult, the survival of firms so hazardous in an environment increasingly, unpredictably, competitive and fraught with danger, that their continued existence depends on the day-to-day mobilization of every ounce of intelligence.
>
> (Newby 1992)

While Japanese industry has undoubtedly succeeded in harnessing the skills and energies of its workers, the total quality management (TQM) approach which this has entailed is not the only possibility, and enskilling may be considered an alternative.

There is overwhelming evidence that the UK work force is inadequately trained in comparison with major industrial competitors. In 1985, for example, 35,000 individuals qualified at craft level in engineering and technology in the UK; the comparable figures for France and Germany were, respectively, 92,000 and 120,000 (CBI 1989). Similarly, while 24 per cent of top managers in the UK are graduates, in France and Germany the percentage is more than twice that, and in Japan and the USA 85 per cent of top managers have degree-level qualifications. Recognizing the need to stimulate training, during the 1980s the UK government opted to deregulate training organizations and establish a revolutionary system of work-based qualifications. Statutory Industry Training Boards have (in all but two cases) been replaced by employer-led Industry Training Organizations (ITOs), and in 1986 the National Council for Vocational Qualifications (NCVQ) was established to develop a nationwide unified system of work-based qualifications. The NCVQ accredits National Vocational Qualifications (NVQs) relating to standards identified by the employer-led Industry Lead Bodies (ILBs) in each industry, which may be the same organization as the ITO. The NVQs are based upon competences rather than the completion of training, and the focus is on the results of learning rather than the process. In Scotland similar arrangements exist for Scottish Vocational Qualifications (SVQs) accredited by the Scottish Vocational Education Council (SCOTVEC). It was widely recognized that the level of training was inadequate to meet the demand for skilled workers in the 1990s, and an increase in the volume and in the standards of training is still required if future demand for skilled labour is to be met. The re-emergence of skills shortages is a result of supply deficiencies (Marsden and Ryan 1990), but also deficiencies in demand have been important in preventing the emergence of a better-trained and more productive work force (Glynn and Gospel 1993). Job growth is expected to be in technical, professional and managerial occupations, but changing skill requirements will not be confined to these groups. Moreover, demographic trends predict that:

> eight in ten of the people who will make up the labour force in the year 2000 are already in the labour market. Thus there is a need to focus urgently on boosting the skills of those adults who are currently in employment or seeking work, as well as the learning needs of young people.
>
> (IPM 1992: 5)

The TUC focus on training shifted from national and industry levels to the workplace, with proposals to create a statutory basis for worker consultation through the formation of Workplace Training Committees (WTCs). The WTCs were to be formulated along the same lines as health and safety committees established under the Safety Representatives and Safety Committees Regulations, 1977 (TUC 1989: 11). The WTCs would have a statutory responsibility to develop a training plan for the enterprise, establishing a minimum annual number of hours of training for each employee. The TUC Guidance Note *Joint Action over Training* argued that in the absence of statutory rights over training, union negotiators were to put training on the bargaining agenda and develop a joint approach with employers (TUC 1990). The TUC response to the National Commission on

Education reiterated the unions' view that statutory underpinning of the training system was needed to give individuals a right to training (TUC 1992: 31). In order to promote bargaining over training and the acquisition of skills, the TUC established briefing sessions for full-time and lay officials and encouraged the negotiation of training agreements with employers (TUC 1993: 5), but it is difficult to assess the extent to which unions have succeeded in engaging employers on the issue. The TUC strategy of negotiating New Technology Agreements in the early 1980s, for example, enjoyed little success in practice as workplace negotiators were unable to make inroads into technology, the sacrosanct area of managerial prerogative (Winterton and Winterton 1985).

The unions have apparently made limited progress in negotiating training agreements, and one possible explanation is that despite training often being regarded as consensual within industrial relations, the interests of the different parties are not entirely congruent. In the abstract, employers and employers' associations, along with employees and trade unions, will pronounce themselves 'in favour of' training, but their motives invariably encompass more than an attachment to a highly educated work force for its own sake. For employers, the major issue is having a work force with the competences to perform in accordance with business objectives. For employees, training and its validation represent a means of having their skills and competences acknowledged, which in turn should provide a route to higher earnings, improved job satisfaction and security, and increased labour market mobility. The representative bodies, employers' associations and trade unions, support these two parties' objectives, but may each have a wider agenda. The employers' associations may take a strategic view of training as a mechanism to support job restructuring through promoting multi-skilling and functional flexibility. The trade unions may see training as a route to increasing employee autonomy and control over the job, as well as maintaining pay rates. While all parties have modified their views considerably in recent years, there is still potential for conflictual objectives over training. However, this should not be seen as an argument against collaborative arrangements involving unions because differences are best resolved through consultation and negotiation.

Skill is a potentially contentious area because it forms a link between the consensual issue of training and the conflictual question of pay. Measures to promote multi-skilling or functional flexibility are most likely to reveal the tensions between training and industrial relations. Skills and competences are at the centre of training arrangements but also feature on the industrial relations agenda as a question of additional remuneration for the acquisition of new skills.

The problems stem from a confusion between the two processes. Rainbird (1990: 90), for example, claims that 'up-grading and de-skilling are social relationships rather than empirically measurable phenomena.'

This approach conflates two separate dimensions of skill: the genuine foundation, which is related only to the competences required to undertake the tasks, and the socially constructed skill labels manifest in the grading structure, which reflect also, and on occasions primarily, the power relations and social values of the parties to negotiation. Leaving aside the perennial problems of the measurement of genuine skill, it is clear that this is the province of training, while grading is a matter for the bargaining system. The questions of upskilling and deskilling (changes in the genuine skill foundation) are analytically distinct from those of upgrading and downgrading (socially constructed skill labels).

The training issues raised by multiskilling depend upon which of three generic forms of functional flexibility are envisaged. The most significant efficiency gains are probably associated with craft–craft multiskilling among maintenance workers, which typically entails electricians gaining mechanical craft skills and vice versa (Cross 1985). Where process–craft multiskilling is involved, if process workers gain significant maintenance skills and increased responsibility this should represent job enrichment, whereas craft–process multiskilling, where craft workers take on additional routine process tasks, amounts to lateral job enlargement. Process–craft multiskilling, designed to equip process workers with craft skills, albeit usually over a relatively narrow range of tasks, presents the greatest training challenge and has the greatest potential for improving the quality of working life.

Significant progress has been made towards multiskilling in recent years through negotiation over demarcation and training. Seven enterprise case studies recently undertaken for the European Commission revealed a high degree of concordance between a highly skilled workforce, significant job restructuring underpinned by employer attitudes conducive to responsible autonomy, and the involvement of trade unions in training (Winterton and Winterton 1994).

Empowerment

The notion of empowerment is equally important in the design of jobs to promote QWL, and can involve developments at the level of superstructure or substructure.

At the superstructure level, the most obvious example is codetermination, whereby worker representatives are elected to company boards. Codetermination developed in the German steel industry after the First World War, and was reintroduced in the post-Fascist reconstruction after the Second World War. Under these arrangements, workers were given representation on company supervisory boards and workers' councils with defined powers were established in each plant. All German companies above a certain size are required by law to have similar arrangements

(Hartmann 1975). Other European countries introduced legislation to support codetermination (Batstone and Davies 1976), as should Britain in accordance with EEC Directive V and the draft statute for the European company. In the British steel industry limited codetermination was also introduced in the form of worker directors (Brannen *et al.* 1976), but these arrangements ended with the privatization of British Steel in 1988.

Sweden's Codetermination Act which came into force in 1977 was the result of strong pressure from the Swedish unions, especially the central federation Landsorganisationen, although the main provisions were supported by all sections of the Riksdag (Ministry of Labour 1988). The Swedish Employers' Confederation (1987) later claimed that expectations had been exaggerated by references to codetermination provisions as 'joint decision making' or 'workers' control', preferring instead to use the term 'consultation'. Similarly, the duty to negotiate before implementing change has not been enforced as a duty to reach agreement. While the 1982 Agreement on Efficiency and Participation made between Svenska Arbetsgivareföreningen (Swedish Employers Federation), Landsorganisationen (Swedish Trade Union Confederation) and Privattjänstemannakarttellen (Swedish Federation of Salaried Employees) built upon the Codetermination and Work Environment Acts to encourage the development of new forms of work, the return of the first Conservative government since the interwar years has, predictably, reduced the effectiveness of these provisions.

The TUC and Labour Party added their support to EEC pressure for more widespread codetermination in Britain, and a private member's bill brought by Giles Radice, a GMWU-sponsored MP, prompted the government to establish a Committee of Inquiry. The Bullock Committee was established to 'see how such an extension [of industrial democracy] can best be achieved' in the UK. The employers' representatives were opposed to this reference and produced a Minority Report.

The Majority rejected the EEC two-tier model of codetermination and argued for a unitary board, with duties modified under company law, reconstituted according to the $2x + y$ formula. The x component represents equal numbers of management and worker representatives, while the y component represents an odd number of co-opted members who the parties agree are independent. The Majority argued that a single channel of representation through the independent recognized trade unions involved would minimize any potential conflict between collective bargaining and codetermination and make such representation more effective.

The Minority argued that there was little to commend any extension of industrial democracy, but that if this were forced upon industry it would be better to have the European model of a two-tier structure. The Minority saw no necessity to restrict representation to the trade union channel and stressed the negative effect of codetermination upon managerial prerogative.

Opposition to Bullock was not confined to management circles. The left of the trade union movement opposed the proposals as incorporation, although some viewed board representation as appropriate in the public sector. Flanders (1968), a leading pluralist, had earlier voiced objections to worker directors, claiming that 'putting a few workers on boards of directors only divorces them from the rank and file.' Union moderates stressed the conflict between board representation and collective bargaining.

The Post Office was encouraged by the Labour government to introduce an experimental Bullock scheme of board-level union representation at the beginning of 1978. An academic study of the Post Office experience, noting that the overall impact of union nominees was marginal, concluded: 'the Bullock model pays insufficient attention to the specific contexts in which board representation is located. "Strong" schemes of worker directors tend to reflect, rather than resolve, the underlying patterns of conflict and co-operation in industry' (Batstone, Ferner and Terry 1983: 177).

A White Paper was introduced later in 1978 which largely ignored the recommendations of the Bullock Majority; it proposed giving unions a right to discuss company strategy and, after a specified period, to representation on supervisory boards. The White Paper represented a compromise between the Minority proposals and the European model. The return of a Conservative government in 1979 effectively put an end to further developments in industrial democracy, although Britain remains obliged to introduce some form of statutory worker representation as a member of the European Community.

Whereas empowerment at superstructure level will depend upon wider political developments, at substructure level enterprises may independently introduce innovations which can contribute to raising QWL.

Marchington *et al.* (1992) describe a hierarchy of forms of employee involvement (EI) according to the degree of employee influence:

- information;
- communication;
- consultation;
- codetermination;
- control.

They note an increasing interest in EI at the lower levels (information, communication and consultation) and show how the systems operate in a selection of cases. The EI initiatives taken by UK companies in recent years are consistent with the voluntary approach advocated by the government and could be seen as a prophylactic against the imposition by the European Parliament of more extensive forms of participation such as codetermination.

Worker autonomy entails a greater degree of worker control than the above forms of participation. Participation means that management redesign jobs in consultation with workers, whereas worker autonomy entails workers themselves redesigning their own work and assuming responsibility for their own activities. Many examples of worker autonomy come from Scandinavian countries, where local job autonomy complements a highly developed form of codetermination.

The motor vehicle plant opened by Volvo at Kalmar in 1974 was designed from the outset around team-working, rather than a rigid machine-paced line for final assembly, which had been the classical approach to making cars since Henry Ford. Job rotation is practised within each work team, which is the fundamental unit of organization. Research after ten years of operating the Kalmar plant showed improvements in quality and efficiency, while over 80 per cent of workers interviewed preferred team working (Aguren *et al.* 1984). Other companies have followed Volvo's lead; one of the subsidiaries of Electrolux has a factory operating with autonomous work groups because the work does not lend itself to traditional mass production techniques. Stockholm's public transport enterprise also introduced a degree of autonomy in decentralizing shift allocation to bus depots, thus reducing absenteeism significantly.

The Swedish Work Environment Fund (Arbetsmiljofonden) has financed a number of projects to introduce worker autonomy and improve the nature of work, usually through collaborative teams of researchers, managers, trade union lay officials and workers. The Swedish Centre for Working Life (Arbetslivscentrum) has pioneered such work since the early 1970s. As a result, nine basic principles for rewarding jobs were identified: security of employment; equitable share of the results of production; codetermination; work organization to promote cooperation; specialist craft knowledge in all jobs; training integral to all jobs; working hours on the basis of social requirements; equality at workplaces; and a work environment free from the risks of ill-health and accidents (Work Environment Fund 1987).

CONCLUSIONS

This chapter has dealt with theories of motivation, measures of QWL and job design. It has been argued that by designing jobs to meet human needs, individuals will be more motivated to perform at the standards required to maintain competitive advantage and will remain committed to the enterprise. The design of jobs to promote skill and autonomy has been shown to be key to the development of a high-trust relationship between a motivated work force and a management committed to improving QWL.

FURTHER READING

Goodman, P.S. and Atkin, R.S. (eds) (1984) *Absenteeism: New Approaches to Understanding, Measuring and Managing Employee Absence*, San Francisco: Jossey Bass.

Hellriegel, D., Slocum, J.W. and Woodman, R.W. (1992) *Organizational Behaviour*, Saint Paul, Minn.: West (6th edition).

Steers, R.M. and Porter, L.W. (eds) (1989) *Motivation and Work Behaviour*, New York: McGraw-Hill (5th edition).

QUESTIONS FOR DISCUSSION

1 Is there any need to pay attention to job satisfaction issues in a situation of demand deficiency for labour?
2 What are the implications for training of a programme of QWL which emphasizes enskilling and empowerment?
3 'Any extension of employee involvement inevitably implies an erosion of managerial prerogative.' Discuss.

Chapter 11

Collective bargaining

INTRODUCTION

This chapter is concerned with one of the major mechanisms by which terms and conditions of employment are established. Collective bargaining is concerned with the effort-reward bargain, with working arrangements and conditions, with discipline and grievances, and with the development of effective procedures for negotiation and consultation. An understanding of the complexities of collective bargaining structures and processes is therefore essential for the effective management of human resources. After outlining the nature and dimensions of collective bargaining, the chapter explores the changing structure of bargaining in the private and public sectors, and introduces key principles of the bargaining process.

DIMENSIONS OF COLLECTIVE BARGAINING

Before trade unions were established, wage rates were either set unilaterally by the employer or through bargaining between an individual worker and the employer. Collective bargaining developed with the growth of trade union representation in order to compensate for the inherent inequality in the employment relationship. Collective bargaining may be regarded as a rule-making process, generating both substantive rules – covering the substance of negotiation, wages, hours, manning levels, etc. – and procedural rules – like disputes procedures – that govern the relations between the parties. These rules include formally codified (written) collective agreements, unwritten (and sometimes unspoken) informal understandings, and unilateral regulation by either party. Thus management rules and work group custom and practice rules are as much products of collective bargaining as are collective agreements.

The structure of collective bargaining is both a product and a major determinant of patterns of industrial relations. Clegg (1976), for example, relates variations between six countries in terms of their union density, union structure, union government, workplace organization and strikes, to differences in collective bargaining structure. The theory is developed further in Clegg's (1979) analysis of British industrial relations. Manufacturing industry is characterized by decentralized collective bargaining, highly developed workplace organization, and many small, short strikes. The public sector is characterized by centralized collective bargaining with less developed workplace organization and strikes that are few, large and protracted. In private services collective bargaining is underdeveloped, workplace organization is weak, and there is a dependence upon statutory maintenance of minimum terms and conditions.

In addition to the level of collective bargaining (the point at which it is conducted), there are other dimensions of the bargaining structure. The scope of bargaining refers to the range of issues negotiated at a particular level, while the depth of bargaining is concerned with the extent to which the parties are involved in the interpretation and application of rules. For a given level, the bargaining unit is defined in terms of the categories of workers covered; the coverage is a measure of the proportion of employees in the bargaining unit whose terms and conditions are determined by the collective agreement; the form of an agreement refers to the degree of formalization (from an informal understanding to a formal written agreement); and the control of an agreement refers to the degree to which it is enforced. In terms of these dimensions, the structure of collective bargaining in Britain has evolved significantly since the 1960s.

PRIVATE SECTOR BARGAINING

The Donovan Commission (1965–8) was established to investigate perceived problems of industrial relations: unofficial strikes, restrictive labour practices and wages drift. Although the terms of reference were wide and the whole economy was within the scope of the inquiry, the Commission focused attention on the private sector manufacturing industries, especially engineering and motor vehicles.

The famous Donovan analysis concluded that the economic problems associated with labour were symptoms of the disorder caused by the extension of the informal system (reflecting the actual behaviour of shop stewards and managers), which was in conflict with the formal system (embodied in the official institutions). Flanders characterized workplace bargaining as 'largely informal, largely fragmented, and largely autonomous', a view confirmed by the Donovan Commission. The informality derived from the prevalence of unwritten understandings and custom and practice rules. Both substantive agreements and procedural arrangements at the workplace were informal; formal procedures were often short-circuited. Workplace bargaining was fractional, with different groups getting different concessions at different times, leading to competitive sectional wage adjustments and disorderly pay structures. Such bargaining was autonomous in that it was outside the control of external institutions and effectively undermined the regulatory effect of industry-wide agreements.

The growth of workplace bargaining both reflected and enhanced the power of work groups (hence of shop stewards) under tight labour market conditions. Where workplace trade unionism was highly developed, as in manufacturing and, especially, the engineering and motor vehicles industries, shop stewards were able to exploit local labour shortages, employing unofficial, unconstitutional stoppages and contributing to the wages drift associated with the problems of the British economy from the mid-1960s.

The Donovan prescription was 'to introduce greater order into factory and workshop relations', i.e. the formalization of the informal system through the codification of local agreements and the adoption of agreed procedures at plant level. The formalization of plant bargaining increased the importance of shop stewards and conveners, but also incorporated them into the formal system of written procedures and union bureaucracy. Changes in the structure of collective bargaining have had a major impact on the power structure of unions (Boraston, Clegg and Rimmer 1975).

Productivity bargaining began to formalize workplace negotiations before Donovan's recommendations and shifted the focus from workshop to plant bargaining. The formalization of plant bargaining enhanced the status of shop stewards and undermined further the authority of front-line supervision (who had acquiesced in granting informal concessions that effectively reduced the control of senior management). It also encouraged the development of joint shop stewards committees (JSSCs) to promote cooperation between different unions represented at a plant. While the JSSCs reduced inter-union conflict, they institutionalized the divisions between shop stewards and full-time union officials; shop stewards on a JSSC could find themselves committed to JSSC majority decisions that conflicted with the official policies of their union. The development of shop steward hierarchies in the big plants may also be viewed as a process of bureaucratization, where the lay official workplace organization replicates the external structures of the formal union.

The threat of companies playing off one plant against another and the discord which developed between JSSCs and union full-time officials led to the creation of inter-plant combine committees, where senior stewards from JSSCs would regularly meet. Companies avoided recognizing combine committees for the purposes of collective bargaining; their main function has been the exchange of information between JSSCs. Where company bargaining was introduced, managements preferred to involve full-time union officials rather than legitimize the combine committees.

Consequences of reform

The Fawley productivity deal (Flanders 1964) is often cited as a model for the reform of collective bargaining in the Donovan style. Productivity bargaining at the Esso Fawley refinery began in 1960 with a series of agreements designed to increase pay and productivity through relaxing demarcation and introducing flexible working arrangements. For Flanders, productivity bargaining was a route to workplace democracy; it extended the collective bargaining agenda and integrated shop stewards into management decision-making. In the long run, productivity bargaining proved more difficult, as Ahlstrand (1990) has shown. At Fawley, the productivity agreements often failed to achieve their stated objectives of reforming working practices. The high-pay/high-effort scenario was never fully realized, and in place of labour market 'internalization', in the 1980s management opted for 'externalization' with an increased use of contractors. Moreover, in the 1980s, Fawley management adopted a strategy of de-unionization through a staff status programme designed to individualize employment relations and eliminate collective bargaining on the site. Ahlstrand concluded that Fawley management never adopted productivity bargaining as a pluralist strategy to integrate unions and workers into management decision-making. Such findings do not invalidate the reformist prescription of integration, only the notion that Fawley represents an adequate empirical test of its effectiveness.

One consequence of the formalization of plant procedures and the elevation of bargaining from workshop to plant level was an increase in the average duration of unofficial strikes. The settlement rate of unofficial stoppages is far higher than that of official strikes, but has deteriorated with formalization; the informal system is probably more efficient at resolving disputes because it is more flexible and because it involves those with most intimate knowledge of local circumstances (Newby and Winterton 1983).

Batstone (1988) reached a similar conclusion that the informal system offered flexibility and that professional personnel managers introduced rigidities which led to strikes. Dunn (1993) suggests that managers were incorporated into the shop steward system: 'stewards defined the terms of the truce and management rationalized its compliance.' While Dunn uses Batstone's evidence to refute the shop steward incorporation thesis, it is not necessarily contradictory to see the incorporation of both parties in Donovan-pluralist institutionalization.

A reversible reform?

Whereas the 1970s may be characterized by institutionalization and the reform of private sector collective bargaining, since the 1980s the emphasis has been more on restricting the scope of bargaining, though with less deconstruction of the institutions than has occurred in some public sector enterprises (see p. 165).

Without doubt, the 1980s witnessed a reassertion of managerial prerogative. This was facilitated by, but was not an automatic outcome of, labour market changes, and was brought about by a departure from the pluralist structures and bargaining norms associated with the Donovan era. Brown (1993) uses data from the Workplace Industrial Relations Survey to demonstrate a significant contraction in the coverage of collective agreements, a narrowing in the scope of bargaining and a decline in the depth of union involvement. The coverage of collective agreements throughout the economy (private and public sector) appears to have fallen from 72 per cent of all employees in 1973 to 64 per cent in 1984 and 47 per cent in 1990 (although the bases of these estimates are not strictly comparable).

The structure of bargaining has also altered. Brown characterizes the 1970s system as one of two-tier pay fixing with multi-employer agreements (industry-wide) being explicitly supplemented by single-employer (company and plant) additions. Surveys showed that of those workers in manufacturing whose terms and conditions were established by collective bargaining, about 75 per cent were covered by single-employer agreements and 25 per cent depended solely upon multi-employer agreements. Since then, two-tier bargaining has declined: in 1984, of those private sector employees covered by collective bargaining arrangements (about 60 per cent of the total), 67 per cent were under single-employer agreements, while multi-employer agreements covered 33 per cent. By 1990 of all multi-establishment firms engaging in single-employer bargaining, corporate bargaining accounted for 66 per cent of manual and 80 per cent of non-manual workers in manufacturing and 90 per cent of all in private services. Bargaining has become less fragmented and there has been a shift towards national single-employer (corporate) bargaining, rather than national multi-employer (industry-wide) bargaining.

PUBLIC SECTOR BARGAINING

The origins of, and motives for, a public sector have influenced its industrial relations characteristics. Public sector activities may be classified into public services, public utilities and public enterprises. The public services, such as health, social security, education and the police, are socially necessary facilities which the state acknowledged would not be provided under market capitalism, either because they would not be profitable, or because the pursuit of profit would be inconsistent with the idea of providing a service to all, according to needs and irrespective of means. The utilities, like gas, water and electricity, were taken into public ownership in order to rationalize local services (most of which were already municipally controlled), take advantage of economies of scale, and to control natural monopolies which would otherwise operate to the detriment of the consumer. The public enterprises, like coal, rail, steel and docks, were nationalized for strategic reasons as the ‘commanding heights of the economy' which were to play a major role in developing the nation's industrial base, especially as part of post-war reconstruction.

The organizational form chosen for nationalization was based on the principles established by Herbert Morrison for the London Passenger Transport Board created in 1933. Morrison's objectives for socialized industries were to ensure that strategic industries were operated efficiently in the public interest, and that political and operational control would be kept separate. To achieve these objectives, industry boards of leading industrialists were established with responsibility for day-to-day operation and management, while government ministers were empowered to give 'general direction'. Thus the public enterprise manages its own finances but is broadly accountable to the relevant government minister, and thus to Parliament and the public. The nationalized industries were expected to be 'model employers', maintaining the highest standards for terms and conditions. The principle of workers' control was rejected in favour of having the 'best business brains' on the boards, although for some years it was customary for the board member specializing in labour relations to be a (retired) union official.

The special characteristics of labour relations in the public sector related to the way labour was managed, conflict was resolved, and the health, welfare and skills of employees were promoted. The public sector institutions were required by statute to conclude agreements with trade unions representing their employees, establishing procedures for negotiation and consultation over terms and conditions of employment. In contrast with most of the private sector (with the exceptions of footwear, furniture and chemicals), the negotiating arrangements were highly regulated, and contained provision for conciliation and arbitration by independent parties.

Manual workers were highly unionized in most of the enterprises before nationalization, but collective bargaining arrangements encouraged the growth of white-collar unionization. In 1948 all the nationalized industries together had a union density of 60 per cent, compared with an average for all industries of 45 per cent. By 1979 public enterprise union density was typically above 90 per cent, compared with an average for all industries of 53 per cent. There was some multi-unionism, but generally few jurisdictional problems between different organizations.

Public sector collective bargaining

Clegg (1979) characterizes public sector bargaining arrangements in general as centralized, with little or no local negotiation on pay. Certainly centralized bargaining became the norm for the public utilities, public administration and services, but public enterprise arrangements were more varied.

In public services, bargaining arrangements are normally based on

Whitley Councils. Civil service conditions, for example, are established centrally through a National Whitley Council, with Departmental Whitley Councils covering issues confined to particular departments. A Civil Service Arbitration Tribunal considers failures to agree, and the government may veto awards 'on grounds of policy'. The National Health Service negotiating arrangements are similarly centralized with representatives of area and district health authorities meeting with representatives of the unions concerned. The Minister for Health must confirm agreements, demonstrating that while the government does not negotiate directly with the unions, it nevertheless controls the level of settlements. Burnham Committees comprising representatives of Local Education Authorities and representatives of teachers' unions used to negotiate pay and conditions for teachers, but these arrangements were disbanded by government following industrial action by the teachers' unions. Local authority workers have their terms established between the management coordinating the Local Authorities Conditions of Service Advisory Board and the relevant unions; the negotiations for manual and white-collar workers are separate. The government has no formal control over local authority agreements but can exert a powerful influence through budgetary constraints.

In many public enterprises, terms and conditions had been negotiated nationally before nationalization, either at industry level (electricity and water) or company level (rail and post). Centralized arrangements therefore continued and were reinforced. Negotiating arrangements for railway workers, for example, involve Local Departmental Committees (LDCs) which discuss local issues such as working arrangements, rosters and links. Sectional Councils in each BR region cover each of the five sections into which grades of workers are divided; the application of national agreements and failures to agree at LDC-level are discussed. National (industry-wide) negotiating arrangements entail a Railway Staff Joint Committee, a Railway Staff National Council and a Railway Staff National Tribunal.

Employee representation was particularly powerful in steel, coal and the docks at both national and local level, and the traditions of local bargaining survived nationalization. Pay rates tended to be determined nationally, while actual earnings were affected by local negotiation on overtime and bonuses (especially in the docks). Fluctuating earnings and strong union organization translated local bargaining opportunities into a relatively high level of conflict in coal, steel and docks, which contrasts markedly with the generally peaceful industrial relations which have characterized the public utilities and other public enterprises.

The public sector norm of peaceful industrial relations may be explained by reference to the 'model employer' idea, the existence of career structures and 'lifetime employment'. However, at least as important have been effective procedures to deal with discipline and grievances, highly developed collective bargaining and consultation arrangements which served to institutionalize industrial conflict, and attractive redundancy arrangements when employment was run down in the public sector. Above all, there is the political contingency argument: governments wanted to keep the trains running and the lights on, as they would be blamed for stoppages. The postwar public sector consensus came under increasing strain as a result of incomes policies, the breakdown of comparability as the main principle of pay determination, limitations on public expenditure and the restructuring and privatization of state enterprises.

Coal mining

Coal mining is unique among the public sector industries in having undergone several major changes of collective bargaining structure since the industry was nationalized in 1947.

Before nationalization, daywage workers (about 57 per cent of the work force) had been paid according to minimum rates established on a district basis between the miners' county unions and local employers. District arrangements continued after nationalization but the National Coal Board and the National Union of Mineworkers wanted to reform the wages structure. In 1950 there were 6,000 different job titles and the 750 remaining after job analysis eliminated duplicates were rationalized into nine industry-wide grades in the Revision of the Wages Structure Agreement, 1955. Pieceworkers remained on price lists negotiated for each seam on a pit basis. While price lists were seldom altered in the life of a face, faceworkers raised their earnings through bargaining over special allowances for changing conditions.

The NCB originally planned to rationalize the pieceworkers' pay structure but this proved impossible and less important with the introduction of powerloading. Between 1947 and 1965 special agreements were negotiated on a district basis covering the pay of faceworkers on powerloaded faces in various District Power Loading Agreements. The Scottish and Durham PLAs provided for a basic daywage, with a completion-of-task bonus which added a further 11 per cent. Most other PLAs were on a measured daywork basis with shift payment for completion of the agreed task and piecerate payments for performance in excess of this. A Comprehensive Agreement in Yorkshire (1958) gave the option of working according to two earlier district agreements or according to the system established in most other districts. Face negotiation continued to be important, but on manning levels and task norms rather than on wages directly.

The National Power Loading Agreement, 1966 (NPLA), introduced standard shift rates for each coalfield in place of the rates established by district PLAs, and left the number of men to comprise a powerloading team and task norms to be established by method study at pit level. The

NPLA covered faceworkers (including craftsmen and rippers) on power-loaded faces during a production shift. NPLA rates also became minima on old faces working according to district PLA rates. The NPLA brought a further 21 per cent of the work force, including the most militant workers, under the scope of national agreements. It is therefore widely credited with bringing about the decline of strike-proneness in the period 1966–71. It certainly reduced the proportion of strikes over allowances, and there was a corresponding increase in the proportion of strikes over working arrangements. Most importantly, the NPLA encouraged the use of the pit conciliation machinery because money could no longer be conceded in face negotiation (Winterton 1981).

The NCB proposed a pit productivity scheme in 1974 as part of a wider strategy to restore influence to moderate area union leaders in the face of increasing rank-and-file militancy and the emergence of a leftist national leadership. The NUM resisted the scheme, rejecting incentives in several membership ballots and delegate conferences, but following legal action brought by the Nottinghamshire and Lancashire areas, an agreement was concluded that established a framework within which NUM areas could agree to local incentive schemes. The model Area Incentive Scheme agreement allowed incentive pay for those covered by an installation agreement whose work was assessed by method study. Others were paid a bonus based on the average pit incentive or the average for the area: 65 per cent for any shift worked between the face line and the gate end; 50 per cent for any shift elsewhere underground; 40 per cent for any shift worked on the surface. For any shift spent at the face, miners received 100 per cent bonus. The Area Incentive Scheme fragmented bargaining, making a national strike in support of a pay claim unlikely, and re-established divisions which were to prove critical in the 1984–5 strike against pit closures. Since the 1984–5 strike, however, pay bargaining has become more fragmented with modifications to the original incentive agreement (so-called options where pay is related directly to tonnage rather than effort as under the original work measurement scheme) and the reintroduction of *ad hoc* contracts, whereby work teams tender for jobs competitively without any involvement of the local union. At the same time, the institutions of collective bargaining established when the industry was nationalized in 1947 have been dramatically deconstructed (Winterton and Winterton 1989).

Government–public sector relations

Government is better able to control pay settlements in the public sector, so public sector workers have suffered more from the application of incomes policies than have workers in, for example, private sector manufacturing. The pay of railway workers fell behind average earnings when the industry contracted during the 1950s, as did that of miners between 1957 and 1972. In the 1970s successive groups of public sector workers were brought into direct conflict with governments in an effort to obtain settlements comparable with those obtaining in the private sector. Incomes policies resulted in a wave of strikes involving postal workers, local authority workers, fire-fighters, railway workers, civil servants, health service workers, teachers and miners (Winchester 1983).

Whereas the public sector confrontations of the 1970s were concerned primarily with wages, those of the 1980s were caused by public sector borrowing requirement (PSBR) limits, operational restructuring and privatization. Although the 1980 steel strike was ostensibly about wages, it formed the prelude to massive restructuring. Similarly, the water workers' pay strike involved wider issues related to privatization. The 1984–5 miners' strike was, of course, the most dramatic example of a conflict over restructuring. Throughout the Thatcher years, the major source of instability in British industrial relations was the relationship between government and public sector trade unions.

Although the Conservative Party has always had a degree of ideological hostility towards nationalized industries, Conservative governments before Thatcher rarely contemplated denationalization (in 1951 road transport and steel were denationalized, the latter being renationalized by Labour in 1967). The Heath government (1970–4) actually brought some enterprises into public ownership in order to save them from bankruptcy. The critique of the nationalized industries became most highly developed in the Thatcher years. The arguments were primarily ideological: the government should leave economic decisions to the market; individuals should be allowed greater choice; bureaucratic control stifles response to consumer preferences. Economic reasons included: the need to control PSBR to reduce inflation; the exclusion of the private sector; assumed inefficiencies arising from subsidies, protectionism and weak profit motive. The industrial relations reasons included: the unions were perceived as too powerful; the 'good employer' obligation had artificially encouraged union membership; workers were insulated from market pressures by monopoly, so pay was unrelated to performance and restrictive practices were difficult to remove.

During the Thatcher years, the prescription to change the public sector began with initiatives to raise efficiency and productivity through exposure to market competition, and ended in wholesale privatization, first of the public utilities, then other public enterprises including the 'commanding heights', and ultimately the public services (Foster 1992). The mechanisms employed included financial reform, deregulation, and the restructuring of industrial relations. Financial pressure was exerted through limiting the funds which public enterprises could raise externally, progressively reducing operating subsidies and imposing profit targets. Deregulation took the form of a relaxation of statutory protections in product and labour markets, and the abolition of the National Dock Labour Scheme, for example. The restructuring of labour relations was in marked contrast with non-intervention; since 1979, intervention has been direct and designed to strengthen managerial resolve in effecting permanent change.

The most obvious result of the decade of change was a dramatic reduction in employment in the public enterprises. Between 1979 and 1992, railways lost 52,000 staff (29 per cent), electricity supply 32,000 (32 per cent), and water approaching 19,000 (28 per cent). The decline was especially marked in coal where the work force was reduced by 193,000 (82 per cent), and steel where 104,000 jobs (66 per cent) were lost. On the docks, 8,000 registered dockworkers (88 per cent) were made redundant, while the bus industry work force contracted by 20–30 per cent. The cutbacks were accompanied by a dramatic increase in productivity and the nationalized industries outperformed the private manufacturing sector from the mid-1980s onwards (Beaumont 1992: 174). As well as a general contraction of operations and withdrawal from less profitable activities, other causal factors of this growth of labour productivity include reforms of working practices, functional flexibility (especially among craft workers), temporal flexibility, and numerical flexibility via subcontractors and casualization.

The major changes in public sector industrial relations (apart from the altered power context) have been in the institutions and structures of collective bargaining (Pendleton and Winterton 1993). In the cases of water, electricity supply, buses and docks, the dismemberment of organizations and industries into several separate companies on privatization led to the replacement of industry bargaining by single-employer bargaining. In other cases the transition to sub-national bargaining occurred whilst the industries were still in public ownership, as with the Post Office and British Coal. Single-employer bargaining has not been automatic with privatization. In the water and electricity supply industries, many senior managers favoured retaining the existing pattern of national bargaining. The primary impetus for changing the structure of bargaining came from organizational restructuring rather than explicit industrial relations strategies. In this sense there are similarities with private manufacturing, though industrial relations factors were by no means absent and in some cases were even predominant: British Rail's proposed reforms in 1989 were explicitly aimed at correcting industrial relations problems whilst British Coal's recent changes can be perceived as an element of the strategy to marginalize the NUM.

Most public and recently privatized enterprises have sought to introduce performance-related pay, and to improve communications with employees, independent of union representatives. One of the main features of the Thatcher years was the willingness of management to force through change in the face of union and workforce opposition, resulting in several major confrontations including the 1980 steel strike, railway strikes in 1982, 1985 and 1989, the Post Office strike in 1988, the strike over the abolition of the National Dock Labour Scheme in 1989, and the coal miners' strike of 1984–5. Nevertheless, some sectors, such as electricity supply, water and docks, continued to be largely free of overt conflict throughout the 1980s (the 1983 water strike notwithstanding). Railways experienced a number of major national disputes but the pattern of strike-free relationships at the workplace persisted, and confrontational management was at most episodic and intermittent.

The extent to which novel and consistent industrial relations strategies have been pursued varies considerably between different public and recently privatized enterprises. In both coal and docks there seem to have been more or less consistent strategies guiding managerial actions for much of the 1980s. The port employers sought to break the stranglehold imposed by the Dock Labour Scheme and to weaken the power of the stevedores. Beyond this they appear to have aimed to return to the situation in the 1950s where much of the activity associated with unloading ships was conducted by sub contractors rather than direct employees. In coal, the 1984–5 strike was the outcome of a long-term strategy held by sections of British Coal management who came into the ascendant in the 1980s, and since then it has been their strategy to marginalize the NUM and reassert managerial prerogative at pit level.

In the other industries remaining in public ownership the situation is not so clear cut. Although there is some evidence of a new approach to industrial relations, leading to national strikes in British Rail and to an increase in local disputes in the Post Office, it is not clear that management actions were guided by a radically new industrial relations strategy. In the recently privatized utilities, water and electricity, there have been major structural reforms of collective bargaining institutions, but for much of the decade management's approach to industrial relations was broadly unchanged. Privatization *per se* has been relatively insignificant in accounting for the changes experienced by public enterprises, compared with the effects of organizational restructuring (partly in response to commercialism).

In evaluating the extent of change since 1979, it is clear that some industries have changed almost beyond recognition in terms of their size and patterns of union representation, others have experienced changes in bargaining structures, and in some there has been considerable institutional continuity but at the same time major changes to working practices. Public enterprises underwent considerable changes, especially in their working practices, before the Thatcher years, and on occasion have been at the forefront of innovation (as in the adoption of operational research in the 1950s). While some parts of the public sector underwent major changes to their structures, their technology and their working practices without conflict, in others conflict was the primary means of securing such changes.

THE BARGAINING PROCESS

The principles of the bargaining process are common to collective bargaining at all levels, although they are more likely to be adhered to in formal bargaining conducted by experienced negotiators. It is useful to view the bargaining process as entailing five distinct stages. In the first stage, the parties formulate their overall bargaining objectives, identifying priorities and issues that may be sacrificed later. Next, the parties must assess the relative bargaining power and either adjust their objectives or alter the balance of power as required. The third stage, where negotiators prepare their case and brief the team, is critical to the success of subsequent negotiations. The negotiations are only the fourth stage of the process, which does not end with the successful conclusion of an agreement, since agreements need to be continually monitored, the fifth stage.

The bargaining process and its outcome are influenced above all else by bargaining power, itself influenced by various economic, social and political factors. It is relative, rather than absolute, power which is important, and this balance of power changes. Power determines the position that can be adopted in negotiation after the opponents' concessions have been exhausted. Power must be perceived as real by the opponent, and the threat of its use as realistic if credibility is to be maintained. Bargaining power is usually defined by the equation:

$$\text{power of A} = \frac{\text{cost to B of disagreement with A's terms}}{\text{cost to B of agreement with A's terms}}$$

Established conventions or ground rules are very important in bargaining; while these vary with time and place, some are universal. Past bargaining determines the issues for future bargaining; a precedent is established to negotiate in the future on topics which have been negotiable in the past. If an issue is to be kept non-negotiable in the future, do not enter into discussion on it in the present. Existing agreements should be upheld; this is essential for trust and to promote stable bargaining relationships. It is also necessary to control slippage. There should be a time scale for settlement. The parties need to acknowledge that the issue will not be discussed indefinitely and that sanctions will not be imposed before reaching a failure to agree. For the bargaining process to operate effectively, each side must be prepared to make concessions. Final offer openings create conflict, and give the other side no room to be accommodating, so the parties should identify their own ideal settlement, realistic settlement and fall-back position. The overlap between the demands and concessions of the two sides constitute the parameters of bargaining.

The means of achieving movement should not be abused. Movement is encouraged by linking issues, hypothesizing about reciprocal movement and using adjournment, usually to consider an offer or make a concession, but these should only be used when one side is genuinely ready to move its position. All bargaining involves the implicit or explicit use or threat of sanctions, but sanctions are no substitute for bargaining, and should be seen as complementary to the bargaining process rather than as an alternative mechanism.

Most importantly, bargaining should be in good faith. This means that an offer once made should not be withdrawn later unless it was explicitly made conditionally, and the conditions have not been fulfilled. Neither side should deny what has previously been unambiguously agreed (although this does not prevent discussion of the interpretation of an agreement). Negotiation should not be circumvented until it has failed and the procedure (see Chapter 12) has been exhausted. Both sides must be willing to bargain on negotiable issues, but information obtained in an off-the-record meeting (which often facilitates effective negotiation) should not be used to get formal commitment. The opposition must be allowed to retain credibility with its own side, even where it has been defeated in the negotiations, in the interests of maintaining stable bargaining (for which reason it is often necessary to create a face-saving solution). The final agreement should contain no deliberate ambiguity or trickery and should be implemented in its entirety, even if the situation alters, until such time as it becomes renegotiable.

Bargaining strategies and tactics

Bargaining strategy refers to the overall plan for obtaining objectives, while tactics refer to techniques for putting the plan into practice in negotiation. The strategies available to the parties depend upon their relative power and involve a combination of defensive and offensive ploys. The opening moves, or initial demand and offer positions, are most important; they must allow room for manoeuvre if bargaining is to proceed. If the demand is too high, then equal movement becomes impossible and one side will eventually have to make considerable movement with little in return; therefore a demand with many facets allows more opportunity for trading. There are special situations where a zero movement position is encountered. In such cases one party has no movement available at the start of negotiation either because a principle is at stake or because there cannot be equal movement.

When negotiations are underway, several strategies may be employed to encourage movement by the other side. By linking issues, negotiators aim to suggest that the opposition will gain their demand by granting yours; the link is established, therefore, as a prelude to joint movement between one of your issues and one of your adversary's. There are several ways of increasing bargaining power during negotiations. These may involve strengthening your own position or weakening the opponent's, delaying negotiation or confrontation to the most favourable time, or increasing the costs to the opponent of disagreement to your demands. Sanctions are often more effective when threatened than when applied, although the use of empty threats is counter-productive. If sanctions are used, they should impose costs on the opposition sufficient to alter their bargaining spectrum. Spontaneous sanctions may also be employed when the status quo is threatened or the other party is deviating from the ground rules. Sometimes sanctions need to be applied to maintain the credibility of bargaining power: weapons grow rusty if never used.

Preparation for negotiation is at least as important as the negotiations themselves. Particular attention needs to be paid to the case and to the negotiating team. A good case alone will not win, but a bad case will invariably lose. The case should support the bargaining objectives. Weaknesses should be identified and either declared or concealed, depending upon your tactical approach (show reasonableness or make opposition work for every concession). The full strength of a case should not be revealed at once, allowing scope to compensate for weaknesses targeted by the opponent. The demand should represent the ideal settlement and the case should justify the demands made. Division of labour within the bargaining team is also important, since three tasks are to be undertaken during negotiations: negotiation itself, recording negotiations and analysing. It is normal for each side to have one lead negotiator, who does all, or most, of the talking. Communication between team members is maintained by passing notes or brief consultation, but this should be kept to a minimum.

Stages in negotiation

The negotiation process can be considered as comprising four stages. In the first stage, the objective is to clarify the opponent's position, obtaining as much information as possible about their realistic settlement and fall-back position, whilst revealing a minimum amount about your own. At the second stage the objective is to restructure the opponent's perception, changing their expectations so that when movement takes place it will be in your favour. This is done by undermining the opposition's argument and credibility, supporting your own argument and credibility, and preventing the opponent from settling prematurely. It is important to identify the optimum timing to move to the third stage of moving towards settlement. The objective here is to get the maximum movement from the opponent while minimizing your own movement, so tactics are employed which encourage movement and the abandonment of commitment. The negotiations end with closure: here the objective is to finalize an agreement, as much in your favour as possible in the circumstances, and close the deal. The opponent needs to be convinced that their position will only deteriorate with further delay and the negotiator may need to offer an incentive to the other party, if only as a face saver.

FURTHER READING

Atkinson, G. (1977) *The Effective Negotiator* London: Quest (2nd edition).
Batstone, E. (1988) *The Reform of Workplace Industrial Relations*, Oxford: Clarendon.
Dunn, S. (1993) 'From Donovan to . . . Wherever', *British Journal of Industrial Relations*, 31, 2, pp. 169–87.
Pendleton, A. and Winterton, J. (eds) (1993) *Public Enterprise in Transition: Industrial Relations in State and Privatized Corporations*, London: Routledge.

QUESTIONS FOR DISCUSSION

1 What were the key elements of the Donovan Commission's recommendations for the reform of collective bargaining? Are they still valid?
2 The most dramatic changes to collective bargaining since 1979 have been in the public sector. Why?
3 'The key to effective negotiations is the development of stable bargaining relationships.' Discuss.

Chapter 12

Discipline, grievances and disputes

INTRODUCTION

In employment, as in any other relationship, there are occasions when one party is dissatisfied with the behaviour of another, and when conflictual situations arise. This chapter is concerned with the maintenance of effective human resource strategies in an enterprise when such difficulties occur and with how differences can be most efficiently resolved. Conflict is an inherent part of the employment relationship, so if human resources are to be adequately developed, conflict must be recognized and anticipated as an operational contingency. To do this most successfully, managers must understand the nature of conflict, its manifestations, motives and meanings, and be prepared to acknowledge that there will always be diverse points of view and different interests expressed within the work situation. After considering forms of conflict and recent trends, this chapter examines the management of discipline, grievances and disputes, emphasizing the role of effective procedures.

CONFLICT: FORM AND MEANING

Industrial conflict is clearly an important industrial relations issue, but one that receives more attention from the media than from serious students of the subject. As a consequence, industrial conflict is often regarded as synonymous with strikes and is inevitably portrayed in negative terms. While no one would deny that stoppages of work are damaging to output, little account is taken of the role of conflict as a safety valve providing an opportunity for frustrations to be vented in order that work can continue. Conflict generally has a bad press, but as Coser (1956) has shown, it can also perform valuable social functions. External conflict generates internal cohesion within work groups and management teams which extends beyond the conflict situation and contributes to more effective working relationships. Conflict also creates relationships between antagonists which can form the basis of constructive associations to resolve the current problem and avoid its recurrence.

The range of alternative expressions of conflict is virtually unlimited and can be classified into *individual* forms (absenteeism, labour turnover) and *collective* forms (strikes, overtime bans, working to rule). Some forms can be individual or collective and are best distinguished by their *covert* expression (sabotage, pilferage). The evidence on whether these forms are alternative or complementary is inconclusive, but some industries have their characteristic forms of conflict. Strikes are rare on the railways and in newspapers; the work to rule is more effective in both cases because the product or service is perishable. Similarly, while conflict among male manual workers is likely to take the form of striking, working to rule or other collective action, conflict among female and white-collar workers is more often expressed in individual forms such as absenteeism or labour turnover.

There have been many attempts to explain industrial conflict, none of which is entirely adequate alone. Perhaps the best known, and still the most widespread, is the theory, or assumption, that strikes are fomented by agitators or militant leaders. The evidence contradicts such a view, since it is impossible to agitate successfully without widespread grievances. The Donovan Commission (1968) described shop stewards as 'more of a lubricant than an irritant', and found that managers and union members did not believe stewards were any more militant than other trade unionists. In many conflict-prone situations, such as the docks and car plants, local union leaders are as likely to be a source of moderation, persuading workers not to take 'wildcat' action in breach of agreed procedures. Nevertheless, grievances alone do not automatically result in expressions of conflict, and someone has to give a lead to discrete discontents before workers become galvanized into action. Research by Batstone *et al.* (1978) has illuminated the complex role of shop stewards in the organization of conflict at the workplace, involving the articulation of collectivist vocabularies among unions members and the management of discontent in the bargaining process.

One of the most notable features of inter-industry patterns of conflict is their consistency across very different industrialized nations. Kerr and Siegel (1954) explained the uniformly high strike-proneness of certain industries by the location of workers in society. According to their community integration thesis, workers with high strike-proneness are often formed into an 'isolated mass', whereas those with a low propensity to strike are 'integrated' into wider society. Thus coal miners living in isolated pit villages, or dockers living close to the harbour, are isolated from wider public opinion and form part of a cohesive community with shared experiences: this reinforces their solidarity in a dispute situation. Printers, or factory workers, by contrast, are more likely to live in a more heterogeneous community so are denied the support of neighbours and are exposed to wider societal pressures. The theory has been criticized for its failure to explain variations within strike-prone industries, although it does explain the patterns of strike breaking in Yorkshire during the 1984–5 miners' strike (Winterton and Winterton 1989: 178–82, 200–6).

While community cohesion is clearly important, so too is cohesion at the level of the individual work group. Kuhn (1961) argued that the cohesion of work groups was a major determinant of propensity to take action, while Sayles (1958) demonstrated how technology influenced work group structure and identified technological circumstances conducive to strike action. Such 'contingency' explanations are valuable to a human resource analysis because it is important to recognize that factors conducive to effective team working and high morale, crucial for maintaining motivation, are equally likely, given adverse circumstances, to facilitate solidaristic responses antagonistic to management.

Economic conditions clearly influence the likelihood of industrial action. When business is booming union demands are higher, while during a recession workers' aspirations are more modest. At the same time, employers more readily meet demands in buoyant economic circumstances and will seek concessions from workers to maintain competitive advantage when product markets are declining. The net effect on strike activity is not therefore straightforward. In the past, econometricians correlated various economic measures with strike activity or other indices of conflict, often without any conscious theory of bargaining. Ashenfelter and Johnson (1969) were the first to produce a coherent model for their regressions, and their conclusions are based on a highly tendentious interpretation of 'time' as a proxy variable for the institutionalization of industrial conflict. Whatever the abstract logical appeal of economic factors, an econometric analysis is limited by its attempt to reduce such complex social phenomena as strikes to statistical measures in which all stoppages are treated as homogeneous.

The role of payment by results (PBR) in the generation of conflict has been widely acknowledged, particularly where changes in the conditions of work cause fluctuations in earnings, as at the coalface (Scott *et al.* 1963) and on the docks (Durcan, McCarthy and Redman 1983). Workers under PBR systems have ample opportunities for fragmented bargaining over special allowances for adverse circumstances; for example, face workers would take action over water, dirt in the coal, heat, cold, dust, faults in the seam, inadequate supplies of materials, and anything else beyond their control which affected earnings (Winterton 1981). Claims for allowances were often supported by unofficial strikes, which were also used by engineering pieceworkers to remedy inequities between effort and reward and to restore disturbed differentials.

Clegg (1979) argues that the structure of collective bargaining is the major determinant of strike patterns. Centralized bargaining is associated with few large strikes, whereas decentralized bargaining is associated with many small strikes. Hence small short strikes were typical of fragmented workplace bargaining in the motor industry, while large, and often protracted, strikes occurred in public sector enterprises where pay was centrally determined. Where disputes procedures are efficient, these resolve grievances which are otherwise expressed as unofficial stoppages. Clearly the patterns of conflict are closely related to patterns of bargaining, although the causality is not unidirectional: the use of local sanctions has in many cases been a catalyst to establishing decentralized bargaining.

STRIKES

With little reliable information on other forms of conflict (see Brown 1981; Edwards and Scullion 1982), quantification is limited to strikes, despite the inadequacies of the official statistics provided by the Employment Department. Firstly, lockouts (where the action is taken by the employer) are not distinguished from strikes (where the action is taken by the workers). In practice, the distinction is often meaningless because workers can provoke lockouts just as employers can cause strikes, and action is usually the result of a longer-running dispute. Secondly, only strikes over terms and conditions are included; thus strikes defined as political are discounted. While relatively few strikes are defined as political, they do occasionally account for substantial losses, as in the protests against the Industrial Relations Act in 1972 and more recently against the abolition of the National Dock Labour Scheme. Thirdly, the series excludes small, short stoppages, some by definition, others by default. A stoppage must involve ten workers and last at least one day, or incur a loss of one hundred or more working days, to qualify for inclusion. Coupled with the fact that there is no obligation on the parties involved to report stoppages of work, this means that as many as 60 per cent of stoppages (mostly small and short, but not all below the qualifying size) pass unrecorded. Most large, protracted stoppages are recorded, so the bulk of working days lost are covered, even if the number of stoppages is underestimated. Even so, the statistics largely ignore knock-on losses because workers indirectly involved are only counted if they are employed at establishments affected by workers directly involved in strike action.

Provided these limitations are borne in mind, strike statistics can be taken as a crude barometer of the level of industrial conflict. There are, however, some further caveats which should be made explicit at this point. Firstly, to reiterate, there are other forms of conflict besides strike action, some of them notoriously difficult to monitor. Secondly, the absence of observable conflict, whether as strikes or in some other form, does not necessarily mean that relations are good; it may simply indicate the lack of opportunity for the conflict to be expressed. (Of course, the converse does not hold; we can fairly assume that where conflict is openly expressed, relations are not good.) Thirdly, and most significantly, despite the popular image, Britain as a whole is not particularly strike-prone in comparison with other major industrialized nations. Even during the period 1972–81 when Britain's strike activity was at its peak, national strike-proneness was half that of France and one-quarter that of Australia and New Zealand (Poole 1986: 129). Moreover, most workplaces in Britain have always been free from industrial conflict. Strike activity in particular is heavily concentrated in certain industries and regions and, within them, in particular workplaces (Smith *et al.* 1978).

Postwar strike trends in Britain

None of the theories of conflict outlined above provides a satisfactory explanation for the temporal or inter-industrial variations in British strikes since the war. Clearly many factors influence strike activity, so monocausal explanations are inadequate.

Table 12.1 shows the annual statistics for stoppages of work since 1950. The annual aggregate number of stoppages has followed a cyclical trend roughly inverse with unemployment until 1967; but since 1968 there has been increased strike activity, unemployment and inflation. The relatively constant number of strikes from 1957 to 1967 obscures a continuous decline in the number of coalmining strikes and a simultaneous increase in those in all other industries. The decline of coal miners' strikes is explained by the contraction of the industry, changes in the bargaining structure and payment systems, and the increased use of the conciliation machinery (Winterton 1981).

The most significant change after 1968 was the enormous increase in working days lost; from a postwar annual average of about 3 million the number rose to a peak of 24 million in 1972, with subsequent peaks in 1974, 1977, 1979 and 1984. Despite the much-publicized decrease in the number of strikes since 1979, aggregate strike losses only returned to the levels of the 1960s. The strike wave of the 1968–74 period can be accounted for by a collision between public sector wage demands and government incomes policies (Hyman 1972). The large official strikes over public sector pay claims (from local authority manual workers in 1970, post office workers in 1971, miners in 1972 and 1974, firefighters in 1977, health workers in 1979) were also more protracted, so strike duration as well as magnitude increased.

Strikes and Donovan

The famous Donovan analysis (1968:12) held that Britain had two systems of industrial relations, and that the informal system undermined the

Table 12.1 Annual statistics of stoppages of work

Year	*Number*	*Workers ('000s)*	*Days lost ('000s)*
1950	1,339	303	1,389
1951	1,719	379	1,694
1952	1,714	416	1,792
1953	1,746	1,374	2,184
1954	1,989	450	2,457
1955	2,419	671	3,781
1956	2,648	508	2,083
1957	2,859	1,359	8,412
1958	2,629	524	3,462
1959	2,093	646	5,270
1960	2,832	819	3,024
1961	2,686	779	3,046
1962	2,449	4,423	5,798
1963	2,068	593	1,755
1964	2,524	883	2,277
1965	2,354	876	2,925
1966	1,937	544	2,398
1967	2,116	734	2,787
1968	2,378	2,258	4,690
1969	3,116	1,665	6,846
1970	3,943	180	10,980
1971	2,263	118	13,551
1972	2,530	173	23,909
1973	2,902	153	7,197
1974	2,946	163	14,750
1975	2,332	81	6,012
1976	2,034	67	3,284
1977	2,737	117	10,142
1978	2,498	104	9,405
1979	2,125	461	29,474
1980	1,348	83	11,964
1981	1,344	151	4,266
1982	1,538	210	5,313
1983	1,364	57	3,754
1984	1,221	146	27,135
1985	903	79	6,402
1986	1,074	72	1,920
1987	1,016	89	3,546
1988	781	79	3,702
1989	701	73	4,128
1990	630	30	1,903
1991	369	18	761
1992	253	15	528
1993	211	39	649

Source: *Employment Gazette*, London: HMSO, annual strike articles

regulatory effect of the formal system. Conflict between the formal and informal systems was demonstrated in the fragmented work group bargaining which led to an increase in the incidence of small, short stoppages that were usually both unofficial (not sanctioned by the relevant authority in the trade union) and unconstitutional (in breach of agreed procedures). The Commission viewed the increasing number of unofficial strikes outside coal mining as symptomatic of the disorderly, informal workplace arrangements and recommended the reform of collective bargaining at plant and company level.

A study of the probability density functions of strike duration demonstrated that official and unofficial strikes (which can be broadly associated with the formal and informal systems of industrial relations) are governed by different bargaining processes (Newby and Winterton 1983). Moreover, the process of settlement in the case of unofficial stoppages is more efficient, suggesting hidden costs of the Donovan prescription for the formalization of industrial relations.

Much of the reform proposed by Donovan was accomplished by the early 1970s. Clegg (1979: 279) argued that 'there is no evidence that the incidence of strikes in manufacturing since 1972 is lower than before 1968.' The Donovan reforms would have elevated bargaining to plant level: this should be reflected in changes in strike duration and magnitude rather than the number of stoppages. Durcan and McCarthy (1972) explained the growth of duration and magnitude since Donovan by the emergence of plant-wide stoppages which they termed the 'post Donovan strike'. Certainly there has been a real increase in the duration of unofficial strikes, which may be attributed to formalization, but the growth of magnitude is more a result of the greater number of large *official* strikes.

The Thatcher era

The 1980s were marked by significant changes in strike activity. In the first place, the level of strike activity was generally lower, with far fewer stoppages and, in aggregate, lower losses than in the 1970s. There were, nevertheless, significant stoppages in steel (1980), coal (1984–5), telecommunications (1987), post (1988), local government and docks (1989) and engineering (1990).

The reduction in strike-proneness was a function both of economic conditions, which provided a much less permissive environment for the frequent, small, short strikes characteristic of fragmented bargaining, and of the package of legal restrictions introduced after 1980. The law reinforced economic constraints, and probably had more impact on the behaviour of trade union officials than on the lay activists normally at the fore of any strike mobilization. Nevertheless, the increased use of injunctions by employers is a factor to be taken into account.

The second key change has been in the reasons for large confrontations in the public sector. Such strikes became a major feature of the British scene in the 1970s largely owing to the collision of pay claims and incomes policies, but the Callaghan government's public spending cuts represented a turning point. All the public sector stoppages of the 1980s involved issues other than pay, as governments systematically dismantled key parts of the public sector and introduced greater market competition to the rest. Thus even strikes in which pay was the overt issue also involved other latent factors concerning industrial restructuring (e.g. steel) or the removal of bargaining rights (e.g. teachers).

Much of the legislation directed at strike activity was designed to regulate official strikes. Despite the government's rediscovery of unofficial strikes, the legal remedies still assumed a 'top-down' model of trade union government and showed little awareness of the processes of strike action. In the 1990s, despite the recession, some of the old pattern of industrial conflict began to reappear, with unions winning ballots in favour of strike action in the coal and motor vehicle industries. Any sustained recovery in the economy could leave employers vulnerable to the wildcat stoppages which typified the tight labour market of the 1960s. Any future Labour government may well face the perennial problem of using its influence with the TUC to restrain local pay bargaining and maintain a corporatist consensus at national level.

THE MANAGEMENT OF DISCIPLINE AND GRIEVANCES

When management are unhappy with the behaviour or performance of particular workers, they may wish to discipline those involved. Workers' grievances represent their dissatisfaction with something management has, or has not, done. When the problems are generalized, involving a whole section or workforce and the company, or when the differences between the parties are not readily resolved, the situation is described as a dispute. In each case, examined in turn below, an effective procedure is the key to resolving problems promptly, fairly and consistently.

Discipline

The maintenance of discipline is essential for the day-to-day operation of any enterprise. Old-style ('theory X') management viewed discipline in negative terms as a means to enforce external demands, expecting workers to conduct themselves in a particular manner as a result of their fear of penalties. This approach was taken to extremes in nineteenth-century Britain when workers could be fined or dismissed for careless work or for failure to attend church on Sunday. The arbitrariness of managerial discipline, a major spur to independent trade union organization, was, and still is, a significant cause of industrial disputes. Management with a more participative style ('theory Y') view discipline constructively as action designed to promote mutual understanding and responsible behaviour contributing to optimum efficiency. All managers are concerned with maintaining and improving the level of performance of individuals. Performance improvement may be accomplished through initiatives to develop individuals who are performing satisfactorily (see Chapter 6) and by actions to bring unsatisfactory performers up to standard, which is a concern in this chapter.

An individual's performance may be unsatisfactory in terms of the quantity or quality of output (whether of physical commodities produced, information processed or service provided), attitude (such as rudeness to customers) or behaviour (for example, poor timekeeping or alcohol abuse). It is important from the outset to identify precisely how an individual's performance falls short of what is desired (the 'performance discrepancy') and to explore factors which may be contributing to the problem. The root causes of unsatisfactory performance are complex and may include an interaction of structural deficiencies in the work or external environment and personal attributes of the individual.

Workplace conditions contributing to unsatisfactory performance include inadequate task specification or training, poor supervision and low intrinsic rewards in the job. External structural conditions which are often reflected in underachievement at work include domestic problems such as marital discord or inadequate infrastructure (housing and transport, for example), and tight labour market conditions in which particular skills are scarce. Personal attributes which affect performance range from lack of motivation or ability to drug dependency or deviant behaviour. The interactions between these various factors make it difficult to disentangle separate effects and distinguish between precipitating and underlying causes. For example, persistent absenteeism or lateness may be the result of alcohol abuse, which in turn could be the result of an individual's attempt to cope with an unhappy marriage and an unrewarding job.

Only when the performance discrepancy has been established and the contributory factors identified is it possible to initiate actions to improve performance. The manager should define a subordinate's performance problem in terms of acts and omissions rather than in terms of personal attributes. Clear goals for improvement should be established. Wright and Taylor (1989: 127) offer a checklist for improving work performance, pairing reasons for performance problems with potential solutions. The purpose of such an approach is to encourage managers to explore a variety of causes of and solutions to unsatisfactory performance, avoiding simplistic solutions based on 'punishment'.

When a disciplinary procedure is integrated into such a developmental context of performance improvement, it promotes a constructive use of discipline by regularizing arrangements, removing scope for arbitrariness and giving prominence to the needs of the organization rather than the failings of the individual. For the procedure to be effective, it should be fair and be seen to be fair. Typically, a disciplinary procedure will involve verbal warnings, a written warning for repeated misconduct, followed by a disciplinary interview with management. Employees should have an opportunity to improve and the record should be wiped clean after a specified period (6–12 months). Dismissal should be confined to serious offences (smoking in a hazardous environment, violence against other employees) but can be justified for relatively minor but frequently repeated misconduct (poor timekeeping every day, unscheduled absence every month) when no mitigating circumstances are established, provided the procedure is adhered to properly.

The authority to dismiss should not rest with an immediate supervisor, who may harbour resentment against an individual over unrelated issues and whose relationship with other subordinates would suffer if the action taken was perceived to be arbitrary or unfair. There should be an appeals procedure and provision should be made for union (or other) representation at every stage. Disciplinary action against local (lay) union officials is invariably sensitive since it may be viewed as an attack upon effective union organization. In such cases, it is recommended in the Code of Practice published by the Advisory, Conciliation and Arbitration Service that procedures contain provision for the automatic involvement of the appropriate external full-time union official.

Grievances

Complaints and grievances may be a source of irritation to management, but they can provide vital information about employee morale, the quality of supervision and the emergence of wider discontent. Grievances will only fulfil this role if an upward channel of communication is established in the form of a grievance procedure.

A grievance procedure is a set of agreed rules for solving individual and collective grievances. The issues may be raised by an individual worker or local union representative, and discussions will proceed according to predetermined arrangements. A comprehensive grievance procedure will define the levels at which particular classes of issues will be discussed. It should specify time limits at each level, and any status quo conditions should be defined.

It is important to solve day-to-day problems as they arise. The first stage of a grievance procedure should therefore involve the immediate supervisor and the aggrieved worker. A local union representative may be involved automatically or exceptionally at this stage, or their involvement may represent the second stage. The majority of grievances should be resolved at this level but it should be clear that the absence of grievances going beyond the first stage is the result of their satisfactory resolution and is not because undue pressure has been exerted by the supervisor.

Some grievances cannot be resolved satisfactorily by the parties immediately involved. The circumstances may be beyond the control of the immediate supervisor, or the supervisor may be the perceived problem. In such cases, or where there is failure to agree, the procedure will specify who else is to be involved. Normally there will be reference to a higher authority on the management side and a senior shop steward or convener on the union side. If the issue is more serious or the parties fail to agree at this level, the grievance procedure may specify the involvement of a senior manager and external full-time union official. At this stage, the grievance is becoming a dispute.

Time limits are specified for each stage of a grievance procedure so that issues can be resolved quickly. Workers are obviously keen to have a reply to their complaints and it is in management's interest to respond before relatively minor complaints erupt into more widespread disputes. If managers believe they are too busy to deal with problems because they have a business to run, they may find they are creating the problem of running a business without a motivated work force.

Typical time limits will require a response at the supervisor level within twenty-four hours, a meeting with the senior shop steward and departmental manager within a further three days, and a meeting of senior management and full-time union official within a further seven days. Some grievances may, by their very nature, demand more flexibility in these arrangements. Also, time limits should not prevent emergency meetings called by either side at twenty-four hours' notice when the seriousness of a situation demands such action.

A status quo clause in a grievance procedure means that neither party can vary a practice or agreement existing prior to a difference arising without the express consent of the other party. Typically, collective agreements contain a clause to the effect that:

> It is agreed that in the event of any difference arising which cannot be immediately disposed of, then whatever practice or agreement existed prior to the difference shall continue to operate pending a settlement or until the agreed procedure has been exhausted.

For the union, a status quo clause is an essential safeguard to ensure that no changes take place without union agreement. For management, this may at first sight appear to restrict managerial prerogative and could provide an opportunity for unions to extend their influence over management operations. For the participative manager, however, such a challenge represents an opportunity to establish a high-trust relationship with the workforce. Status quo clauses are embodied in the statutory framework of codetermination in Sweden and this has facilitated workplace change rather than impeded it (see Chapter 10).

Disputes

A disputes procedure is often an extension of a grievance procedure, and in many situations all grievances and disputes are dealt with under the same agreement. The distinction may, however, be made between questions that are resolved internally at plant or company level (grievances) and those which either are not settled internally or which originate beyond the workplace (disputes).

In industries which experienced a high number of disputes, procedures were negotiated as part of the formal collective bargaining machinery. The experience of two such disputes procedures in the UK engineering and coalmining industries contains important lessons.

The procedure devised by the Engineering Employers' Federation (after a lockout in 1898) survived with a few amendments until 1971 and has been widely criticized. This procedure sought both to resolve disputes over the interpretation of national agreements and to prevent the unions from picking off local associations or individual employers by selective industrial action. The procedure functioned slowly because of the employers' fear that settlements would cause repercussions elsewhere; hence many cases were referred back to the plant from the central conference, which was unable to rule on 'local issues'. Under the pressures of plant bargaining and tight labour markets in the late 1960s, workers increasingly circumvented what was seen as an inefficient procedure, and it was suspended in 1971.

The Engineering Employers' Federation and the Confederation of Shipbuilding and Engineering Unions attempted to negotiate a new procedure, but failed to agree on a status quo clause. For five years disputes were discussed at plant level by a works conference at which full-time union officials were present, and by local conferences organized by the local employers' associations. Effectively the engineering procedure continued informally but without recourse to the central conference formerly held at York. These arrangements were reflected in the new procedure agreed in 1976, which provided also for industry-wide discussion on matters concerning the interpretation of national agreements. The 1976 procedure also contained a robust status quo clause, recognized conveners and provided guidelines on the facilities to be afforded shop stewards.

The use of the conciliation machinery in the nationalized coalmining industry demonstrates another aspect of the effectiveness of procedures. From 1949 to 1965 there were about 11,000 disputes each year referred to the conciliation machinery, and only 12 per cent of that number resulted in stoppages of work. In other words, over 88 per cent of disputes were resolved peacefully using the disputes procedure. The number of disputes and the number of stoppages both declined with the coal industry's contraction and changes in bargaining arrangements and pay structures, so from 1966 there were approximately 4,000 disputes per year on average, and only 6 per cent of these resulted in stoppages of work (Winterton 1981).

The coalmining conciliation procedure had become more effective and was resolving 94 per cent of disputes. The improvement was brought about by the reform of pay bargaining with the National Power Loading Agreement under which additional earnings could no longer be conceded at the face. The procedure had to be invoked to raise pay issues to a level at which they could be settled. In the aftermath of the defeat of the 1984–5 miners' strike, British Coal management unilaterally withdrew the conciliation machinery. Despite the altered bargaining power, there was a significant increase in unofficial action.

These examples show that a procedure will only be used where it is efficient and that it is most effective where it cannot be circumvented. These cases also demonstrate that the structural features of procedures embody the power contexts in which they are created, and that significant power shifts therefore necessitate changes in procedures. Thus the engineering procedure, imposed after an employers' lockout had defeated the union, embodied a power relativity unfavourable to the unions, a relativity which had become obsolete under powerful workplace organization in 1971. By contrast, the power relativity embodied in the coalmining conciliation machinery, established during the wartime consensus and postwar corporatist settlement, was seen to confer too many advantages on the union in the altered conditions arising out of the miners' defeat in 1985.

CONCLUSION

A few summary observations may be made in conclusion. We have seen that conflict is an intrinsic part of employment and that the proactive manager should not seek to suppress its manifestation but should understand the reasons for dissent, discontent and inadequate performance. Managed properly, conflict need not be wholly destructive and can be a catalyst for changes benefiting the organization. Since the absence of overt expressions of conflict does not necessarily mean the absence of underlying discontent, it is sometimes better for conflict to be expressed and resolved than to smoulder beneath the surface, damaging motivation and commitment. In this chapter the role of procedures in the efficient resolution of discipline, grievances and disputes has been emphasized. It has also been argued that problems should be addressed in the context of developing human resources and maintaining constructive relationships, the theme of much of this book. Finally, it is suggested that managers should avoid excessive focus on reacting to manifestations of conflict and invest more time in reducing underlying grievances through sound HRM practices. Such an approach has the merit of producing tangible benefits irrespective of whether conflict is openly expressed.

FURTHER READING

Edwards, P.K. (1983) 'The Pattern of Collective Industrial Action', in G.S. Bain (ed.) *Industrial Relations in Britain*, Oxford: Blackwell, Chapter 9.

Hyman, R. (1971) *Strikes*, London: Fontana.

Torrington, D. and Hall, L. (1991) *Personnel Management*, Hemel Hempstead: Prentice Hall, Chapter 30.

Winterton, J. and Winterton, R. (1989) *Coal, Crisis and Conflict: the 1984–85 Miners' Strike in Yorkshire*, Manchester: Manchester University Press.

QUESTIONS FOR DISCUSSION

1 'Industrial conflict is endemic and attempts to suppress it will always simply replace overt action with covert forms of expression.' Discuss in relation to recent legislative initiatives.

2 Outline the key features of an effective procedure for the resolution of grievances or disputes.

3 What are the objectives of a disciplinary procedure? How can disciplinary arrangements best support a progressive human resource management strategy?

Chapter 13

The working environment

INTRODUCTION

This chapter examines issues of health, safety and welfare, and considers how an integrated approach to HRM can contribute to the maintenance of a congenial working environment. The importance of industrial injuries has long been recognized, but the broader effects of work upon health have only been acknowledged relatively recently. This chapter traces the development of working environment concerns and the progressive extension of legislation reflecting a dynamic area so often neglected by HR specialists. A major reassessment made during the 1970s, in response to evidence of a deterioration in occupational health and safety, resulted in a new legal framework and a more formal role for the trade unions. The approach to involving unions which was advocated in Chapter 4 is consistent with the statutory support which union lay officials have in promoting health and safety at workplace level. The policies and arrangements made by employers are shown to form a link between this union role and the HR strategy. Using the example of accidents at work as a universal problem, theories of their causation and methods of analysis are shown to relate closely to other elements of HRM. Finally, we consider what future provision may be made for health and safety in order to remedy perceived weaknesses in current arrangements and to address contemporary concerns such as psycho-social work hazards.

DEVELOPMENT OF WORKING ENVIRONMENT CONCERNS

Since the first personnel departments were established, health, safety and welfare have been among the responsibilities of those managing human resources, and they remain part of the HRM area even though the emphasis has altered over time and within different work contexts. Before the Second World War concerns with the prevention of accidents and the maintenance of welfare facilities reflected the prevailing hazards responsible for more lost production than strikes and the generally low standard of living for workers which contributed to problems such as fatigue. As living conditions improved in the postwar era, the welfare aspects of the personnel manager role became increasingly marginal and by the 1970s were seen as a distraction from more 'strategic' activities like training and industrial relations. By contrast, health and safety issues became more important from the 1970s as they were brought to the bargaining table by trade unionists as part of a new bargaining agenda which had already invaded areas of managerial prerogative such as corporate planning. A key element of this new awareness was the changing role which was perceived for legislation.

Legislation on health and safety was first enacted in the nineteenth century following pressure from social reformers and was initially confined to children working in cotton mills. The Factory Act of 1833 applied only to textile mills but later versions established regulations for fencing factory machinery (1844) and extended the provisions to other trades (1864). The consolidating Factory Act of 1878 provided the basis for the modern code of regulations for conditions in factories laid down in the Factories Act, 1961.

In the period immediately after the Second World War a number of union activists were involved in attempts to establish an occupational health service and provide for stricter legislation than the Factories Act of nineteenth century origin. Only in the early 1970s, however, were health and safety issues achieving prominence because of the worsening record of occupational health and safety. The inadequacies of existing legislation gradually became apparent. Legislation had focused upon the 'safety' aspects in laws that had evolved from attempts to control nineteenth-century hazards, but accidents were increasing. 'Health' aspects had been neglected so that existing legislation could not regulate chemical hazards or the physical and psychological hazards arising out of work organization. Moreover, there was a chronic problem of enforcement of the law.

The Robens Committee of Inquiry on Safety and Health (1972), established to consider how best to promote industrial health and safety, argued that there was 'no greater identity of interest between management and workers than in respect of health and safety'. The paternalistic consensus image of health and safety presented by Robens was challenged by the experience of workplace struggles over health and safety issues, as writers like Nichols and Beynon (1973), and Kinnersley (1973) were quick to demonstrate. In the event the Act which was introduced in the Labour government's legislative package under the Social Contract owed more to the labour movement's post-war occupational safety campaign than to the recommendations of the Robens Committee.

The Health and Safety at Work etc. Act, 1974 (HSWA), imposed general duties on employers (and others) in place of specific provisions so that all workplaces, hazards and persons at risk were covered. While 'personal injury' was taken to include 'any disease and any impairment of a person's physical or mental condition', in the application of the law psychosocial issues became marginalized, if not ignored entirely. Under HSWA, a new Health and Safety Commission (HSC) was established as a policy-making authority and a Health and Safety Executive (HSE) with more extensive powers than the Factory Inspectorate was created to undertake inspection and enforcement.

The 1974 Act was enabling legislation designed to create new procedures for dealing with health and safety issues rather than impose new substantive standards. The separate inspection agencies (such as the Factory Inspectorate and Inspectorate of Mines and Quarries) are gradually being brought closer together under the HSE. All existing statutes remained in force under the umbrella of the new Act, which allowed for both increasing the coverage of existing standards and improving upon them. As a consequence over 8 million workers and 3 million others at risk (e.g. the public, customers, students) were covered for the first time by legally enforceable health and safety provisions.

UNION SAFETY REPRESENTATION

Traditionally unions had left arrangements relating to health and safety to management; bargaining was often directed at obtaining special allowances for working in dangerous or unpleasant conditions rather than seeking to eliminate these conditions. Most major unions had a full-time officer pursuing claims for compensation for members long before they appointed an officer with responsibility for campaigning to improve working conditions. Even now the majority of unions do not have a national officer with exclusive responsibility for health and safety matters.

Perhaps the most significant difference between HSWA and previous health and safety legislation was its departure from the 'careless worker' approach in favour of the concept of workplace hazards. The new Act therefore provided for the Secretary of State to make regulations for the appointment of safety representatives with specific legal rights from among the work force. Such regulations were written by the HSC but their introduction was delayed mainly because of pressure from the local authorities. The local authorities claimed that it would cost £80 million to allow safety representatives to use their powers, but the HSC estimated the cost to be approximately £2.75 million. After a vigorous campaign launched by the trade unions and autonomous health and safety groups the government relented, and the Safety Representatives and Safety Committees Regulations, 1977 (SI 500), became effective from 1 October 1978.

Under the Coal Mines Act, 1954 (s.123), union-appointed inspectors were empowered to examine conditions and investigate accidents and dangerous occurrences in coal mining. The new SRSC Regulations extended a similar provision to all other industries where workers were unionized. Originally, the 1974 Act contained provision for representatives to be elected in non-union workplaces also, but this was subsequently repealed on the grounds that effective trade union organization was a prerequisite for employees to play an effective role in workplace safety organization; hence the rights are extended only to trade unions which are independent of the employers and recognized by them for collective bargaining purposes. Once safety representatives in other industries had statutory support workplace attitudes on health and safety were transformed. However, in many workplaces existing safety representative powers are not effectively used and a number of inadequacies have become apparent. The provision of information relating to health and safety is one area where safety representatives have faced similar difficulties to those experienced by shop stewards seeking information about planning from employers. For example, the Act requires manufacturers to maintain and make available information on substances for use at work and employers have a general duty to maintain such information. The regulations, however, only obliged management to make available to safety representatives information that is within the employer's knowledge. While ignorance is no defence for failing to comply with the general duty, one survey found that less than a quarter of manufacturers contacted had provided adequate information and suggested that because employers did not normally put pressure on chemicals suppliers, safety representatives were rarely able to obtain adequate information at the workplace (Winterton 1984). This paucity of information meant that safety representatives tended to seek outside advice only once a chemical hazard had become apparent from ill-health among members, preventing them from taking a more proactive role. The recent introduction of regulations on Control of Substances Hazardous to Health (COSHH) has improved the situation in the case of chemical hazards, but safety representatives still may not always be provided with basic information like records of sickness absence with which to analyse independently health trends among members.

The second weakness is that safety representatives have no legal right to stop a job. Although there was some discussion in the trade union movement in favour of gaining such a statutory right, the majority view was that such dependence upon legal rights is less reliable than traditional trade union methods and runs the risk of divorcing safety representatives from the rank and file. In theory safety representatives can alert the Factory Inspectorate (or other appropriate enforcement authority), who are empowered to prohibit work. In practice, safety representatives' rights and powers, like those of other lay representatives, derive from the strength of workplace organization. In the present economic climate the weakness of unions in the workplace relegates action over many issues to 'after the event', just as in the case of chemicals and other chronic health hazards.

Thirdly, the Act requires employers to consult with safety representatives but imposes no duty to bargain over changes in work organization. In the absence of an effective status quo clause, safety representatives are unable to modify new working arrangements introduced by management and need not receive adequate notice of planned changes (see Chapter 12).

EMPLOYERS' HEALTH AND SAFETY ARRANGEMENTS

As a result of the 1974 Act, the arrangements which employers are required to make in order to secure the health, safety and welfare of their employees at work include the preparation of a safety policy, the establishment of a safety committee and the introduction of safe systems of work. Each will be considered in turn.

Under s. 2(3) of HSWA employers are required to prepare and revise as often as necessary a written statement of policy relating to the health and safety of employees, covering both general policy and the detailed organization and arrangements for carrying this out. While policy is the employer's responsibility, it is consistent with good practice for union safety representatives to be consulted. The policy should relate to specific organizational features and safety problems of the employer: general statements of intent are inadequate. It is a common failing of safety policies that they do not adequately specify how the policy is to be translated into action, nor define the responsibility for carrying out the policy. Typically such policies define the same responsibilities at different levels or emphasize employees' responsibilities under s.7 HSWA above the more comprehensive duties imposed on employers under s.2.

In addition to a general policy statement to the effect that the employer intends to seek to provide the safest and healthiest working conditions possible, the policy should outline safety organization and arrangements. The statement should give the name and business address of the executive responsible for fulfilling the safety policy. Overall responsibility should be at the highest management level, and main areas of responsibility delegated to senior management posts. Where the expertise exists to advise management, then the relationship of these functions (such as safety officer, plant engineer) should be made clear. The role of HR managers in the safety organization should be commensurate with their qualifications and experience; it would be inappropriate, for example, for HR managers to have technical responsibility for safety in chemical plants unless they were also qualified chemical engineers.

The arrangements outlined in the safety policy should include the mechanisms for making all who are at risk aware of the health hazards and of their own role in maintaining a safe and healthy working environment. Adequate training and supervision are fundamental to health and safety arrangements, and the HRM department should ensure that these aspects are integrated into the broader training provision. The main hazards should be identified and rules to be observed publicized with details of systems of work to be followed. The safety arrangements should also include procedures for reporting accidents and dangerous occurrences.

An employer is required to establish a safety committee if requested to do so by a safety representative of an independent, recognized trade union. Employers should consult union representatives on the formation of the committee and post details of its composition in the workplace; the committee must be established within three months of the request from a safety representative. The composition of the committee is a matter for local determination through the usual bargaining and consultative machinery, but representatives of TUC-affiliated unions will not normally welcome the participation of non-affiliated organizations. The committee should be kept small enough to operate efficiently while allowing adequate representation of all interest groups. The number of management and union representatives should be equal and the Chair of the committee agreed by the two sides. Senior management should be represented on the committee along with relevant specialists (company doctor, safety officer, HR manager) to ensure the committee has access to relevant expertise and its decisions have adequate authority within the organization.

The functions of the safety committee are defined in s. 2(7) of HSWA as 'to keep under review the measures taken to ensure the health and safety of employees and such other functions as may be prescribed'. Agreed objectives may include:

- studying accident and illness statistics;
- considering reports from HSE inspectors;
- considering reports of safety representatives;
- providing guidance in the development of works safety rules;
- monitoring the safety content of training programmes.

Regular meetings should be held at stipulated intervals, and it is practical to link these with statutory three-monthly workplace inspection.

While there is no legal requirement for this, a formal safety agreement between the employer and the trade union side of a safety committee can reduce uncertainty and avoid disputes. Such an agreement cannot be used to restrict the statutory rights of safety representatives; thus if safety representatives are granted the right to stop dangerous work, this cannot be at the expense of their immunities from legal liability granted under the SRSC Regulations. Where a safety agreement is negotiated, this may include a status quo provision to the effect that no substantial change in conditions of work will be made before full consultation and agreement.

Safety representatives have a statutory right to undertake a formal inspection of the workplace every three months, after an accident or dangerous occurrence, after any substantial change in working conditions, and when new information becomes available on hazards. Unsafe or unhealthy conditions should be notified to the employer in writing and remedial action taken to the satisfaction of the safety committee (or representatives if no committee has been formed).

Employers are required under s.2 (2) HSWA to provide such information as is practicable to secure the health and safety of employees. The Code of Practice on the SRSC Regulations provides further details of information to be provided: the main exclusions are individual health records (unless the individuals concerned give their consent); and information that would cause substantial injury to the employer's undertaking.

Agreed actions to control hazards should be underpinned by a defined safe system of work, which should entail monitoring, inspections and adequate training. As part of a safe system of work, safety procedures such as a 'permit to work' system should be designed to ensure control over personnel working in hazardous areas and to prevent others entering the area. When personnel are working on an electrical installation, for example, the power is isolated and can only be turned on again when the individual returns the permit, indicating that work is complete and no one is at risk.

ACCIDENTS AT WORK

An accident may be defined as an unexpected and unintended event which results in one of three outcomes:

- major accident: injury causing loss of working time;
- minor accident: injury causing no (serious) loss of working time;
- near miss: damage to equipment without injury.

Major accidents are fortunately far less common than minor accidents, and near misses are much the most frequent. Various studies have shown that for every major accident there are 60 minor accidents and 400 near misses. As a result, for any analysis of accident trends or distribution to be reliable, all three categories should be taken into account.

Accidents have been viewed by some authorities as a form of withdrawal from the work situation analogous to uncertified absence and labour turnover (Hill and Trist 1953). Certainly the level of accidents is a measure of working environment problems which are likely to impact upon QWL, even if they are not the result of low morale among employees. Like the measures of job dissatisfaction considered in Chapter 10, the costs of accidents are greater than might be assumed from the actual time lost by an individual suffering an injury, although this is of course a major component of costs. In estimating the true costs of accidents account must also be taken of the costs of safety administration, the costs (whether or not directly incurred by the company) of medical, welfare and emergency services, the production lost directly and indirectly, for example when training a replacement to cover for the injured employee, and any materials or equipment losses involved. Even ignoring the social costs, which cannot readily be quantified, the cost-benefit equation weighs heavily in favour of preventing accidents.

There are three sets of explanations for accidents, each of which may help in identifying fruitful avenues for reducing their incidence: environmental; behavioural; and physiological. Of the three, the work environment itself must be seen as the major determinant of workplace safety and health. Clearly some industries and occupations entail an inherently greater degree of risk than others, hence the much higher accident rates in deep-sea fishing, coal mining and construction than in manufacturing industries. While there are always liable to be some risks associated with the sorts of jobs found in these industries, it is often possible to reduce risk through the use of safety equipment, appropriate training and supervision, and by designing safe systems of work. The same is true for less hazardous industries and occupations which, in absolute terms, account for more accidents than the high-risk industries. Responsibility for these environmental factors should rest with a safety manager or director with the necessary technical expertise, rather than with the HRM specialist, although in addressing the other two areas HR strategy will need to complement the activities of the safety team.

Behavioural explanations for accidents should not be confused with a 'careless worker' philosophy. Even though the environmental causes are accorded primacy, there are invariably behavioural factors which have contributed to a particular set of events leading to a specific accident. Learning theories are among the most powerful behavioural models of accidents. According to this explanation, when people learn unsafe methods of working as ways of 'cutting corners' to facilitate earlier completion of tasks or to increase bonus earnings, there is no negative reinforcement of the methods taught in training until an accident occurs. Another behavioural explanation focuses upon lapses of memory which result in accidents. The skilled operative having a more varied and complex set of operations to perform is thought to be more prone to error as a result of memory lapse, although for an individual performing highly repetitive, boring tasks with a very low cycle time, concentration is even more likely to lapse. It has also been suggested that the 'accident-proneness' of certain workers is explicable in terms of their personality traits, with those who score highly on aggression being inherently more accident-prone. There is rather more evidence for the view that accident-proneness is a temporary condition arising from an individual's psychological state at a particular time. Similarly, workers who are subject to more life stress (such as divorce, bereavement, fear of redundancy) are held to be more disposed to have an accident.

The most important of the physiological models of accident-proneness relates to the body's 'circadian rhythms', twenty-four hour and monthly biological cycles, which explain the timing of some accidents and accounts for their concentration in particular shifts. The taking of prescribed drugs and any substance abuse, whether alcohol, drugs or solvents, increases greatly the likelihood of an individual having an accident. Judgement is impaired and reactions slowed down, which interferes with the execution of skilled tasks, so that 'problem drinkers' have been shown to have far higher accident rates than other workers. The implications for HRM strategy are clear: for employees who have drink or drugs problems adequate supervision, counselling and support must be available and underpinned by an effective disciplinary procedure.

Like labour turnover and absence, accident statistics can provide a wealth of information, but given the ratio of near misses to minor and serious accidents, all three types of events need to be reported using a uniform return which requires sufficient information to be provided at the time of the occurrence. Such information should be regularly collated and analysed by department, time of occurrence, and category of personnel involved, in order to identify areas for action such as training, the provision of additional break times, or the removal of a payment-by-results system. Individuals may falsify reports or make untrue statements in order to cover their own, or others', misdemeanours, so for the statistics to be accurate, valid and reliable, witnesses should be interviewed independently. Even when reliable information has been obtained, the analysis of accidents is not without difficulties. Accidents are (fortunately) comparatively rare events, so the data on which analysis is based are seldom extensive. Comparisons are difficult to make because of the need to take into account the exposure to risk of accidents in terms of the frequency and duration of an operation as well as the number of undesirable occurrences. It is often difficult to reconstruct events because of dependence on individual recall and, in extreme cases, because the most important witness may actually have died in the accident. Moreover, the remedy is not always obvious from the analysis of an accident because the event is invariably caused by a combination of factors.

While the analysis of a major accident such as an explosion in a chemical plant is obviously a matter for investigation by a team of technical experts, the HR manager should be able to undertake an analysis of routine accidents and near misses, none individually serious but which collectively represent a substantial loss of working time and a source of labour inefficiency. There are several techniques which can be readily applied in addition to a simple statistical breakdown of accidents over the quarter. Using the critical incident technique, a large number of people who use a particular machine are asked about errors or mistakes they have made. This can lead to the discovery of difficulties which really are critical and may lead (or may have led) to an accident. Change analysis focuses on changes in time, technology, personnel, sociological, organizational and operational factors. The underlying assumption is that something must have changed from when the operation was carried out without a mishap. Fault-tree analysis is a system for analysing failure using logic statements to work backwards from the undesired event to contributory factors. The causal factors identified in the fault tree thus identify areas for remedial action. With multi-linear events sequencing (MES), the times of events are plotted from when a stable situation was disturbed to when the last injurious or damaging event occurred. The MES flowchart produced breaks an accident down into a sequence of events each comprising an actor and an action. Finally, managerial oversight and risk tree (MORT) diagrams can be used to analyse how an event has resulted from the management system overseeing the job, specific oversights and omissions, and known events beyond human control.

FUTURE HEALTH AND SAFETY ORGANIZATION

The perceived inadequacies of existing health and safety legislation in Britain were also apparent in Scandinavia and have been tackled by a novel application of the law which may yet become a model for future British legislation. The Norwegian Work Environment Act was introduced in 1977 and the Swedish equivalent in the following year. Both Acts specify general work environment standards, which represent an extension of existing health and safety law, but depart from legal tradition in fundamental ways. The first section of Chapter 2 of the Swedish Act demonstrates the novelty of the approach:

> The Work Environment shall be kept in a satisfactory state having regard to the nature of the work involved and the social and technological progress occurring in the community at large. Working conditions must be adapted to human physical and mental aptitudes. The aim must be for work to be arranged in such a way that the employee himself can influence his work situation.

There are important innovations contained in this approach. It abandons the principle of static standards; conditions should advance with social and technological progress. It moves the emphasis further from the 'careless worker' approach towards the 'unsafe workplace' approach by introducing the requirement that the working environment be adapted to human physical and mental aptitudes. This is expanded by a later provision:

> The employer must give consideration to the particular aptitudes of each employee for the work in hand. In the planning and arrangement of

work, due regard must be had for the fact that individual persons differ in their aptitudes to perform tasks.

This law is especially innovatory in requiring that employees should be able to influence their work situation. The thinking behind this is outlined in the guide to the Act published by the Swedish Ministry of Labour:

> It is axiomatic that, in order to achieve a working environment which is satisfactory to those directly concerned, the viewpoints of employees must play an important part in the assessment process . . . the ability of the employee to play a personal part in the design of his work place and tasks and to assume professional responsibility is an important pre-requisite of job satisfaction.

FURTHER READING

Beaumont, P.B. (1983) *Safety at Work and the Unions*, London: Croom Helm.

Drake, C.D. and Wright F.B. (1983) *Law of Health and Safety at Work: the New Approach*, London: Sweet & Maxwell, Chapters 3, 8.

Goodman, M.J. (1988) *Health and Safety at Work: Law and Practice*, London: Sweet & Maxwell.

Health and Safety Commission (1977) *Safety Representatives and Safety Committees Regulations* (SI 500), London: HMSO.

QUESTIONS FOR DISCUSSION

1 Discuss the proposition that where safety is a charge on profit, a degree of risk is acceptable.
2 What role should the HR manager play in promoting health, safety and welfare in an enterprise?
3 How can trade union safety representatives contribute to the implementation of an effective health and safety policy?

Bibliography

Adams, J.S. (1963) 'Towards an Understanding of Inequity', *Journal of Abnormal and Social Psychology*, 67, 422–36.

Aguren, S., Bredbacka, C., Hansson, R., Ibregren, K. and Karlsson, K.G. (1984) *Volvo Kalmar Revisited*, Stockholm: Efficiency and Participation Development Council.

Ahlstrand, B.W. (1990) *The Quest for Productivity: A Case Study of Fawley after Flanders*, Cambridge: Cambridge University Press.

Alderfer, C.P. (1972) *Existence, Relatedness and Growth: Human Needs in Organizational Settings*, New York: Free Press.

Allen, V.L. (1966) *Militant Trade Unionism*, London: Merlin.

Armstrong, M. and Murliss, H. (1991) *Reward Management*, London: Kogan Page.

Ashenfelter, A. and Johnson, G.E. (1969) 'Bargaining Theory, Trade Unions and Industrial Strike Activity', *American Economic Review*, 59: 35–49.

Atkinson, G. (1977) *The Effective Negotiator*, London: Quest.

Babbage, C. (1833) *On the Economy of Machinery and Manufactures*, London: Charles Knight.

Bain, G.S. (1970) *The Growth of White Collar Unionism*, Oxford: Oxford University Press.

Batstone, E. (1988) *The Reform of Workplace Industrial Relations*, Oxford: Clarendon.

Batstone, E., Boraston, I. and Frenkel, S. (1978) *The Social Organization of Strikes*, Oxford: Blackwell.

Batstone, E. and Davies, P.L. (1976) *Industrial Democracy: European Experience*, London: HMSO.

Batstone, E., Ferner, A. and Terry, M. (1983) *Unions on the Board: an Experiment in Industrial Democracy*, Oxford: Blackwell.

Beaumont, P.B. (1979) *Safety Legislation: the Trade Union Response*, Occasional Paper in Industrial Relations No. 4, Universities of Leeds and Nottingham/Institute of Personnel Management.

——— (1983) *Safety at Work and the Unions*, London: Croom Helm.

——— (1992) *Public Sector Industrial Relations*, London: Routledge.

Beckhard, R. (1969) *Organization Development: Strategies and Models*, Reading, Mass.: Addison-Wesley.

Behrend, H. (1959) 'Voluntary Absence from Work', *International Labour Review*, 79, February, 109–40.

Bell, D.J. (1974) *Planning Corporate Manpower*, London: Longman.

——— (1989) 'Why Manpower Planning Is Back In Vogue', *Personnel Management*, July.

Blyton, P. and Turnbull, P. (1994) *The Dynamics of Employee Relations*, London: Macmillan.

Boraston, I., Clegg, H.A. and Rimmer, M. (1975) *Workplace and Union*, London: Heinemann.

Bowey, A. and Thorpe, R. (1986) *Payment Systems and Productivity*, London: Macmillan.

Boyatsis, R. (1982) *The Competent Manager*, New York: Wiley.

Braddick, W. and Smith, P. (n.d.) 'The Design of Appraisal Systems', undated occasional paper, Ashridge Management College.

Brady, L. and Wright, V. (1990) 'Performance Related Pay', Fact Sheet No. 30, London: Institute of Personnel Management.

Braham, P., Rhodes, E. and Pearn, M. (eds) (1981) *Discrimination and Disadvantage in Employment*, London: Harper & Row.

Bramham, J. (1989) *Human Resource Planning*, London: Institute of Personnel Management.

Brannen, P., Batstone, E., Fatchett, D. and White, P. (1976) *The Worker Directors*, London: Hutchinson.

Braverman, H. (1974) *Labor and Monopoly Capital*, New York: Monthly Review Press.

Brown, Wilfred (1962) *Piecework Abandoned*, London: Heinemann.

Brown, William (ed.) (1981) *The Changing Contours of British Industrial Relations*, Oxford: Blackwell.

——— (1993) 'The Contraction of Collective Bargaining in Britain', *British Journal of Industrial Relations*, 31, 2, 189–200.

Brown, W., Ebsworth, R. and Terry, M. (1978) 'Factors shaping shop steward organisation in Britain', *British Journal of Industrial Relations*, 16, 2.

Bullock, A. (chairman) (1977) Report of the Committee of Inquiry on Industrial Democracy, Cmnd.6706, London: HMSO.

Burgoyne, J. and Stuart, R. (1978) 'Management Development Programmes: Underlying Assumptions about Learning' in J. Burgoyne and R. Stuart (eds) *Management Development. Context and Strategies*, London: Gower Press.

Butler, R. (1991) *Designing Organizations*, London: Routledge.

Campion, M.A. and McLelland, C.L. (1991) 'Interdisciplinary examination of the costs and benefits of enlarged jobs: a job design quasi-experiment', *Journal of Applied Psychology*, 76, 245–52.

Cannell, M. and Long, P. (1991) 'What's Changed About Incentive Pay?', *Personnel Management*, October.

Castles, S. and Kosack, G. (1973) *Immigrant Workers and Class Structure in Western Europe*, Oxford: Oxford University Press.

CBI (1987) *Absence from Work*, London: Confederation of British Industry.

——— (1989) *Towards a Skills Revolution*, London: Confederation of British Industry.

Child, J. (1984) *Organization: A Guide to Problems and Practice*, London: Harper & Row.

Claydon, T. (1989) 'Union Derecognition in Britain in the 1980s', *British Journal of Industrial Relations*, 27, 2, 214–24.

Clegg, H.A. (1976) *Trade Unionism under Collective Bargaining*, Oxford: Blackwell.

——— (1979) *The Changing System of Industrial Relations in Great Britain*, Oxford: Blackwell.

Coser, L. (1956) *The Functions of Social Conflict*, London: RKP.

Cox, A. and Tapsell, J. (1991) 'Graphology and its Validity in Personnel Assessment', Paper read at BPS Conference, Cardiff.

Craft, J. (1988) 'Human Resources Planning and Strategy' in Dyer, L. (ed.) *Human Resources Management: Evolving Roles and Responsibility*, Washington, DC: Bureau of National Affairs.

Cross, M. (1985) *Towards the Flexible Craftsman*, London: Technical Change Centre.

Crumbaugh, J. and Stockholm, E. (1977) 'Validation of Graphoanalysis by Global or Holistic Method', *Perceptual and Motor Skills*, 44.

Davis, L.E. (1971) 'Job Satisfaction Research: the Post-industrial View', *Industrial Relations*, 10, 176–93.

Deming, W.E. (1986) *Quality, Productivity and Competitive Position*, Cambridge, Mass.: Centre For Advanced Engineering Study.

——— (1988) *Out of the Crisis: Quality, Productivity and Competitive Position*, Cambridge: Cambridge University Press.

Donovan (chairman) (1968) Royal Commission on Trade Unions and Employers' Associations 1965–1968, *Report*, Cmnd. 3623, London: HMSO.

Drake, C.D. and Wright, F.B. (1983) *Law of Health and Safety at Work: the New Approach*, London: Sweet & Maxwell.

Drucker, P.F. (1961) *The Practice of Management*, London: Mercury Books.

Dummett, A. (1973) *A Portrait of English Racism*, Harmondsworth: Penguin.

Dunn, S. (1993) 'From Donovan to . . . Wherever', *British Journal of Industrial Relations*, 31, 2: 169–87.

Durcan J.W. and McCarthy, W.E.J. (1972) 'What is Happening to Strikes?', *New Society*, 2 November, 267–9.

Durcan J.W., McCarthy, W.E.J. and Redman, G.P. (1983) *Strikes in Post-war Britain: A Study of Stoppages of Work due to Industrial Disputes, 1946–73*, London: Allen & Unwin.

Edwards, P.K. (1983) 'The Pattern of Collective Industrial Action', in G.S. Bain (ed) *Industrial Relations in Britain*, Oxford: Blackwell.

Edwards, P.K. and Scullion, H. (1982) *The Social Organization of Industrial Conflict*, Oxford: Blackwell.

Equal Opportunities Commission (1978) *Guidance on Equal Opportunity Policies and Practices in Employment*, Manchester: EOC.

Eva, D. and Oswald, R. (1981) *Heath and Safety at Work*, London: Pan.

Fatchett, D. (1982) 'Postal Ballots – Some Practical Considerations', *Industrial Relations Journal*, 13, 4, 13–17.

Fayol, H. (1949) *General and Industrial Management*, London: Pitman.

Flanders, A. (1964) *The Fawley Productivity Agreements*, London: Faber.

——— (1968) *Management and Unions*, London: Faber.

Fletcher, C. and Williams, R. (1985) *Performance Appraisal and Career Development*, London: Hutchinson.

Forrester, K., Thorne, C. and Winterton, J. (1984) 'Workers' Investigations into the Working Environment', *Industrial Relations Journal*, 15, 4, 28–37.

Foster, C.D. (1992) *Privatization, Public Ownership and the Regulation of Natural Monopoly*, Oxford: Blackwell.

Fowler, A. (1988) 'New Directions in Performance Pay', *Personnel Management*, November.

Fox, A. (1966) *Industrial Sociology and Industrial Relations*, Research Paper No. 3, Royal Commission on Trade Unions and Employers' Associations, London: HMSO.

——— (1971) *A Sociology of work in Industry*, London: Collier-Macmillan.

——— (1974) *Beyond Contract: Work, Power and Trust Relations*, London: Faber & Faber.

French, W. and Bell, C. (1978) *Organization Development: Behavioural Science Interventions for Organization Improvement*, New Jersey: Prentice Hall.

Gill, J. and Molander, C.F. (1970) 'Beyond Management by Objectives', *Personnel Management*, 8, 2, 18–22.
Glynn, S. and Gospel, H. (1993) 'Britain's Low Skill Equilibrium: a Problem of Demand?', *Industrial Relations Journal*, 24, 2, 112–35.
Goodman, M.J. (1988) *Health and Safety at Work: Law and Practice*, London: Sweet & Maxwell.
Goodman, P.S. and Atkin, R.S. (eds) (1984) *Absenteeism: New Approaches to Understanding, Measuring and Managing Employee Absence*, London: Jossey Bass.
Gospel, H.F. and Palmer, G. (1993) *British Industrial Relations*, London: Routledge.
Green Paper (1983) *Democracy in Trade Unions*, Cmnd. 8778, London: HMSO.
Guest, D.E. (1987) 'Human Resource Management and Industrial Relations', *Journal of Management Studies*, 24, 5, September.
——— (1989a) 'Human Resource Management: its Implications for Industrial Relations and Trade Unions', in Storey, J. (ed.) *New Perspectives on Human Resource Management*, London: Routledge.
——— (1989b) 'Personnel and HRM: Can You Tell the Difference?', *Personnel Management*, January.
Hackman, J.R. and Oldham, G.R. (1980) *Work Redesign*, Reading, Mass.: Addison-Wesley.
Hamblin, A.C. (1974) *Evaluation and Control of Training*, London: McGraw Hill.
Hartmann, H. (1975) 'Codetermination Today and Tomorrow', *British Journal of Industrial Relations*, 13, 1, 54–64.
Health and Safety Commission (1977) *Safety Representatives and Safety Committees Regulations* (SI 500), London: HMSO.
Hellriegel, D., Slocum, J.W. and Woodman, R.W. (1992) *Organizational Behaviour*, Saint Paul (Minn.): West (6th edn).
Herzberg, F. (1968) *Work and the Nature of Man*, Clevcland: World Publishing.
Herzberg, F., Mausner, B. and Snyderman, B. (1959) *The Motivation to Work*, New York: Wiley (2nd edn).
Hill, J.M.M. and Trist, E.L. (1953) 'A Consideration of Industrial Accidents as a Means of Withdrawal from the Work Situation', *Human Relations*, 6, 357–80.
Honey, P. and Mumford, A. (1986) *The Manual of Learning Styles*, London: P. Honey.
Hughes, J. (1967) *Trade Union Structure and Government*, Donovan Research Paper 5, London: HMSO.
Hyman, R. (1971) *Strikes*, London: Fontana.
——— (1972) *Disputes Procedures in Action*, London: Heinemann.
Industrial Relations Review and Report (1989) 'NFC Contact Distribution: a Move to Staff Status', *Industrial Relations Review and Report*, 435, 12–14.
IPM (1992) *Towards a National Training and Development Strategy*, London: Institute of Personnel Management.
Jackson, M.P. (1991) *An Introduction to Industrial Relations*, London: Routledge.
Kelly, J. (1988) 'The Decline of Trade Unionism?', *Industrial Tutor*, 4, 7, 5–17.
Kerr, C. and Siegel, A. (1954) 'The Interindustry Propensity to Strike – an International Comparison', in Kornhauser, A., Dubin, R. and Ross, A.M. (eds) *Industrial Conflict*, New York: McGraw Hill, 189–212.
Kinnersley, P. (1973) *The Hazards of Work*, London: Pluto.
Kolb, D.A., Rubin, I.M. and McIntyre, J.M. (1984) *Organizational Psychology*, Englewood Cliffs, NJ: Prentice Hall (4th edn).
Krieger, J. (1984) *Undermining Capitalism: State Ownership and the Dialectic of Control in the British Coal Mining Industry*, Princeton: Princeton University Press.
Kuhn, J. (1961) *Bargaining in Grievance Settlement*, New York: Columbia.

Leggett, J.C. (1963) *Class, Race and Labor: Working Class Consciousness in Detroit*, New York: Oxford University Press.

Lester, A. (1958) *As Unions Mature*, Princeton, NJ: Princeton University Press.

Lester, A. and Bindman, G. (1972) *Race and Law*, London: Sweet & Maxwell.

Locke, E.A. and Latham, G.P. (1990) *A Theory of Goal Setting and Task Performance*, Englewood Ciffs, NJ: Prentice Hall.

Lockwood, P.A. (1986) 'Human Resource Planning: the Role of the Practitioner', *Health Services Management Review*, 12, 2, August.

Lupton, T. (1963) *On the Shop Floor*, Oxford: Pergamon.

——— (ed.) (1972) *Payment Systems*, Harmondsworth: Penguin.

Lupton, T. and Bowey, A.M. (1975) *Wages and Salaries*, Harmondsworth: Penguin Books.

McCarthy, W.E.J. and Parker, S. (1968) *Shop Stewards and Workplace Relations*, Donovan Research paper 10, London: HMSO.

McGivering, I. (1987) 'Organisational Development', in Molander, C.F. (ed.) *Human Resource Management*, Bromley: Chartwell Bratt.

MacKay, L. and Torrington, D. (1986) *The Changing Nature of Personnel Management*, London: Institute of Personnel Management.

McMullen, J. (1978) *Rights at Work*, London: Pluto.

Marchington, M., Goodman, J., Wilkinson, A. and Ackers, P. (1992) *New Developments in Employee Involvement*, Employment Department Research Series No. 2, Sheffield: ED.

Marsden, D. and Ryan, P. (1990) 'Institutional Aspects of Youth Employment and Training Policy in Britain', *British Journal of Industrial Relations*, 28, 3, 351–69.

Marsh, A.I., Evans, E.O. and Garcia, P. (1971) *Workplace Industrial Relations in Engineering*, London: Engineering Employers Federation.

Martin, R. (1968) 'Union Democracy: An Explanatory Framework', *Sociology* 2, 205–20; reprinted in McCarthy, W.E.J. (ed.) (1985) *Trade Unions*, Harmondsworth: Penguin (2nd edn), 224–42.

Maslow, A.H. (1943) 'A Theory of Human Motivation', *Psychological Review*, 50, 1, 370–96.

——— (1970) *Motivation and Personality*, New York: Harper Row.

Mayfield, E.C. (1964) 'The Selection Interview: A Reevaluation of Published Research', *Personnel Psychology*, No. 17.

Metcalf, D. (1989) 'Water Notes Dry up: the Impact of the Donovan Reform Proposals and Thatcherism at Work on Labour Productivity in British Industry', *British Journal of Industrial Relations*, 27, 1, 1–31.

Michels, R. (1911) *Political Parties*, Glencoe, Ill.: Free Press (1949 edn).

Ministry of Labour (1988) *The Swedish Act on Co-determination at Work*, Stockholm: Arbetsmarknadsdepartementet.

Molander, C.F. (1986) *Management Development, Key Concepts for Managers and Trainers*, Bromley: Chartwell Bratt.

——— (1994) 'Coming to Terms with Empowerment', *Management Development Journal of Singapore*, 3, 1, February.

——— (ed.) (1989) *Human Resource Management*, Bromley: Chartwell Bratt.

Muir, J. (1981) *Industrial Relations Procedures and Agreements*, Aldershot: Gower.

Newby, M. (1992) Personal communication.

Newby, M. and Winterton, J. (1983) 'The Duration of Industrial Stoppages', *Journal of the Royal Statistical Society A*, 146, 1: 62–70.

Nichols, T. and Beynon, H. (1973) *Safety or Profit*, Bristol: Falling Wall Press.

Offe, C. (1976) *Industry and Inequality*, London: Edward Arnold.

Parker, S. (1968) *Workplace Industrial Relations*, Report SS402, Government Social Survey, London: HMSO.

Parker, S. (1974) *Workplace Industrial Relations, 1972*, Report SS472, Social Survey Division, London: HMSO.

Parker, S. (1975) *Workplace Industrial Relations, 1973*, Report SS1020, Social Survey Division, London: HMSO.

Parkin, F. (1971) *Class, Inequality and Political Order*, London: MacGibbon & Kee.

Pendleton, A. and Winterton, J. (eds) (1993) *Public Enterprise in Transition: Industrial Relations in State and Privatized Corporations*, London: Routledge.

Pigors, P. and Myers, C.A. (1956) *Personnel Administration*, New York: McGraw Hill.

Pinder, C.C. (1984) *Work Motivation*, Glenview, Ill.: Scott Foresman.

Plumbley, P.R. (1985) *Recruitment and Selection*, London: Institute of Personnel Management (4th edn).

Plumer, A. (1992) *Equal Value Judgements: Objective Assessment or Lottery?*, Warwick Paper No. 40, Coventry: Industrial Relations Research Unit.

Poole, M. (1986) *Industrial Relations: Origins and Patterns of National Diversity*, London: RKP.

Rainbird, H. (1990) *Training Matters: Union Perspectives on Industrial Restructuring and Training*, Oxford: Blackwell.

Randell, G., Packard, P. and Stater, J. (1984) *Staff Appraisal – A First Step to Effective Leadership*, London: Institute of Personnel Management.

Revans, R.W. (1972) 'Action Learning – a management development programme', *Personnel Review*, autumn.

Revans, W. (1989) *Action Learning*, London: Blond & Briggs.

Rimmer, M. (1972) *Race and Industrial Conflict*, London: Heinemann.

Robens, A. (chairman) (1972) Committee on Safety and Health at Work, *Report*, Cmnd. 5034, London: HMSO.

Rodger, A. (1974) *The Seven Point Plan*, London: National Foundation for Educational Research.

Sayles, L.R. (1958) *Behaviour of Industrial Work Groups*, New York: Wiley.

Scott, W.H., Mumford, E., McGivering, I.C. and Kirkby, J.M. (1963) *Coal and Conflict: A Study of Industrial Relations at Collieries*, Liverpool: Liverpool University Press.

Sisson, K. (ed.) (1989) *Personnel Management in Britain*, Oxford: Blackwell.

Smith, A. (1776) *The Wealth of Nations*, London.

Smith, C.T.B., Clifton, R., Makeham, P., Creigh, S.W. and Burn, R.V. (1978) *Strikes in Britain*, Manpower Paper No. 15, Department of Employment, London: HMSO.

Smith, D.J. (1974) 'Racial Disadvantage in Employment', *Political and Economic Planning*, Vol. XL, 544, reprinted and enlarged 1976.

Smith, P. and Morton, G. (1991) 'A Change of Heart: Union Exclusion in the Provincial Newspaper Sector', *Work, Employment and Society*, 4, 1, 105–24.

Stainer, C. (1971) *Manpower Planning*, London: Heinemann.

Steers, R.M. and Porter, L.W. (eds) (1989) *Motivation and Work Behavior*, New York: McGraw-Hill (5th edn).

Storey, J. (1989) *New Perspectives on Human Resource Management*, London: Routledge.

Storey, J. and Sisson, K. (1993) *Managing Human Resources and Industrial Relations*, Buckingham: Open University Press.

Swedish Employers' Confederation (1987) *Functioning and effects of Worker Participation in Sweden*, Stockholm: Svenska Arbetsgivareforeningen.

Taylor, F.W. (1911) *The Principles of Scientific Management*, New York.

Thompson, N. (1993) *Pay and Performance: the Employer Experiment*, Report No. 258, Brighton: Institute of Manpower Studies.

Tiernan, A. (1988) 'The Man Who Taught the Japanese About Quality Management', *Works Management*, May.

Torrington, D. (1988) 'How Does Human Resources Management Change the Personnel Function?', *Personnel Review*, 17, 6.

Torrington, D. and Chapman, J. (1983) *Personnel Management*, London: Prentice Hall International (2nd edn).

Torrington, D. and Hall, L. (1991) *Personnel Management: A New Approach*, Hemel Hempstead: Prentice-Hall (2nd edn).

Torrington, D. and Weightman, J. (1989) *The Appraisal Interview*, Manchester: UMIST.

Trist, E.L. (1968) 'The Professional Facilitation of Planned Change in Organizations', Reviews, Abstracts, Working Groups, XVI International Congress of Applied Psychology, Amsterdam: Suets and Zeitlinger, 1968, 111–20, in Vroom, V.H. and Deci, E.L. (eds) *Management and Motivation: Selected Readings*, Harmondsworth: Penguin, 1970, 349–63.

TUC (1989) *Skills 2000*, London: Trades Union Congress.

——— (1990) *Joint Action over Training*, London: Trades Union Congress.

——— (1992) *Opportunities for All*, London: Trades Union Congress.

——— (1993) *Learning for Life*, London: Trades Union Congress.

Turner, H.A. (1962) *Trade Union Growth, Structure and Policy*, London: Allen & Unwin.

Ungerson, B. (ed.) (1975) *Recruitment Handbook*, Aldershot: Gower Press.

Ure, A. (1835) *The Philosophy of Manufactures*, London: Charles Knight.

Vroom, V.H. (1964) *Work and Motivation*, Chichester: Wiley.

Waddington, J. (1992) 'Trade Union Membership in Britain, 1980–1987: Unemployment and Restructuring', *British Journal of Industrial Relations*, 30, 2, 287–324.

Wainwright, D. (1981) 'A Programme for Change', in Braham, P., Rhodes, E. and Pearn, M. (eds) (1981) *Discrimination and Disadvantage in Employment*, London: Harper & Row, 351–62.

Walters, B. (1983) 'Designing and Resourcing Training' in D. Guest and T. Kenny (eds) *A Textbook of Techniques and Strategies in Personnel Management*, London: Institute of Personnel Management.

White, M. (1985) 'What's New in Pay?', *Personnel Management*, February.

Whyte, W.F. (1972), 'Economic Incentives and Human Relations', in Lupton, T., and Bowey, A.M. (eds) (1983) *Wages and Salaries*, London: Gower (2nd edn).

Winchester, D. (1983) 'Industrial Relations in the Public Sector', in Bain, G. (ed.) *Industrial Relations in Britain*, Oxford: Blackwell.

Winterton, J. (1981) 'The Trend of Strikes in British Coal Mining, 1949–1979', *Industrial Relations Journal*, 12, 6, 10–19.

——— (1984) *The Control of Hazardous Substances at Work*, Working Environment Research Group, Report No. 3, Bradford: University of Bradford.

——— (1994) 'Social and technological characteristics of coal-face work: a temporal and spatial analysis', *Human Relations*, 47, 1, 89–118.

Winterton, J. and Winterton, R. (1985) *New Technology: the Bargaining Issues*, Leeds: Universities of Leeds and Nottingham/Institute of Personnel Management

——— (1989) *Coal, Crisis and Conflict: the 1984–85 Miners' Strike in Yorkshire*, Manchester: Manchester University Press.

——— (1994) *Collective Bargaining and Consultation over Continuing Vocational Training*, Paper RM.7, Sheffield: Employment Department.

Work Environment Fund (1987) *Rewarding Work*, Stockholm: Arbetsmiljofonden.

Wright, P. (1989) 'Motivation and Job Satisfaction', in Molander, C. (ed.) *Human Resource Management*, Bromley: Chartwell-Bratt, 96–118.

Wright, P. and Taylor, D. (1989) 'Managing Unsatisfactory Performance', in Molander, C. (ed.) *Human Resource Management*, Bromley: Chartwell-Bratt, 119–42.

Index

absence rates 141
absenteeism 140–2
abstract conceptualization 90–1, 92
accident-proneness 192–3
accidents at work 191–4
action learning 82
active experimentation 90–1, 92
Adams, J.S. 135
advertising, job 67–8
Advisory, Conciliation and Arbitration Service (ACAS) 180
affirmative action 102–6
Afro-Caribbean immigrants 96
age scale salary systems 124
Ahlstrand, B.W. 158
alcohol abuse 193
Alderfer, C.P. 133–4
Allen, V.L. 50–1
anti-union perspective 49
application forms 69
appraisal *see* performance appraisal
aptitude testing 70–3
Area Incentive Scheme 163
Amalgamated Electrical and Engineering Union (AEEU) 51, 54
Amalgamated Engineering Union (AEU) 54
Amalgamated Society of Engineers (ASE) 56, 60
Amalgamated Union of Engineering Workers (AUEW) 59
Armstrong, M. 126
Ashenfelter, A. 173
Asian immigrants 96
assessment centres 72
assignments 82–3
attitudes: employee attitude surveys 138–40; job specification 80
automated mining 146–7
autonomy, worker 153
average duration of absence 141

Babbage, C. 144
Bain, G.S. 54, 55
bargaining power 167, 168–9
bargaining strategies/tactics 168–9
Batstone, E. 62, 151, 158, 172
Beckhard, R. 26–7
behaviour, job 85
behaviour change, individual 87, 87–8
behavioural explanations for accidents 192–3
Bell, D.J. 38
Beynon, H. 186
blank form appraisal 117
bonus payments 125
Boraston, I. 62, 157
Bowey, A. 25, 122, 123
Boyatsis, R. 81
Braddick, W. 108, 109
Brady, L. 126
Brannen, P. 151
Braverman, H. 144, 145
British Coal 147, 165, 166, 183; *see also* National Coal Board
British Gas 33
British Rail 165, 166
British Steel 151
British Telecom 33
Brown, Wilfred 122
Brown, William 61, 159, 174
budget 34, 35
Bullock Committee 151–2
bureaucracies: appraisal 112; compared with mature problem-solving organizations 26–7

Burnham Committees

cafeteria payment systems 125
Campion, M.A. 144
Cannell, M. 126
case study 83
Castles, S. 96
Central Arbitration Court (CAC) 99
centralization: collective bargaining 156, 160–1; organization design 18
change: achieving organizational change 25–6, 31; EO policies and need for 104; external environment 1–3; internal environment 3–7; levels of and management development 87, 87–9; methods of introducing 89–90; structural 13, 25
change analysis 194
Chapman, J. 73
Chapple, F. 59
Child, J. 25
Civil Service Arbitration Tribunal 161
class consciousness 46, 47
classical conflict 46–8
Claydon, T. 55
Clegg, H.A. 62, 155–6, 157, 173–4, 177
closed shops 51–2
closed unions 57
clothing industry 143
coaching 83
Coal Mines Act (1954)] 187
coalmining: Area Incentive Scheme 163; collective bargaining 162–3; conciliation machinery 182–3; miners' strikes 54–5, 163, 164, 166, 173, 175; National Power Loading Agreement 162–3, 183; Revision of the Wages Structure Agreement 162; socio-technic systems 145–7
codetermination 150–2
cohort analysis 38, 39
collective bargaining 155–70; dimensions of 155–6; pluralist values 50; private sector 156–9; process 167–70; public sector 159–66; scope 51, 55, 156; structure 60, 155–6, 173–4
collective expressions of conflict 172
Combination Acts 44
combine committees 157
commission 125
Commission for Racial Equality (CRE) 101–2, 102
commitment 18, 25
Communist Party 59
community cohesion 172–3
Community Relations Council (CRC) 101–2, 102
company-level bargaining 157
competency-based training 81
competition 2
composite longwall mining 146
computer-based learning 83
computer-based modelling 36
conceptualization, abstract 90–1, 92
conciliation machinery 182–3
Confederation of British Industry (CBI) 126, 142
Confederation of Shipbuilding and Engineering Unions 182
confidentiality 70
conflict 140, 171–84; classical 46–8; discipline 178–80; disputes 182–3; form and meaning 171–4; grievances 180–2; strikes 174–8
consultation 114
consultative management development 87, 89–90
content theories of motivation 133–4
continuous challenge relations 47, 48
control, span of 20
Control of Substances Hazardous to Health (COSHH) Regulations 188
conveners 61
cooperation 5–6
core workers 6
corporate planning 9; HRP and 33–4, 35, 42–3, 65; management development and 86
Coser, L. 171
covert expression of conflict 172
covert needs in appraisal 108, 109
Craft, J. 33
craft-craft multi-skilling 150
craft unions 55, 56
critical incident technique 193–4
criticism 115; *see also* feedback
cultural change 1–3
culture, organization *see* organization culture

Davies, P.L. 151
Davis, L.E. 144

decentralization: collective bargaining 60, 156, 159; organization structure, 4, 18
deductive learning 91
demand-driven culture 6
demand for labour: forecasting 35–7; reconciliation with supply 41–2
demarcation rules 52
Deming, W.E. 130
democracy 58–60
demonstration 83
development planning 116–17; *see also* management development
direct discrimination 100
direct reporting relationship 24
direction 115
Disabled Persons (Employment) Acts 74
discipline procedures 140, 178–80
discrimination 94; direct and indirect 100; legislation to deter 98–102; *see also* equal opportunities
dismissal 180
disputes 140, 181, 182–3
divisional organization structure 21–2, 22
do-it-yourself learning 83
docks 166, 174
dominant value system 46, 47
Donovan Commission 45, 50, 60, 61, 172; private sector bargaining 156–7; strikes 175–7
Drucker, P.F. 14
drug abuse 193
dual labour market 96–7
dual reporting 23–4, 24
Duffy, T. 59
Dummett, A. 97
Dunn, S. 158
duration of absence, average 141
Durcan, J.W. 173, 177

earnings *see* payment systems
Ebsworth, R. 61
Edwards, P.K. 62, 142, 174
effective organizations 26–7
elections, union 59
Electrical, Electronic, Telecommunication and Plumbing Union (EETPU) 51
employee attitudes *see* attitudes
employee involvement 18, 25, 31; hierarchy of forms 152–3; *see also* empowerment
employee stability index 38; *see also* labour turnover
employers: health and safety arrangements 189–91; objectives in training 149
Employment Appeal Tribunal 101
empowerment 6, 143, 150–3
Engineering Employers' Federation 182
enskilling 143, 147–50
environment: external 1–3, 30–1, 37; internal 3–7; role in health and safety 192; working *see* health and safety
equal opportunities (EO) 94–107; basis of inequality 95–8; human resource practices and 102–6; legislation to deter discrimination 98–102
equal opportunities clauses 105
Equal Opportunities Commission (EOC) 101
equal opportunities policies 102–6
Equal Pay Act (1970) (EqPA) 74, 98–9
equity theory of motivation 135
ERG (existence-relatedness-growth) theory 133–4
Esso Fawley refinery 157–8
ethnic minorities 95, 96
ETU 59
evaluation: in appraisal 110; of training 84–6, 93
Evans, E.O. 61
exit interviews 142–3
expectancy theory 134–5
experience, practical 90–1, 92
experimentation, active 90–1, 92
external environment 1–3, 30–1, 37
external supply forecasting 40–1
extinction 136
extrapolation 36

Factory Acts 186
factory consciousness 46, 47
Factory Inspectorate 188
Fatchett, D. 59
fault-tree analysis 194
Fawley productivity deal 157–8
Fayol, H. 20
feedback 110, 115; levels of in training 84–6
Flanders, A. 60, 152, 156, 157–8
flat organization structure 19, 20

flat rate salary systems 124
flexibility 4
flexible incremental scales 124
flow of labour 40, 41
forecasting: labour demand 35–7; labour supply 37–41
Foster, C.D. 164
Fowler, A. 125
Fox, A. 45, 46, 46–8
Frenkel, S. 62
functional flexibility 149–50
functional organization structure 20–1
functional reporting relationship 24
Furniture, Timber and Allied Trade Union (FTAT) 51

Garcia, P. 61
gender roles 97
General Motors 141
General, Municipal, Boilermakers and Allied Trades Union (GMB) 54, 56
general unions 55, 56
Germany 150
Gill, J. 117
Glynn, S. 148
goal setting *see* targets
Gospel, H. 148
government–public sector relations 163–6
grading 149–50
graduates 78
grievance procedures 140, 180–2
groups *see* leaderless group activities, work groups
Guest, D.E. 8, 48–9

Hackman, J.R. 145
Hall, L. 122
Hamblin, A.C. 84–6
handwriting analysis 72
harmonization 123
Hartmann, H. 151
head hunters 68
health records 140
health and safety 14, 185–95; accidents at work 191–4; development of concerns 185–7; employers' arrangements 189–91; future organization 194–5; union representation 187–9
Health and Safety Commission (HSC) 187
Heath and Safety Executive (HSE) 187
Heath and Safety at Work Act (1974) (HSWA) 186–7, 188, 189, 190, 191
height 19, 20
Hellriegel, D. 134
Herzberg, F. 121, 133, 144
Hill, J.M.M. 191
Honey, P. 91
Hughes, J. 57
human resource management (HRM) 1–16; activities/issues 9–14; analysis of accidents 193–4; audit of policies/procedures 102–4; changing external environment 1–3; changing internal environment 3–7; EO and 102–6; and health and safety 189, 193–4; new pragmatism 15; and pay 11, 129–30; and performance-related pay 127; role in selection 75–6; strategic and functional aspects 7–9; and unions 48–50
human resource management officers 8
human resource management policy 9–10
human resource planning (HRP) 10, 32–43; demand forecasting 35–7; place of 33–4; purpose of 32–3; reconciliation 41–2; recruitment 64–5; stages of 34–5; supply forecasting 37–41
human resource professional, role of 30–1
hybrid organization structure 22–4
hygiene factors 133
Hyman, R. 60, 175

incentive schemes 123, 126, 163
incentives 134–5
incomes policies 163–4, 175
incremental payment systems 124
indirect discrimination 100
individual behaviour change 87, 87–8
individual expressions of conflict 172
individual withdrawal 140–3
inductive learning 91
industrial relations 13; multi-skilling 149–50; two systems 175–7; *see also* collective bargaining, conflict
Industrial Relations Act (1971) 52, 174
Industrial Relations Review and Report 123
industrial unions 55, 56

industry boards 160
Industry Lead Bodies (ILBs) 148
Industry Training Organizations (ITOs) 148
informal systems 104; collective bargaining 156–7, 158; strikes 175–7
information, provision of 188, 191
Institute of Personnel Management (IPM) 111–12, 148
instruction 83
integration 4, 9
intelligence testing 70–3
intergroup relations 28–30
internal environment 3–7
internal labour supply forecasting 38–40
interpersonal relationships 28
interviewing, selection 73–4; interviewing skills 74–5
inventories 70–3
involvement *see* employee involvement
Irish immigrants 95, 96
'iron law of oligarchy' 58–60

Jewish immigrants 95, 96
job avoidance 140, 142–3
job behaviour 85
job description 65, 66–7
job design 143–53; empowerment 150–3; enskilling 147–50; job enrichment 144–5; socio-technic systems 145–7
job enlargement 144
job enrichment 143, 144–5
job evaluation system 67
job rotation 83–4, 144
job satisfaction *see* quality of working life
Johnson, G.E. 173
joint shop stewards committees (JSSCs) 61, 157
judgement, managerial 36–7

Kalmar Volvo plant 153
Kelly, J. 54
Kerr, C. 172
Kinnersley, P. 186
Knapp, J. 59
knowledge 80
Kolb, D.A. 90
Kosack, G. 96
Krieger, J. 62
Kuhn, J. 173

Labour Paty 45, 151
labour productivity 137–8, 164–5
labour turnover 38–9, 140, 142–3
lapses of memory 192
Latham, G.P. 135–6
leaderless group activities 72
learning: cycle 90–1, 92; level of feedback 85; theories and explaining accidents 192; *see also* management development, training
lecture 84
legislation: equal opportunities 98–102; strikes 177–8
Lester, A. 59
Local Authorities Conditions of Service Advisory Board 161
Locke, E.A. 135–6
lockouts 174
Lockwood, P.A. 32
London Passenger Transport Board 160
Long, P. 126
longwall mining 146
lumpen proletariat 95–6
Lupton, T. 62, 122, 123

Mackay, L. 118
Management By Objectives (MBO) 116
management development 12–13, 86–91; focus 87–9; how managers learn 90–1; performance appraisal and 110–12; style 89–90; *see also* training
management–employee relations 6, 46–8
managerial judgement 36–7
managerial oversight and risk tree (MORT) diagrams 194
managers: appraisal process 113–14; attitudes to appraisal 111–12; behaviour during appraisal 114–15; HRM issues 10, 11, 12; and selection 74, 75–6
manpower planning *see* human resource planning
Mansfield Hosiery 98
Manufacturing Science Finance (MSF) 56
Marchington, M. 152
Markov chain 40, 41

Marsden, D. 148
Marsh, A.I. 61
Martin, R. 59
Maslow, A.H. 133
matrix structure 24–5
Matsushita, K. 147
mature rational problem-solving organization 26–7
Mayfield, E.C. 73
McCarthy, W.E.J. 61, 173, 177
McLelland, C.L. 144
McGivering, I. 26
measured day work (MDW) 122–3
memory lapses 192
merit rating systems 124–5
Michels, R. 58
militancy, paradox of 50–1
mining *see* coalmining
mixed organization structure 22–4
Molander, C.F. 3, 6, 93, 116, 117
Morrison, H. 160
Morton, G. 55
motivation 110, 132–6; content theories 133–4; process theories 134–6
motivators 133
multi-employer bargaining 159
multi-linear events sequencing (MES) 194
multi-skilling 149–50
Mumford, A. 91
Murliss, H. 126

National Coal Board (NCB) 146, 162, 163; *see also* British Coal
National Dock Labour Scheme 166, 174
National Health Service (NHS) 126, 161
National Power Loading Agreement (NPLA) 162–3, 183
National Union of Mineworkers (NUM) 51, 56, 68; collective bargaining 162, 163, 165, 166; membership losses 54; party factions 59
National Union of Railwaymen (NUR) 59
National Vocational Qualifications (NVQs) 148
nationalization 159–60, 164
needs: in appraisal 108, 109; content theories of motivation 133–4; training 78–81
negotiation 167–70; performance appraisal 115; stages of 169–70
New Technology Agreements 149
Newby, M. 147, 158, 177
Nichols, T. 186
Norway 194

objective labour forecasting methods 36
objectives: payment systems 120–1; performance 115–18; training 81; *see also* targets
observation, reflective 90–1, 92
occupational unions 55, 56
Oldham, G.R. 145
oligarchy 58–60
'on the job' training 11, 83
open unions 56–7
organization analysis 78–9
organization culture 3–7; performance appraisal and 112
organization design 13–14, 17–26; current designs 20–5; key issues 17–20; organizational change 25–6
organization development (OD) 13–14, 26–7; techniques 27–31
organization structure 4; divisional/product 21–2; functional 20–1; hybrid/mixed 22–4; matrix 24–5; structural change 13, 25; *see also* organization design
organizational level of management development 87, 88–9
organizational level of training evaluation 85–6
output measures of QWL 137–8
outward bound activities 72
overt needs in appraisal 108, 109

Packard, P. 119
paradox of militancy 50–1
Parker, S. 61
participation *see* employee involvement, empowerment
party factions 59
payment by results (PBR) 121–2, 173
payment systems 5–6, 120–31; equal opportunities 103; government–public sector relations 163–4; HRM and 11, 129–30; likely future trends

129; objectives 120–1; performance appraisal and 108–10; performance-related pay 103, 126–9; salaries 124–5; shop stewards' power 62; wages 121–3
Pendleton, A. 165
performance appraisal 103, 108–19; competencies of 114–15; in context 108–12; group-based 117–18; and management development 110–12; and organization culture 112; performance objectives/targets 115–18; process 112–14; training for 118–19; as training method 82
performance orientation 4–5
performance-related pay 103, 126–9; difficulties 127–9
peripheral workers 6
personal skills 27–8
person specification 66, 67
personality inventories 70–3
personnel management 7–8
physiological explanations for accidents 193
piecework 121–2, 173
Pinder, C.C. 133
planning: corporate *see* corporate planning; human resource *see* human resource planning; strategic 9, 33–4, 35; training provision 81–2
plant-level bargaining 157, 158, 177
plant-wide incentive schemes 123
Plumer, A. 99
pluralist values 45–6, 47, 48–50
Poole, M. 175
post-entry closed shops 51–2
Post Office 152, 165, 166
postal ballots 59
power, bargaining 167, 168–9
power loading 146, 162–3
practical experience 90–1, 92
pre-entry closed shops 51–2
pre-interview tests/inventories 70–3
prescription 114–15
prescriptive management development 87, 89
private sector bargaining 156–9
privatization 164, 166
procedural rules 155
process-craft multi-skilling 150
process theories of motivation 134–6
product structure 21–2, 22
productivity 137–8, 164–5
productivity bargaining 157, 157–8
profit-sharing systems 123, 125
profitability 136–7
public sector 159–66, 175; coalmining 162–3; collective bargaining 160–2; government–public sector relations 163–6
public sector borrowing requirement (PSBR) 164
punishment 136

qualifications 147–8
quality 33, 131; consciousness 5; work force 2–3; *see also* Total Quality Management
quality of working life (QWL) 132–54, 191; employee attitudes 138–40; individual withdrawal 140–3; job design 143–53; measures of 136–43; output measures 137–8; theories of motivation 132–6
quit rate 38–9, 140, 142–3

Race Relations Act (1976) (RRA) 74, 101–2
racism 97–8
radical value system 46, 47
Radice, G. 151
railways 161
Rainbird, H. 149
Randell, G. 119
rational problem-solving organization 26–7
reactions to training 84
reconciliation 41–2
recruitment 10–11, 32–3, 64–8
Redman, G.P. 173
redundancy 32–3, 42; equal opportunities 103–4
references 69–70
reflection 114
reflective observations 90–1, 92
reinforcement 136
relationships: intergroup 28–30; interpersonal 28; management-employee 6, 46–8
reliability of tests 71
reporting accidents 193
reserve army of labour theory 96–7
Revans, R.W. 82

reward systems 11, 120–1; *see also* payment systems
Rimmer, M. 96, 157
Robens Committee of Inquiry on Safety and Health 186
Rodger, A. 66
rules, collective bargaining and 155
Ryan, P. 148

safe system of work 191
safety *see* health and safety
safety agreement 190
safety committee 190
safety policy 189–90
safety representatives 187–9, 190–1
Safety Representatives and Safety Committees (SRSC) Regulations (1977) 187–8, 191
salaries 123, 124–5; *see also* payment systems
sanctions 168, 169
Sayles, L.R. 173
Scargill, A. 59
scientific management 144
Scott, W.H. 62, 173
Scottish Vocational Qualifications (SVQs) 148
Scullion, H. 62, 142, 174
segmentation 6
selection 10–11, 64, 65, 69–75; interview 73–4; interviewing skills 74–5; pre-interview tests/inventories 70–3; references 69–70
sensitivity training 85
separation index 38
separations 32–3, 42, 142–3; *see also* labour turnover, redundancy
seven-point plan 66, 74
Sex Discrimination Act (1975) (SDA) 74, 99–101
shop stewards 58, 172; collective bargaining 157, 158; influence 60–2
short listing 69
Siegel, A. 172
single-employer bargaining 159, 165
'sitting next to Nellie' 83
skills: enskilling 147–50; job specification 80; personal 27–8; two dimensions 150
Slater, J. 119
Smith, A. 144
Smith, C.T.B. 175
Smith, D.J. 96
Smith, P. 55, 108, 109
social amenities 14
Social Charter 2
socio-technic systems 143, 145–7
sophisticated modern relations 47, 48
sophisticated paternalist relations 47, 48
span of control 20
staff status schemes 123
Stainer, C. 37
standard modern relations 47, 48
statistical forecasting methods 36, 37
status quo clauses 181–2
strategic HRM staff 8
strategic planning 9, 33–4, 35
strikes 171, 174–8; Donovan Commission 175–7; incomes policies 164; miners' strikes 54–5, 163, 164, 166, 173, 175; postwar trends 175, 176; Thatcher era 166, 177–8; theories explaining 172–4; unofficial 158
structural change 13, 25
structures, systems and 30–1
subjective labour forecasting methods 36–7
subordinate value system 46, 47
substance abuse 193
substantive rules 155
substructure 152–3
superstructure 150–2
supply of labour: forecasting 37–41; reconciliation with demand 41–2
support services 14; *see also* quality of working life
survival rate 39
Sweden 151, 182, 194–5
Swedish Centre for Working Life 153
Swedish Employers' Confederation 151
Swedish Work Environment Fund 153
systems, structures and 30–1

T groups 85
tall organization structure 19, 20
targets: group 117–18, 129; motivation 135–6; performance 115–18
Tavistock Institute of Human Relations 145–7
Taylor, D. 179
Taylorism 144
team development 28, 29, 84; *see also* work groups

technology 145–7
Terry, M. 61
testing, pre-interview 70–3
Thatcher era 165–6, 177–8
Thorpe, R. 25
Tiernan, A. 130
time rates of pay 121
Tolpuddle martyrs 44
Torrington, D. 6, 73, 118, 122
Tory government 126; *see also* government-public sector relations, Thatcher era
Total Quality Management (TQM) 5, 118, 147
Trades Union Congress (TUC) 50, 105, 151; training 148–9
traditional paternalist relations 46, 47
training 78–86, 91–3; clarification of objectives 81; dependence on appraisal 111; enskilling 147–50; equal opportunities 103; evaluation 84–6, 93; HRM issue 11–12; identification of needs 78–81; interests of employers and unions 149; methods 82–4; for performance appraisal 118–19; planning provision 81–2; *see also* management development
transference, problem of 81–2
Transport and General Workers' Union (TGWU) 54
Trist, E.L. 145, 191
Turner, H.A. 56

ultimate value of training 86
underclass 96, 97
Union of Democratic Mineworkers (UDM) 54, 56
union education 52
union officials 180; *see also* shop stewards
Union of Shop, Distributive and Allied Workers (USDAW) 51
unions 2, 44–63; acceptance of 44–5; codetermination 152; collective bargaining *see* collective bargaining; equal opportunities 105–6; government 55, 57–60; growth and decline 52–5; HRM and 48–50; membership 51–2, 52–4; objects and methods 50–2; perspectives on unionism 44–8; racism 97–8; role in workplace 60–2; safety representation 187–9; 190–1; structure 55–7; training 148–9; underclass 97; white-collar 160
unitary values 45–6, 47, 48–50
Ure, A. 144

validity of tests 70
value systems 46–8
Volvo 153
Vroom, V.H. 110, 134

Waddington, J. 54
wages 121–3; *see also* payment systems
Wainwright, D. 105
welfare 14, 185–6
White, M. 11, 130
Whitley Councils 161
Whyte, W.F. 122
width 19, 20
Winchester, D. 164
Winterton, J. 146, 163, 165, 177; miners' strikes 55, 173, 175, 183; safety information 188; training 149, 150; unofficial strikes 158
Winterton, R. 55, 149, 150, 163, 173
withdrawal, individual 140–3
women 95, 96–7, 104
work avoidance 140–2
Work Environment Acts 194–5
Work Environment Fund 153
work groups: cohesion 173; focus for change 87, 88; incentive schemes 123; performance appraisal 117–18; shop stewards and 62; targets 117–18, 129; team development 28, 29, 84
work study 36
worker autonomy 153
worker representation/directors 150–2
workers' aspirations 48–9
working environment *see* health and safety
workplace bargaining 156–7
Workplace Training Committees (WTCs) 148
Wright, P. 133, 179
Wright, V. 126